BROKEN OATHS

NORMAN MOUNTER

BURTON MAYERS

Content compiled for publication by Richard Mayers of Burton Mayers Books. Cover images: Caduceus - a Doctor's sign in the Wellcome Institute; Papyrus text: fragment of Hippocratic oath, also from the Wellcome collection Attribution 4.0 international.

First published by Burton Mayers Books June 2021.
All rights reserved.

A CIP catalogue record for this book is available from the British Library

ISBN: 1-8383484538
ISBN-13: 978-1-8384845-3-8

Typeset in Garamond and Palatino

This book deals with the Holocaust. While the author has taken great lengths to ensure the subject matter is dealt with in a compassionate and respectful manner, it may be troubling for some readers. Discretion is advised. This book is a work of historical fiction based on real events. The likeness of historical/famous figures has been used fictitiously; the author does not speak for or represent these people. All opinions expressed in this book are the author's, or fictional.

www.BurtonMayersBooks.com

ACKNOWLEDGEMENTS

Writing a book of this nature has not been an easy experience, and would not have been possible without the encouragement and support of my best friend, John Wedlake. I dedicate this book to him. He has stood by me through the long months of research and writing, and has been a constant beacon of inspiration. That is true friendship.

A very special thank you must go to Martin Dixon for his scholarly analysis of the historical backdrop, languages and cultures. He has also written a foreword to the novel.

I am greatly indebted to my editor, mentor and publisher, Richard Mayers. I must thank him for believing in me and the book. He has been with me every step of the way during the editing process, and has made the whole experience an enjoyable and enlightening one.

I would also like to thank Chris Malone and Pam Taylor for their beta-reader input which was invaluable.

Last but by no means least, I must say an enormous thank you to my amazing wife, Sarah, for her enduring patience and support during the arduous months of research and writing.

AUTHOR'S NOTE

'Broken Oaths' is not a book for the fainthearted and contains many disturbing passages.

The novel is mainly written in diary format, and concentrates on the harrowing events that occurred at Auschwitz-Birkenau during the summer of 1944. The narrative explores the life of a Hungarian Jewish pathologist, Dr. József Sárkány and his role as Josef Mengele's senior pathologist in Crematorium I (now generally referred to as Crematorium II). Details are drawn from the memoirs of the real life pathologist, Dr. Miklós Nyiszli (1901-1956), who published his 'Auschwitz: A Doctor's Eyewitness Account' in 1946.

I appreciate that many readers are uncomfortable with the concept of 'holocaust fiction'. Whilst this novel is indeed fictional, it draws extensively from firsthand accounts, letters, diaries and biographies of those concerned within the narrative. Indeed, there are very few events described that do not have a direct historical source associated with it.

The reliability of Miklós Nyiszli's account of his time in the crematorium at Auschwitz-Birkenau is of course open to speculation and has been the basis of much academic scrutiny. Despite this, the account remains part of the historical archive and offers a rare insight into the personality and war crimes of Dr. Josef Mengele.

The book explores numerous themes that include anti-Semitism, medical ethics, euthanasia and eugenics. It also attempts to examine the genocide from a German perspective, especially in the context of their rich scientific and medical past. This is especially pertinent in their design of the Birkenau crematoria which became both killing factories and centres of pseudoscientific medical research. This facet of the novel investigates the functioning components of the extermination and cremation processes, specifically addressing some of the arguments of holocaust denial.

Above all, what I hope to have achieved is a thought-provoking look into the heinous crimes of the Nazi doctors, nurses and scientists. These are crimes that cannot be denied; shocking yes, but also informative and forever relevant to the complex world of contemporary medical ethics.

Dr. Norman Mounter, March 2021

To my dear friend from Glenbervie Drive.

'There is no doubt this is the most horrible crime ever committed in the whole history of the world, and it has been done by scientific machinery by nominally civilised men in the name of a great State and one of the leading races of Europe.'

Winston Churchill, July 1944

Foreword

An autopsy of Dr. Norman Mounter's novel *Broken Oaths* reveals a dark tour de force of writing, necrotic at its heart. Against the backdrops of Kristallnacht, wartime Hungary and the Auschwitz dissection table, time quickly accelerates post-war into a constellation of times, locations and characters, familiar and unfamiliar; but all touched by the pervading smell of putrefaction or formaldehyde.

If *Broken Oaths* belongs to any literary tradition, it is to the kaleidoscopic literary sub-category 'Holocaust literature': a term which has been the subject of scholarly debate since the mid-1970s, but which still lacks much value as an analytical category. Texts as diverse as Tadeusz Borowski's misanthropic camp memoirs of Auschwitz[1] and Cynthia Ozick's shocking vignette *The Shawl* (1980) - partial versus pure fictionalisation, Realism versus Lyricism - as well as songs, graffiti and oral histories have all been ascribed to the texture of collective memory of the Holocaust.

The first and foremost concern in Holocaust literature was and always will be ethics and aesthetics, the compassionate memorialisation and description of the indescribable, and the limits of adequate representation through the written (especially fictional) word. An initial current of general scepticism about fictionalising the

---

[1] *Pożegnanie z Marią (Farewell to Maria)*, translated into the English by Barbara Vedder and published in 1962 as *This Way for the Gas, Ladies and Gentleman*.

Holocaust, weighted most heavily in the voice of the Jewish-American literary-critical tradition, was replaced by a greater openness from the turn of the century onwards, and a widening of the discourse on Holocaust literature beyond debates on ethics and national memories. These debates were accompanied by thorough scholarly confrontation of and efforts to analyse, rather than merely memorialise through respectful silence, the events and experiences of the Holocaust – as in Primo Levi's seminal collection of essays, *The Drowned and the Saved* (1986) – and attempts to instil the field with some degree of conceptual unity. Many echoed writer and Holocaust survivor Elie Wiesel's claim in 1977 that a new epoch of literature had been inaugurated by their generation, that a new 'literature of testimony' had risen from the confines of the death camps, as the tragedy as an art form had been born of Ancient Greece, the epistle of Rome, the sonnet of Trecento Sicily,[2] while in 1980 Alvin Rosenfeld defined Holocaust literature in terms of the sense of a 'double dying' – the extermination not just of European Jewry but of Enlightenment Humanism, of the collective values of Humankind.[3]

In *Broken Oaths* these central motifs are refracted through the prism of Medicine, specifically Pathology, which is at the heart of the novel's originality but which still pastiches the works of Borowski and that first generation of writers and survivors who paid testimony to the Holocaust, to the loss of life, to the apparent death of human values (for the second time in that dark European half-century).

The breakdown of humanistic values, or those that might be ascribed vaguely to 'civilisation', appears in *Broken*

---

[2] In: Wiesel, E., Lefkovitz, E. (eds.), *Dimensions of the Holocaust: lectures at Northwestern University*, 2nd ed. (Evanston, IL, 1990).

[3] Rosenfeld, A.H., *A Double Dying: Reflections on Holocaust Literature* (Bloomington, IN, 1980).

Oaths as the breakdown and destruction of the anatomical Body, its metaphorical dissection and evisceration on the pathologist's table. The synecdoche of the human Body as Europe, and of Health and Medicine as emblems of civilisational progress and modernity, has deep roots originating in the Renaissance (when abstract notions such as progress and modernity had wider and very different breadths of meaning than in the 20th century). Rabelais conceived of the corporeal and social as indivisible in a concept Bakhtin later called the 'Grotesque Body', reducing and degrading the metaphysical and the loftily theoretical down to base anatomical elements in the service of satirising the medieval French social élite, in particular the monastic orders.[4]

And yet the essential function of the Rabelaisian grotesque is not to satirise life, but to celebrate it. Renaissance archways and bell-towers swarm with impish figures sporting grotesquely protruding noses or wide-open mouths, the latter being the part of the Grotesque Body that most symbolises and most celebrates excess – the mouth's function is to allow the delights of the outside world an entry into the Body, and after for the byproducts of indulgence to triumphantly belch back outwards. Just as these uppermost regions are associated with life and excess, the nether become symbols of death and decay, but never in tension with the celebration of life: death and the putrefaction of the Body are the natural and victorious conclusion to the great act of living.

This dialectic is eroded in Dr. Mounter's novel by the ironic union of the upper and nether – the mouth, afflicted by starvation, becomes as much imbued with decay as the nether regions ravaged by dysentery – grotesqueing the celebration of life and breaking the Rabelaisian cycle. Renaissance humanist principles and the notion of the

---

[4] Bakhtin, M., *Rabelais and His World*, trans. H.Iswolsky (Bloomington, IN, 1984).

'victory of life' become poignantly quixotic in the context of the concentration camp. If the Renaissance stands for an epoch of cultural revival in human history, Modernity as conceived of in Nazi ideology is the *nouveau mal du siècle*. Gersonides' Rod of Jacob, designed to uncover the arcane knowledge of the stars, is paralleled by the trinity of chamber, gas canister and furnace, designed to destroy human beings with the mechanical efficiency witnessed in the memoirs of Sonderkommando Filip Müller[5] (a leitmotif in this novel also).

For the most prevalent motif in *Broken Oaths* is the travestying of Rabelais's Grotesque: the degradation of the human Body and the corporeal rather than the metaphysical – unforgettable images of the abuse and destruction of the human anatomy and Body, its uppermost and nethermost regions, which in Rabelais stand as a celebration of the cycle of existence – eradication of the semiotic opposite which should exist between life and decay – the grotesqueing of the Grotesque by a 20th century reality where health and medicine, appropriated by an aggressive new nationalist-racial ideology in the name of collective progress, in the name of forging a path to modernity, was invoked to justify the murder of as many as 6 million people.

The central character, pathologist Dr. Sárkány, attends a lecture by a Nazi party ideologue where collective society and the ideal Europe – the Nordic-Aryan nation – is ironically and chillingly conceived of not as a human Body but as a centipede.[6] This grotesque metamorphosis of the Body, the emblem for the celebration of life and human values, mirrors the grotesque transformation of medical science and theory in the moulding (and mouldering) hands

---

[5] Müller , F., *Sonderbehandlung neboli zvláštní zacházení - Tři roky v osvětimských krematoriích a plynových komorách* (Praha, 2018).

[6] p.22-3.

of Nazi ideology.

Like much of the novel, the motif of the travestying of Medicine is imbued with irony, accentuated by the emphasis on Pathology specifically in *Broken Oaths*. Pseudo-medical and medicalised Nazi ideology, notions of so-called racial hygiene drawing on Social Darwinism, were born of a long tradition of German involvement in the vanguard of medical scientific discovery and development; the seminal text *Cellular Pathology* (1858) was written by the prolific German physician and social scientist Rudolf Virchow, often called the Father of Pathology.

Even when intended for its true, humanistic purpose, in the novel Medicine fails to make any impression against the tides of cyclical and ironic fate. The baby son of Sárkány, the half-Jewish doctor, is saved from death in the womb when his wife is rushed to hospital, in an ambulance sent by the man for whom Sárkány will later arrange for that same son to be symbolically sacrificed, in the name, too, of Medicine and of Nazi racial ideology.

Today the intersection between the practice of medicine, medical science and theory, politics, and the course of history is as forefront as it has been since the crystallisation of this ideology. The overarching tension between the practise of humane medicine, questions of medical ethics, society, politics and the idea of an unspoken 'oath' sworn by medical professionals on behalf of humanistic values, resonates in some ways with the contemporary dynamics brought about by the Covid-19 Pandemic. National health, thankfully largely purged of the ethno-nationalist and racial-nationalist connotations it had in the first half of the 20th century, is again central to political discourses, and a renewed meaning has been placed on oaths – of the state to protect the most medically vulnerable, of the individual to protect his fellow individual, of the medical professional to serve society, even at the risk of their own health and lives. Can any rational individual living in the United Kingdom today say that the last of these oaths has been broken?

Like medicine itself, the characters of *Broken Oaths* are swept inexorably towards the death camps by the course of history, which they are powerless to change. The narrative is driven, against a thematic tableaux ranging from the struggle with Jewishness to eugenics, not by the Individual but by the distorting lens of Ideology. Medicine and the concept of the Body are grotesquely appropriated by Ideology, and the central character, Josef Sárkány, ironically parrots the very zeitgeist of racial thought that destroys his career and leads him to internment in Auschwitz-Birkenau. The unseen puppet-strings of Ideology are the novel's antagonists, so pervasive that they erase any trace of heroism, of protagonism from the story.

The most sympathetic character, Eva Sárkány – an idealised Rachel figure who functions as a spiritual-moral foil to her husband – is powerless against the ideologies controlling her husband, and forgives his most unforgivable transgressions against their own family. The theme of forgiveness, and how it links with Jewish memory and spirituality in relation to the Nazis, is central to Holocaust literature. Eva's ultimate forgiveness of her husband alludes to forgiveness as the agency of the powerless – a way for the Jewish people to reclaim their autonomy from the grasps of victimhood, to conceive of the Holocaust in their history not passively as a genocide, but actively as a sacrifice by fire. The theme is not elaborated to the point of conclusion in *Broken Oaths* – Eva's ability to forgive serves as a brief flash of agency which is quickly negated by Ideology, as it neither heals the wounds caused by her husband's crimes in its name, nor leads him to any meaningful repentance.

Josef Sárkány is unheroic, lacking the idealised characteristics of the hero or the moral complexity and aspect of social criticism typical to the antihero. This stems partly from his being modeled on Hungarian pathologist and Sonderkommando, Miklós Nyiszli. Features of Sárkány's story, and episodes such as the finding of a young girl still alive in the gas chamber, are direct analogies to Nyiszli's memoirs – which famously record the horrors of Auschwitz and Mengele's experiments in objective, analytical rather than emotive style.[7]

This intertextual style, with its own modifications in *Broken Oaths*, leaves little room for heroism and ascribes to the narrator an intrinsic passivity, and the quality of an observer at the whim of History and Ideology. However most crucially the character of Josef Sárkány perpetuates rather than fights Ideology, and his own deplorable acts make any claim to sympathy as a victim of Ideology unconvincing, albeit understandable.

The tough prisoner and Nazi hunter Kowalsky is the only character really to strive actively against the forces of Ideology in *Broken Oaths*, yet he too is stained with complicity in horrifying experiments on the pathologist's table at Auschwitz, and later submits to the lasting effects of Nazi ideology when he rejects his own Jewishness.[8] The roster of characters all become collective victims of History and Ideology: 'ordinary men' transformed from the Body into the guise of the centipede by group ideology, like Reserve Police Battalion 101.[9]

The above is not in itself original in Holocaust literature. Collective dehumanisation and powerlessness at the hands of History and Ideology are prominent motifs of Borowksian misanthropy, while the power of discourses of race, nationality, modernity and health – shot through with

---

[7] Nyiszli, M., *Auschwitz: a doctor's eyewitness account*, trans. T.Kremer and R.Seaver (Greenwich, CT, 1960). Scholarship has cast doubt on the full authenticity of his account: see Mattogno, C., *An Auschwitz doctor's eyewitness account: the bestselling tall tales of Dr. Mengele's assistant analyzed* (Uckfield, 2018).

[8] p.290.

[9] Browning, C.R., *Ordinary Men* (New York, 2017).

ideology to motivate human action and history – is central to Foucauldian literary-critical-philosophical thought. The character through whom we mostly view this bleak panorama is, however, quite original as a portrayal of the medical professional in literature.

There are some features to Dr. Sárkány and his story with broad parallels in medical fiction. The figure of the doctor unable to control his sexual desire in Yehoshua's *Open Heart* (1994), a trope so popular because it contrasts with society's ideal vision of the calm, collected, rational medic. The trope of the failed doctor struggling to revive his career or whose career has been irreversibly destroyed, which can be found in fiction as diverse as the medical soap opera and Roger Martin du Gard's epic interwar sequence of novels *Les Thibault* (1922-1940), for which he won the 1937 Nobel Prize for Literature. The cold, even sociopathic guises in which doctors appear in the novels of Graham Greene – in *The Human Factor* (1978) we find a direct parallel with *Broken Oaths*, a doctor committing murder with little evident remorse in the service of state ideology.[10] However Greene's oath-breaker, Dr. Percival, has been recruited by the Secret Service, and thus his deed is without the bleak irony that accompanies Sárkány's crimes against his own family.

In the figure of Dr. Sárkány, Mounter presents us with a doctor who is compelled to travesty the name of Medicine in the name of Ideology, but one who is capable of atrocity on behalf of the Self. Ideology drives Sárkány's actions but to an extent he also appropriates Ideology in turn for himself, rationalising his affair with Dr. Fischer in terms of his wife's racial inferiority (as perceived through the Nazi ideological framework). Even in Auschwitz he still dreams

---

[10] Surawicz, B., Jacobson, B., *Doctors in fiction: lessons from literature* (Oxford, 2009), ch. 1

of reviving his career, of receiving the same acclaim as Mengele, to whom he panders across the dissection table. He *aspires* to the dehumanising forces of Ideology which form the background for the Holocaust, being not just a victim corrupted by Ideology but also its culpable agent.

This element of Mounter's Sárkány is most memorable, and the most defiant of typical representations of the medical professional in literature – but not defiant of the historical context, as physicians were amongst the most represented socioeconomic cohorts in Nazi party membership (half of Weimar Republic registered physicians became early joiners of the party)[11].

Sárkány dashes formaldehyde in the face of George Eliot's Tertius Lydgate, Middlemarch's resident young, naive doctor with ambitions to change the world and practise medicine in its ideal form, in the form for which he believes it was intended: Medicine as the perfect axis uniting Science and Art, intellectual progress and human values. He shames the work of the kind, gifted doctors who save Kostoglotov's life in a small Tashkent hospital 1 year after the death of Stalin, but long before the shadow of Stalinist ideology has gone into remission, in Solzhenitsyn's *Cancer Ward* (1966). The nihilistic Chekhovian doctor has lost his empathy, his passion, his values – but at least his values have not been grotesquely morphed by militant Ideology.

Sárkány is a microcosmic example of Mounter's ability to find a black untouched recess in the category of medical fiction, a literary category which has a cross with oft-sickly historical-romantic fiction as one of its most popular cultural literary off-shoots.

Of course some of the darkness of Sárkány's character emanates from his irrepressible fascination with Pathology

---

[11] Haque, O.S., De Freitas, J., Viani, I., Niederschulte, B., Bursztajn, H.J., 'Why did so many German doctors join the Nazi party early?', *International Journal of Law and Psychiatry* 35/5-6 (2012), p. 473.

and lack of sanctity for the anatomical Body – manifest as a sanctity for the dissected and decayed Body; the body on the pathologist's table rather than the body as an artifact of the 'victory of life'. He is often animated more by the body on the dissection table, and by the medical dimensions to the suffering around him, than by their emotional and psychological pain – though he is not emotionally sterile, like his counterpart Mengele.

Sárkány is – ironically, given he becomes complicit in the travestying of Medicine – the quintessential 'Pathologist'. Though his faith in human values quickly fades in the novel, his fascination for and faith in the science of Pathology never does. It contributes to the chilling clinical aestheticisation of horror in *Broken Oaths* which is so creative and unique from the literary perspective, but one wonders given Mounter's background whether it is also a satire of the archetypal pathologist, of the notion that a pathologist *must* be emotionally retarded or soulless to choose a profession where they consult on a daily basis with the dead. In any case it is the former, in particular the medicalisation of suffering, which leaves the deepest impression on the text and on the reader, impressing on the reader that same combination of clinical, scientific emotional sterility with a pervading sense of mortality which makes hospital corridors inspire a chilling discomfiture in the individual, or evoke searing reminders of past pain and loss.

This dark charge which the text carries, transmitted through chains of visceral images, the grotesque, often hyperbole, throws sparks so often, however, that the reader begins to experience a numbness – but is occasionally still caught off guard, even far into the novel. Aesthetically this desensitisation might give the text a monochromeity, but to say it lessens the force of the book would be to oversimplify: is the reader truly 'desensitised' by relentless, traumatic imagery, or do they begin to process the trauma differently, subconsciously?

Broken Oaths does lack chiaroscuro – humour to contrast the darkness, light to deftly create shadow – but if anything this speaks to Mounter's commitment to the act of testimony, of memorialising that which he knows about the Holocaust; something he could never have experienced firsthand like Borowski or Wiesel. That which he knows is the medicine, evident in his interweaving of pathologist's terminology, imagery and shorthand into the text, and the inhumanity of the ideologies and agents which history has told were complicit in the darkest of stains on collective human memory. The novel is certainly memorable and shocking, but not haunting, like Jiří Weil's *Life With a Star* (1949),[12] where emotional force which lingers long after is created by the intersection of hope and despair.

If the reader feels tempted to accuse Mounter of over-stylising a subject which requires the greatest of compassion and most delicate of handling, they might first ask themselves: does the plot, the aesthetics and the style of the narrative in *Broken Oaths* serve to mystify or demystify, to impress or to dispel ambiguity, to further a representation of the Holocaust or to present historical fact? In every case it is the latter. The stylisation of suffering in *Broken Oaths* is also its affirmation, its medical demystification, forming part of the author's exploration of the complicity and grotesqueing of Medicine during the Holocaust. Nor, it should be added, is employment of the grotesque and other highly stylised aesthetics without precedent in Holocaust literature. Czech poet Radek Malý combines the grotesque and – perhaps even more controversially – Morgensternian absurdism, in his collection of fatalistic poems *Crow Songs* (2002).[13]

---

[12] *Život s hvězdou* in the Czech. Translated into the English in 1989 by Růžena Kovaříková and Roslyn Schloss.

[13] *Vraní zpěvy* in the Czech. As yet un-translated, but see Firlej, A., Heimer, E., Holý, J., Nichtburgerová, H. (eds), *Handbook of*

Despite its overwhelming darkness, *Broken Oaths* sheds historical light. In her speech on International Remembrance of Victims of the Holocaust Day, the 27th of January 2021, Slovak president Zuzana Čaputová highlighted the affinity between disinformation and tacit complicity in the distortion of the truth – towering issues which are as pertinent today as a century ago – and the events which led to the Holocaust.[14] Holocaust denial, the denial of the crimes so painfully analysed in the medical idiom by Dr. Mounter, is still alive in popular forums as well as academic circles with the aim of inculcating Antisemitism and bending History to the will of its racist Ideology; that same Ideology in the shadow of which *Broken Oaths* is set.

Though the contents of the novel take place in the iron grip of Ideology, metatextually *Broken Oaths* is part of the tradition of testimony to the Holocaust which rejects the primacy of Ideology over stories of human experience, rejects the primacy of Ideology over History, rejects attempts to distort historical truth.

The structure of the novel is intrinsically a middle-finger to Ideology, as its events are constructed through a reel of fictionalised diary pages, journals, transcripts of recordings, interviews, autopsy reports – giving it the unique texture of a file presented by the Polish Supreme National Tribunal at the Auschwitz Trials. History is idealised and de-mythologised, presented to the reader through fictionalised primary sources as evidence, as documented truth undistorted by Ideology. The reader is offered the chance to experience History unfold as omniscient spectators.

The author asks something in return: that the reader

Polish, Czech and Slovak Holocaust Fiction (Berlin, 2021) for excerpts in English.

[14] Pravda, 'Čaputová si uctila pamiatku obetí holokaustu' (27 January 2021)

suspend their disbelief when they read diary pages bursting with ornate description, minutiae which a diarist could not possibly recall from memory, direct and indirect speech written down verbatim, clipped and unnatural dialogue hyper-stylised to bear open the characters' empty souls to the reader. Because as much as Mounter's style of writing can be a bludgeoning over the temple with images that affront the mind's eye, it can also be introspective, as fragile and sharp as paper:

"There is no shelter from the elements, and we all sleep huddled together under sheets of tarpaulin. We did manage to get hold of some straw, but this is damp and does little to ease. There's no sanitation, no running water, no heating... no food. In what feels like an irretrievable state of total disintegration – corporeal, psychological and spiritual – death now seems like a release. I crave the ecstasy of nothingness."[15]

What might the reader find, should they indulge in a moment of introspection on finishing *Broken Oaths*? I found, paradoxically given the contents of the book, that the deepest impression I was left with was the assertion of human empathy and compassion, and the endless desire of human beings to understand and connect with one another across space and time.

Piotr Paziński's *The Boarding House* (2009)[xvi] meditates on the Holocaust and postmemory, telling the story of a young Jewish man who listens to the stories of Holocaust survivors, and is able to successfully connect with them emotionally, intellectually and spiritually, culminating in a poignant epiphany about his own identity. The same desire to connect with the true stories of Borowski, Müller, Nyiszli, Levi and thousands of others is not merely *part of*, but *is* the

---

[15] p.67.

[xvi] *Pensjonat* in the Polish original, published in English translation as *The Boarding House* in 2018, translated by MJ Dabrowska.

fabric of *Broken Oaths*, and therefore so is the assertion of the human values which are so ostensibly absent from the book.

Because *Broken Oaths* is also the story of the author coming to terms with the Holocaust, that horrific event which is part of Humankind's collective history, which can never be forgotten, which still and always will have the power to inspire and to move (and it is moving to see in the text, with such clarity, how far the author has been moved by his subject matter). Of the author trying to connect with the suffering of people he can never know or meet. Trying to understand that which seems beyond understanding. Pathology, medicine, the written word, and simple human compassion are the tools in Dr. Mounter's particular arsenal.

Martin Dixon
Liptovský Mikuláš, Slovak Republic
February 2021

Part I
The Road to Auschwitz

BROKEN GLASS & BROKEN WATERS

Diary of Dr. József Sárkány, Heidelberg, 1938

<u>**Sabbath 1st January**</u>

The first *Shabbat* of 1938 has ended as darkness begins to envelope the house. The *Menorah* candles continue to burn, caressing this page in a watery illumination. Éva is next door teaching piano to the girls. The number of dissonant notes emanating from the living room tells me that she's failing abysmally as usual.

The Polish au pair is probably in her bedroom. Lena Herschell is a strikingly beautiful and intelligent girl who has been attending to the twins' education since their dismissal from the public-school system two years ago. Éva detests her, probably for her beauty and youth. She has also caught me staring covetously at her on more than one occasion, but is unaware of our affair.

I am writing in my new leather-bound journal at the dining room table. The Faber-Castell paper is exquisite and allows the ink to glide gracefully from my Montblanc-146. Both diary and pen were *Hanukkah* presents from Éva. The girls got me a luxury hamper of preserves, honey, chocolate and biscuits. Lily and Emilia are growing up fast, having shared a unique childhood together that only identical twins could. But their adolescences will be different, I'm sure.

I have to admit that these thoughtful *Hanukkah* gifts were not reciprocated. Last December was an expensive time for me as I endeavoured to resurrect my career as a Pathologist with a series of financial sweeteners to the non-Jewish medical elite of Heidelberg and beyond. Éva remains ignorant of these bribes, and I pray that they help me to find more permanent and fulfilling work this year.

How could I, one of Germany's most eminent pathologists, lose so much in so short a time? I'm not even fully Jewish. I must accept that I have some Hebrew blood on my paternal side, but my mother was of pure Aryan stock. Surely her bloodline courses through these veins more strongly than the sluggish torrents of a half-Jewish father.

Éva is a Jewess through and through. Our daughters are therefore considered Jewesses and accordingly judged by German society as undesirables. The dirty smear of Jewishness seems to taint everything we do. I've thought of divorcing Éva several times, especially when things got bad at the university. To disassociate completely from her must surely be a step in the right direction for my struggling medical career. But the twins need a father and Éva a husband. She also wants a son. Likewise, I too want a male heir, although a Jewish son again seems like a bitter pill to swallow in the current political climate of racial hygiene.

Sabbath 12th February

Despite all the bribes and clandestine abortions for the rich and influential of Aryan high society, my career has failed to reignite as planned. It makes me swell with rage when I think back to those draconian Nuremberg Laws and the stripping of my German citizenship. The rot actually began two years earlier when I found myself expelled from Heidelberg University. I appealed the decision of course, and was able to show only a tenuous Jewish bloodline on my father's side. But my marriage to Éva Székely of Munkács in 1924 had already sealed my fate.

Why? How? I was Doctor József Sárkány, a renowned Pathologist and Senior Lecturer in Anatomy. I was so sought after, so respected – and so very proud. Hubris was my middle name. I was frequently called upon as an expert witness in high-profile cases where my extensive knowledge of pathology and forensic medicine helped to elucidate a cause of death that was beyond any reasonable doubt.

I was once famous throughout Germany and Europe. My postmortem examinations were second to none, and I was able to shed light upon all manners of deaths, both natural and unnatural. I lectured at Heidelberg University – and with an imminent professorial chair, I'd hoped to conduct research into the hereditary causes of epilepsy, and to explore the roles of certain drugs in the development of the fetal brain. I had already procured ethical approval and funding for this venture, and had hoped to work closely with colleagues at the Kaiser Wilhelm Institute in Berlin.

Then Hitler's Enabling Act scuppered my dreams of academia. My world imploded.

Sabbath 19th March

I've been following the heightened debate on eugenics with great interest and have just finished reading the papers of Brandt, Hoche and Gross. The concept of euthanasia fascinates me, and I've become all too aware of what's going on across many special centres in Germany. The term 'useless mouths' is currently in vogue amongst fashionable doctors and scientists. Usually applied to the cerebrally defective, this *zeitgeist* phrase is not without controversy; with many physicians and psychiatrists arguing that mental capacity is just one aspect of life. The miracle of living, they assert, must surely trump any argument to destroy life – whether it is based on medical, anthropological or even economic grounds. I do not agree with this.

I have lately written on the subject of religion and pseudoscientific sentimentality in medicine, but have been unable to find a publisher under a suitable alias. I have argued that society will soon come to realise that the humane elimination of the mentally sick is a beneficial act for all. Not only is it a merciful emancipation for the victim, but a relief for the long-suffering family and society at large. This new generation of doctors must therefore take the

Hippocratic Oath with a hefty pinch of salt.

The works of Dr. Eberl have inspired me to think more closely about the brains of the sick – Jew and Aryan alike. His latest notion compares German society to a giant centipede: a fascinating analogy for students of medicine and anthropology to explore. The racial pollution and eugenics arguments have, rightly or wrongly, progressed onto the very nature of the Jew and other inferior races that inhabit Germany at this time.

Although Eberl is a staunch anti-Semite, I respect his ideas and would happily collaborate with him if my soiled mantle of Jewish ancestry could be somehow washed clean. He argues, like me, that the new breed of doctors must not only heal, but be equally able to euthanise. And like me, he sees the fundamental importance of scientific experiment. My pathological knowledge and dissecting skills would be an ideal adjunct to this facet of his research. My learned shoulders are patiently waiting to be stood upon by the Aryan doctors of our present and future.

Wednesday 30th March

I returned home after lunching out. I usually liaise with the au pair at a little riverside café, but Lena didn't show up today. This wasn't the first time I'd been stood up as she's occasionally obliged to stay back to perform an extra household chore or pop to the shops. At least it's only Wednesday. A no-show from Lena on Friday would deprive me of more than food alone; for I have an understanding with the café owner on this day in which he rents me out his bedroom for an hour or so. I sometimes give him a little extra money, although his usual recompense is having the girl to himself for the second half-hour whilst I dine with his wife downstairs.

Éva must be aware of my little affair by now, but seems to tolerate it for the children's sake. It doesn't really bother me either way.

I'm back from lunch early today and was surprised to catch Éva and the twins loitering inside my study. My wife flushed and quickly departed, beckoning Lily and Emilia to follow. The girls however hesitated over a pile of papers on my desk. They bore slight frowns and looked both confused and awkward.

"What's the matter?" I asked. "Where is Lena?"

"Nothing's wrong, Daddy," said Emilia. "Well, we're both famished, but Lena's gone out to pick up some bread and jam for our sandwiches. Mummy says that bread and jam are all we can afford."

"Nonsense! Why are you in my private study?"

"Mummy was just giving it a quick dust and we followed her inside looking for biscuits."

"You're an even better liar than me, little madam! But what's caught your eye on my desk?"

"Daddy, what is eu-than-asia?"

"That's something that a young girl who hasn't even had her *Bat Mitzvah* should not be concerning herself about."

Éva must have been eavesdropping outside. She walked in calmly and began to speak in a didactic, impassive tone:

"Your father is reading and writing about things that are unwelcome in my home. His books and scientific papers are never to leave this room. I want no discussion on such matters in any other part of the house. But to answer your question: euthanasia is murder. That's it, end of conversation."

As she turned to leave the study again, I called out to my wife but she blanked me.

"Is it really murder, Daddy?" asked Emilia.

"No, of course not," I replied. "But since you persist in getting an answer from me, I shall say that euthanasia means *good death*. It is dying with dignity and respect."

"Then why does Mummy call it murder?" asked Olivia.

"Imagine Mummy has a terrible accident one day and is left in a permanent coma: would it not be kinder to let her pass away rather than to go on suffering, with no quality of life? Well, allowing her to die mercifully and painlessly is a form of euthanasia – a good death: an important final human right."

"And is this the same as eu-gen-ics, Daddy?" asked Olivia.

"You girls have been nosy little busybodies!"

"I know what eugenics is," interrupted Emilia. "I have skim-read your letter to the German Medical Journal. You believe that some people have better blood than others. You and your doctor friends want to make more of this good blood by getting rid of all the bad."

Sabbath 2nd April

My unexpected association with Dr. Hannah Fischer has been most stimulating, both physically and intellectually. She is developing powerful connections in the German medical hierarchy which can only be good for my own career. One day I may even marry her. A son and heir from a woman such as Hannah would be desirable indeed.

Sorry, Éva: I do still care about you, but cannot contend with career, religion and racial disgrace at this crucial stage of Germany's rebirth under the banner of National Socialism. Blood and honour is everything. Purging my blood of Jewish taint will surely lead to the latter, bringing me reputation and wealth alongside it. I will transform myself from a *Mischling* maggot into an Aryan butterfly. But this glorious metamorphosis will not be complete until the butterfly has taken flight.

To be wholly reunited with my ego fills me with boundless excitement. I want to feel infallible again, untouchable and secure in my academic erudition. Am I pompous and arrogant? Yes, almost certainly. But am I not approaching the zenith of my professional game? Of course, yes, undoubtedly. In the world of pathology, I am Kaiser József Sárkány. Nobody will stand in the way of this destiny. And no man, Aryan or otherwise, comes close to me in skill and intellect.

Sabbath 9th April

This evening has seen my fracturing marriage symbolised in broken glass. For I've just had a gorgeous row with Éva. The woman is pregnant, for God's sake!

I immediately suggested an abortion. She exploded with anger and screamed hysterically. I narrowly evaded the *Menorah* as it whistled past my head before crashing through the dining room window.

Human pathology is the study of sickness and disease in our society: as a pathologist married to a Jewess, the two would appear to go hand in hand.

Wednesday 9th November

It's Éva's birthday. I took her to a nice little Jewish bistro in the Bergheim district, situated on the south bank of the Neckar River. The owner was a familiar patient of mine.

We left shortly after nine and decided not to take a cab back home. The night air was cold, but dry and still. The gloomy streets were bathed in a bluish moonlight and we held each other's hands as we stared up at the stars.

Éva pecked me on the cheek and whispered in my ear: "That was a lovely meal, József." Her warm breath and fringe tickled my ear, making me recoil.

"I'm glad you enjoyed it, my dear. It's so nice to see you devour a rare sirloin with such relish."

"And don't forget that gargantuan pudding. But I'm eating for two, remember: well, that's my excuse for being such a glutton, so there!"

"I'm just glad to see you've got your appetite back, especially after all those months of morning sickness. Not long to go now."

"Baby András will come when he's ready to say hello."

"You're still convinced it's a boy then?"

"After having the twins so long ago now, God will surely

7

bless us with a boy. Lena also agrees."

I looked at her incredulously and asked: "What does a twenty-year-old au pair from Poland know about such matters?"

"Because, my dear József, she happens to have four younger brothers, and reliably assures me that my bump is definitely a masculine shape!"

"Assuming you're right, how do you feel about the holy snip?"

"I know, poor little mite! But the covenant of circumcision is a special bond with God and an integral part of our identity. It doesn't hurt, does it?"

"Now let me see. Nope, I really can't remember."

"Well it couldn't have been that bad then!"

We continued to walk, holding hands. After several minutes of silence, Éva stopped abruptly and turned round to face me. Her eyes were puffy and bloodshot. She had been crying in silence under the veils of her winter hat and scarf. The conversation that followed was contrived and tarnished by my palpable deceit. But lies seemed like the best option for me at that moment, especially with Éva being heavily pregnant and in a fragile mental state.

"Do you love me, József?"

"What do you think? You're my wife and mother to my children."

"But I'm a Jew, am I not?"

"As am I, you silly woman!"

"No, you're not. For a true Jewish man would put his religion before everything else, even his profession. I often feel your frustration and anger, I really do. The twins can sense it too. It upsets them, confuses them."

"What are you talking about? I'm getting cold. Come on, what's your point?"

"You make me feel guilty for marrying you. I feel as if I've somehow poisoned you with my Jewishness and destroyed your career. I wish I could simply wave a magic wand and let all my ancestry disappear. I'm sorry for what I am, József. I have freely given you my body, my womanhood, my unadulterated love. But I am a Jewess – and will always be so."

"O Éva, that's enough! I couldn't ask for a better life. I am proud of my own Jewish heritage and equally proud of yours. I'm a Jew first, and a doctor second. That's really how it is, despite your trivial doubts."

"So, you're a doctor before a husband and father then?"

"Now you're being facetious. What I meant is… Do you smell burning?"

I grabbed Éva's hand. Something was wrong. We hastily entered the Jewish Quarter. There was nobody in sight. Heavy smoke was in the air and a sickly glow hung over the rooftops. The main street before us was strewn with rubble and shattered glass. Several tenements had boarded up windows. Others had been dreadfully vandalised. Crude graffiti adorned many of the shop windows.

Turning a sharp corner, a hideous site then came into full view: the Königsberg Synagogue was ablaze!

Feeling a sense of bewilderment and growing panic, I decided to take a rapid detour through the old Jewish cemetery. To my astonishment, the place was alive with activity. It wasn't long before we came across a group of men dancing merrily around a grave. They were clearly intoxicated and were holding bottles of beer in one hand and lighted torches in the other. On closer inspection, I noticed that the tombstone had been toppled over and cracked. I then discerned two men with spades, half submerged in the mud and shoveling earth at a ferocious pace.

My God! They were exhuming a corpse!

I seized Éva by the arm and hastily turned around. But too late! As we hurried away in the opposite direction, these drunken desecrators caught sight of us and began to hurl abuse. I calmed my wife and told her to keep her head down. We picked up speed and exited through the cemetery gates back onto the lamplit streets.

The men continued to shout and then run towards us. Seizing my overcoat, one man pulled me down onto the concrete pavement. A volley of vicious kicks followed in rapid succession, first to my belly and then to my ribcage. I writhed in agony as a muddy boot struck me under the diaphragm, emptying my lungs and leaving me gasping.

I turned my head desperately towards Éva. She was screaming and pummeling one of my assailants on the back. He swung round and yanked on her long black hair. She lost her balance and stumbled to the hard ground, falling face-first onto her heavily pregnant belly.

"She's with child!" I cried. But it made no difference. A dull thud smashed into the side of my head… then nothing.

I don't know how long I laid unconscious for, but it was still dark when I came around. My head throbbed and I felt dazed and disorientated. A wave of nausea and panic then hit me. I managed to sit up just in time before ejecting my recent meal all over the pavement.

Éva! She was lying beside me, sobbing faintly. Her face was badly grazed and blood trickled from her nostrils. My God, the baby! Was the baby still alive?

"I'm losing it!" she whimpered. I staggered to my feet and just about managed to help her up. There was no one in sight. A nearby car was ablaze and I saw flames in the distance from a row of terrace houses. I called for help. Nobody came. There was nothing I could do except pray for a miracle.

I finally summoned up enough strength to escort my wife down a back-alley. Hammering on every available window pane and door, I shouted for urgent assistance. An elderly woman opened her front door. I begged her to call for a doctor. She beckoned us inside and rushed to the telephone.

Éva was now pale and clammy. She sank into a chair. It was then that I saw the pinkish fluid trickling down her legs. She screamed as a contraction kicked in, causing a gush of sanguine clots to pour onto the rug.

The old woman called me over to the telephone table, explaining that the duty doctor wished to speak to me. He introduced himself. I didn't catch his name, but his voice was somewhat familiar. The exchange that followed was surreal:

"Dispatch an ambulance at once! My pregnant wife has been assaulted and is losing the baby. She's haemorrhaging badly. Please, hurry!"

"You must stay calm. You need to lay your wife on her side and bend her knees up. Don't give her anything to eat or drink; a tiny sip of water at most."

"Yes, fine. But please come quickly!"

"An ambulance has been alerted. I just need to take down your address and personal details."

I began with our location, assisted by the kind lady who had already written down the full address for me. There followed a pregnant pause. The doctor began to speak, then hesitated:

"You're calling from the... Jewish Quarter – yes?"

"That's right. Is there a problem?"

"We are extremely busy tonight. This is a difficult zone for our ambulances to currently access. The hospital must also prioritise resources for our German citizens, you understand."

"So my wife must bleed to death whilst my unborn child asphyxiates, yes?"

"You have to appreciate that the life of a Jewess and her baby is of little or no consequence to German society at this time. Aryan families will always take precedence. Maybe you can contact some of your own kind?"

"Now listen! I may be a Jew – actually a half-Jew – but I still retain a certain influence in the medical fraternity of this country. My name is Dr. Sárkány..."

"József Sárkány, the pathologist?"

"Yes... sorry, who are you?"

"I am Dr. Josef Mengele. We were acquaintances at Frankfurt. You actually tutored me in pathology for a term."

"Yes, I remember you."

"Dr. Sárkány, I'm sorry for our little misunderstanding. I'll dispatch a transport immediately and organise an emergency team to be prepared for your imminent arrival."

I threw down the telephone in anger and disbelief.

"Is the ambulance on its way?" asked the old woman.

I nodded. Éva gave a strained half-smile before apologising to the lady for the dreadful mess on the floor. She tutted and shook her head:

"Don't you worry about that, my dear. I'm far more concerned about you and baby."

"Thank you for your kindness and understanding," I replied.

My wife nodded feebly in agreement before another wave of agony gripped her. She gritted her teeth and began to squeal. Beads of sweat erupted from her brow as a soupy brown fluid dribbled down her ankles.

The ambulance arrived a few minutes later and conveyed us to the nearest hospital. Upon arrival, Éva was taken immediately to theatre. I waited in a side room.

After what seemed like an eternity, a midwife entered, holding a cup and saucer. I arose from my chair.

"How is she? Is the baby alright?"

"Your wife is sick. But she's over the worst of it. She had to have a caesarian section. The placenta had torn away from the womb lining and was starving baby of oxygen."

"An abruption!" I cried. I told her that I was a doctor. She frowned.

"Your wife has lost a great deal of blood and is currently being resuscitated with intravenous fluids and a blood transfusion. Thankfully, the obstetrician has managed to control the haemorrhaging."

"And the child?"

The midwife looked into my eyes and sighed:

"You have a beautiful baby boy. Congratulations to you both. He was very flat when he came out and is still being attended to by our paediatricians. They managed to get him

12

to start breathing on his own, but he was very blue and had inhaled a considerable amount of meconium. It's early days yet, but if he does pull through, well… there may be some… damage."

"I have to see them both – now!"

"All in good time," the nurse replied. "Mother and child will shortly be moving to Intensive Care once they're both stabilised. In the meantime, I would suggest that you see a doctor about your own wounds. That gash on your head certainly needs stitches, and I wouldn't be surprised if you've broken a few ribs by the way you're breathing. Once you've been patched up, I am sure you'll soon be able to see your wife and son. Anyway, drink up your tea while it's hot."

A tall handsome man entered. Groomed and scented, he wore a pristine white coat with a stethoscope round his neck. His black hair was swept back off his ample forehead, his eyes dark and penetrating:

"Hello József. I spoke to you earlier on the phone. I am Dr. Mengele."

I thanked him for his help. He asked after my wife and child. I told him that they were currently stable. A porter then arrived and pushed me to the emergency department in a wheelchair. Mengele followed behind. My head was pounding and my body ached all over.

A nurse met me at the reception desk. She blushed as Mengele ambled over and gave her some brief instructions. I was taken into a side-room where Mengele personally attended to my scalp laceration and closed the wound with a series of extremely neat stitches, thirteen to be precise. After a visit to the X-ray department, I was lucky to have only sustained two broken ribs and a sprained wrist. My abdomen was bruised, but there was no internal damage.

"Thank you for seeing to me so quickly, Josef. I'm sure there are more urgent cases than mine requiring your attention."

"That's what old friends are for, József. I'd be a poor doctor indeed if I didn't look out for my own kind. Anyway,

I'm off duty in a little under an hour. I'm only covering a couple of shifts here this week to help pay for my SS application."

"What's happening tonight, do you know?"

"Haven't you heard? There's a national pogrom. It seems to stem from the assassination of a German diplomat in Paris. He was shot last night by a Polish Jew in revenge for the deportation of his parents."

"But why attack the Jews in Germany? We're not Poles, and have nothing to do with it."

"You know how it is. The nation wants a scapegoat – and shit travels downward."

"What's that supposed to mean?"

"Nothing… look, József – if I were you, I'd take your wife and get the hell out of Germany. It's not safe to be a Jew in this country any more. Go back to Hungary and live in relative peace and safety. There's talk about ghettos and deporting all Jews to work camps in the East. They're already rounding up Jewish intellectuals and sending them into Protective Custody."

"Protective Custody – what are you talking about?"

"Wake up, József! They're building concentration camps all over Germany. Many are already incarcerated in Dachau and Sachsenhausen, and I'm sure there'll be many thousands of new prisoners after tonight."

"You seem to know an awful lot about it, Josef."

"Yes, of course. National Socialism is the future. There are great opportunities ahead."

"Unless you're a Jew…"

"Unless you're a Jew," Mengele murmured. "But let's not talk about such things. You will go back to Hungary and live a comfortable life there. The next time we meet, we'll both be reputable doctors, living our own separate lives but united in one common goal – helping others."

I nodded in acquiescence, but felt an icy chill. Mengele was a good liar: I knew this for certain.

I eventually returned to the maternity suite and decided

to bed down for the night on a comfy chair in the side room. The midwife paid me another visit and brought me a blanket and pillow. I asked her for a pen and some paper to record the harrowing events of tonight whilst they were still fresh in my memory. As if I'd ever forget them!

She was glad to see that my head had been sutured and dressed, and brought me in a mug of hot cocoa, together with paper and pen. We talked a little longer. Her name was Ilka, and she was a native of Heidelberg. She told me to get some rest and reassured me that she'd keep me informed of any updates regarding my wife and baby. I sipped my cocoa and turned to pen and paper.

Thursday 10th November

This morning I was devastated to hear that Éva began to haemorrhage again in the night. Despite rapid transfusions, the only therapeutic option was to perform an emergency hysterectomy.

I met the gynaecologist who explained that the uterus had failed to contract down adequately and how the blood had seeped through the muscle layers of her womb.

The baby is currently in an oxygen tent and incubator. His name is András, after his mother's father. He is just over five weeks premature and has underdeveloped lungs which are hampering his breathing. Various wires and tubes obscure his face and tiny limbs.

I spoke with the paediatrician. She explained that baby András was markedly underweight and had suffered from significant distress *in utero*, with hypoxia secondary to aspiration of meconium. She talked about the possibility of cerebral palsy, and told me that it was too early to assess the severity of any potential handicap.

A MURDER OF CROWS

Diary of Dr. József Sárkány, 1940

Bernburg Railway Station, Friday 22nd November

My medical career is still floundering, although I have made some important contacts on the inside of the Aryan Hippocratic circle. After 18 months of mundane work at the local mental asylum, my less than professional relationship with Dr. Hannah Fischer has granted me an unofficial position at the Bernburg Psychiatric Institute, where she currently works as a research assistant. The job requires me to stay on site for much of the working week, and I'm fortunate enough to be able to lodge with Hannah in her nearby apartment. Returning to Heidelberg on the noon-train every Friday also means that I'm back home just before sunset and the start of *Shabbat*.

My work at Bernburg is of fundamental importance. It gives me access to a wide range of research material, and I've even started to perform a few autopsies for the medical director, Dr. Irmfried Eberl. As a high-ranking SS officer, this brilliant and ambitious young psychiatrist could be my stepping stone onto the higher echelons of the new medical fraternity.

An unreserved and outspoken anti-Semite, Eberl is visibly aware of my Jewish connections. However, he appears to tolerate this, albeit unofficially, and for how long I'm not sure. What is certain is the powerful grip Dr. Fischer holds over him. Hannah has a way with men in authority, and is able to exploit her youth and sexuality in order to advance her own career. This impresses me greatly. But where do I fit into her feminine jigsaw of lovers and advocates? What can I possibly do for her – this deliciously sophisticated fisher of men?

Heidelberg, Sabbath 23rd November

The past two years have been fraught with difficulties for my wife. Éva has never fully recovered from that fateful November night. She suffers from bouts of crippling depression and would no doubt have taken her own life by now if it were not for the children and her strong faith. All of her time and energy goes into the care of our two-year-old son, András. He has a severe form of cerebral palsy, requiring round-the-clock care. He suffers from epileptic seizures on an almost daily basis. He is quadriplegic and has a pronounced scoliosis. His enhanced muscle tone has already led to some contractures in his hands. Bottle feeding requires patience and care in order to prevent choking.

Shabbat ended this evening with another family row. Once András was bathed and settled in his special cot, Éva wasted no time in attacking me. The twins sat quietly by the fire, listening intently:

"Why I married you, God only knows! My mother warned me that you were no good. You're the most self-centred, arrogant man I've ever met. So bloody selfish! I don't see you for most of the week. You've pretty much abandoned me and the twins, and have no interest whatsoever in being a proper father to your handicapped son that needs you more than ever.

"Just look at your girls over there! Have you even noticed them? They're now thirteen, but you treat them as if they were five-year olds. You didn't even come to their *Bat Mitzvahs* last year because you were too damn busy promoting your great comeback into the medical world. I'm so very proud of my daughters. They have shown great compassion and maturity in dealing with their disabled baby brother, and have always been there for their mother in what seems like an inexhaustible supply of love and care. Thank you, Lily. Thank you, Emilia.

"As for you, all you really care about is your bloody career and reputation! Everything else is just a distraction.

Well, I'm sick to the teeth of it! I'm tired of your constant lies, your womanising, your affairs, your ridiculous notions of medical ethics, your half-baked heritage, and your perpetual shame for being married to ME – your WIFE – a full-blooded JEWESS and proud of it!'"

Heidelberg, Sunday 24th November

Before I departed for the train back to Bernburg, Éva showed me a letter that was delivered to our home address last week. It outlined the particulars pertaining to the 'Law for the Prevention of Genetically Diseased Offspring'.

The family is therefore required to undergo preliminary blood tests before attending a Genetic Health Court this Thursday. Here, a panel of racial hygiene experts will determine whether we all qualify for compulsory sterilisation.

The letter went on to state that: '… the individual named András György Sárkány, born on November 10th 1938, is suspected of harbouring the following genetic defects: congenital mental deficiency, hereditary epilepsy and hereditary chorea'. The concluding paragraph explained that both parents and all siblings of the aforementioned may therefore be 'rendered incapable of procreation'. This is ironic in that my wife no longer has a womb.

Bernburg Psychiatric Hospital, Monday 25th November

I told Hannah about the letter. She smiled. We went to see Irmfried and explained that all was going to plan. Eberl is to make contact with Karl Brandt who will be sitting on the panel of judges. They will recommend my son be transferred to Bernburg for a full medical evaluation and further tests.

Hannah has volunteered to do the deed. We agreed upon gentle suffocation.

Bernburg Psychiatric Hospital, Tuesday 26th November

I'm rather out of sorts today. Am I doing the right thing? It's surely for the best. There'll be no pain, no suffering. The whole process will be over in a matter of seconds, and then the Sárkány family can start to rebuild its life again. I'm really doing it for Éva. I need to release her from that yoke of motherhood; a life sentence of round-the-clock caring that is already beginning to grind her down and devour her, body and soul.

Heidelberg, Wednesday 27th November

I returned to Heidelberg and joined my family for some routine blood tests at the hospital. The court hearing is scheduled for tomorrow afternoon.

My wife seemed to be in high spirits today. She kept herself busy with the laundry and ironing. Lena bathed the twins and washed their hair. She then assisted Éva in bathing András and preparing his clothes for tomorrow. I was instructed to clean the pushchair and polish all the metalwork. I picked up my best suit from the dry cleaners before supper. Éva showed off her new grey blouse and jacket. In the evening, she insisted on seeing the twins in their formal outfits. She later went through some German elocution with them, together with the essential do's and don'ts of public etiquette.

Heidelberg, Thursday 28th November

After attending the Genetic Health Court today, the panel concluded that our son's impairments were solely due to prenatal trauma, resulting in acute hypoxic brain injury and cerebral palsy. The healthy nature of our twin daughters further supported the case for a non-hereditary causalogy.

Right on cue, Dr. Karl Brandt proceeded to make a formal request that we visit to Dr. Irmfried Eberl at the Bernburg Psychiatric Institute. He informed us that Eberl was experimenting with pioneering therapies for both epilepsy and muscular contractures. Turning round to Éva, I saw a look of deep mistrust on her face.

Heidelberg, Monday 2nd December

A private ambulance pulled up outside the house at seven this morning. Éva held onto András whilst I took charge of the pushchair and baggage. The girls were at home today with Lena.

Hannah Fischer accompanied us in the back of the ambulance, and I introduced her to my wife as my work colleague at Bernburg. Hannah offered her hand in friendship, but Éva snubbed her. She was angry and stressed, and in no mood for pleasantries this morning:

"I suppose you're another one sleeping with my husband."

I flinched and tried to laugh it off. Hannah blushed, but remained focused and professional.

The journey to Bernburg was a silent one. The two women exchanged glares in the back of the vehicle whilst I helped attend to András. We crossed the River Saale and arrived at the hospital just after eleven. The drive had thankfully been a good one for my son, and he slept for most of the way.

Our appointment with Dr. Eberl was at noon. Punctual as ever, he introduced himself under the guise of Dr. Schneider, and immediately started to interact with our son. Highly groomed and smelling of cologne, he came across as a caring and sophisticated specialist – young and good looking, with penetrating eyes, toothbrush moustache and immaculate Brylcreemed hair. My wife's frosty stance slowly began to thaw as his charming personality and erudition filled the room.

Eberl paused momentarily, glancing over at me. Dr. Fischer was also in the office, sitting quietly in one corner behind Éva. I turned round to look at Hannah. Her short skirt and slip were shifted up to show off her glossy black stockings and suspender belt straps. She gave a gentle nod to Eberl and slowly uncrossed and crossed her legs. He ogled momentarily before composing himself and smirking:

"I would like to keep András at the hospital for a few days to run some rudimentary tests. This will involve small samples of blood, saliva, sweat, urine and stool. I would also like to perform a lumbar puncture to extract some cerebrospinal fluid."

Éva's face instantly bleached. Eberl assured her that her son would be looked after by the very best paediatric doctors and nurse specialists. She looked at me, almost despairingly. I somewhat reluctantly held her hand and told her that everything would be alright. She suddenly fired off some pertinent questions to Eberl who deflected them with the dexterity and ease of a seasoned politician. The three conspirators kept their cool. The façade was maintained. My wife finally submitted.

We agreed to travel back to Heidelberg in a taxi laid on by the hospital, and arranged to collect András on Thursday afternoon. Éva politely asked if she could have a tour of the paediatric wing and meet some of the nurses. Eberl seemed put out by this request and tapped his fat gold Rolex. He explained that he was giving an important lunchtime seminar, and that it would be more convenient for her to have a guided tour upon her return on Thursday.

Éva was clearly troubled by this reply. But what could she do? Hannah Fischer got up from her chair and approached the child. Eberl picked up his telephone and called for a nurse and porter. My wife swooped up András and hugged him tightly, showering his forehead in kisses. She fussed and checked that he'd got his favourite teddy – a motheaten *Steiff* bear called 'Stitch' that had belonged to her younger brother when he was a boy. Éva had inherited the bear after he died from scarlet fever.

A nurse and porter shortly arrived. My wife produced several lists for the nurse, including all sorts of detailed information on feeding times, bath routines, medication schedules and a whole inventory of items she'd packed. As I looked at her going through the particulars of what had become her daily grind, I pitied her love and devotion to such a pitiful specimen of humanity. A Jewish mother's love for her son – however defective he may be – is unconditional, self-sacrificing... sublime.

As I departed the office behind Éva, she halted just outside the doorway and turned around. Her teary eyes looked once more upon her precious little boy as she blew him a kiss and whispered:

"I'll see you very soon, my love. Mummy wants the best for you, and these good doctors will help you to get better."

I suggested that we go to the refectory for lunch. Éva wasn't hungry and took a few sips of black tea only. I tried the beef stew which was very good.

Our transport back to Heidelberg had been booked for three. This delayed departure would allow me to attend Dr. Eberl's seminar and therefore fulfill my final part of the bargain. After two helpings of apple strudel, I made my excuses to Éva and headed off in the direction of the lecture theatre. She seemed fine with me leaving her for an hour or so, saying that she'd take a quiet stroll around the hospital grounds to collect her thoughts and blow out the cobwebs. The weather was cold, but bright and dry.

The lecture theatre was packed to capacity. Hannah Fischer had saved me a seat next to her in the front row. I looked behind me at the animated audience sitting impatiently in the shadows of the brightly illuminated front stage. I pilfered a pen and paper from Hannah as Dr. Eberl entered to a flourish of applause. I took down his lecture verbatim, in my own form of pathologist's shorthand. His introduction was as follows:

"Ladies and gentleman, welcome. My name is Dr. Irmfried Eberl, although I'm generally known to my patients as the good Dr. Schneider. Now, I want you all to think of our society as a gigantic centipede. It is precisely the sum of its healthy individual parts that produces the organism's mobility, strength and wellbeing. Any aberrations must therefore be surgically excised so that new healthy tissue can grow in its place. This has nothing to do with medical ethics, but is about biological and racial hygiene. The health of our Aryan civilisation must always take precedence over that of its individual members. Therefore, we must not only abort these deleterious abnormalities, but be ready to destroy those mutant creatures that currently swarm in our hospitals, sanatoria and asylums."

Eberl now signalled to an assistant who left behind a side curtain and re-entered the auditorium, wheeling in a young child. The gurgles and wheezes were familiar to me. The specimen on display; this gift of my own flesh and blood, was the penultimate sacrifice I had to make in the pact with Eberl and Fischer. Hannah furtively put a hand on my groin and gently squeezed. She then whispered a thank you in my ear. The effect was oddly arousing, but also filled me with conflicting thoughts of pride, guilt and betrayal.

With a look of revulsion, Eberl continued:

"Now, my learned guests – this is precisely what I am talking about. The little monster grunting before us is the end-product of centuries of hereditary degeneracy. Behold, the baby Jew! Such grotesque beings only serve to drain and mutilate the organism as a whole, releasing its parasitic toxins that both paralyse and corrupt.

"It must therefore be the most sacred duty of any doctor to restore balance to society by the application of a merciful death. I stress the word *merciful* here, for we are none of us butchers, but respectable and humane medical scientists. But we must remain vigilant in the fight against this special form of genetic malignancy. In the restitution of public decency, we must learn to adapt our arsenal against the bacillus of racial degeneracy and the throttling mould of world Jewry.

"We physicians must consequently face our own ethical

struggles. In the name of eugenics and public health, we must not only cull, but experiment. There is much to be learned from these creatures, both *in vivo* and postmortem: for ultimately, it is a battle of life and death – the survival and procreation of the fittest over the weak. As future doctors, there is a plethora of opportunities ahead of you, whether it is in the fields of euthanasia and racial pollution, or in the pioneering work of medical experimentation and biological warfare. The prospects are endless. We are all standing on the shoulders of giants!"

András began to cry out before going limp. I sensed another seizure coming on, and decided that I couldn't watch any more. Although I'd been fully complicit in this twisted form of fairground freak show, the emotional impact of seeing my naked and vulnerable son on display was shocking. I hurriedly exited from the auditorium. A handful of others also left with me, mainly women, all weeping. One of them stopped at the exit, turned round and shouted:

"Shame on you all! How many broken oaths sit in this travesty of a lecture hall? First, do no harm!"

But the temple stones at Cos are crumbling and decayed. Like it or not, we are now in the postmodern world of Nietzsche and Schopenhauer. Nihilism is the new medicine of the masses… and nothingness needs no oaths.

As I walked towards the solitary figure of my wife sitting on a bench, I was torn in two about what I should do next. But there was nothing more I could do. The final part of the conspiracy had to play itself out. My son had to die so that my wife could live.

"How was the lecture?" she asked.

"Dull," was my terse reply.

Heidelberg, Tuesday 3rd December

Éva was restless and uneasy this morning, picking up on my own anxieties and growing sense of guilt. I tried to calm her, but she knew something was amiss.

"You've heard something haven't you? Something was said at that lunchtime lecture, and it's made you uneasy. What is it? The last thing I want before *Hanukkah* is a bloody *Shiva!*"

I explained to her that medicine was striving ever forward with new concepts and ideologies, but its moral backbone and ethical foundations remained set in stone. I also reaffirmed my status within the medical community, and explained that no doctor or nurse would dare to harm the child of such an eminent pathologist.

Heidelberg, Thursday 5th December

Today will be the day of liberation for my wife. The euthanasia of our handicapped son must surely set her free.

We arrived back at Bernburg Hospital just before noon. Eberl was officially away at a conference in Austria, but I caught a glimpse of him peering out from a first-floor window in the extermination wing. We were told the news by Dr. Heinrich Bunke, Eberl's deputy medical officer, who went under the pseudonym of Dr. Keller. Hannah Fischer was also present. The official cause of death was 'bronchopneumonia'.

Although I was expecting it, the news hit me hard. I suppose it was the finality of the whole thing. When I inquired about an autopsy, Éva crumpled in my arms and sobbed. Bunke asked Dr. Fischer to escort her out of the office, but she refused to leave and screamed. With a gesture from Bunke, Hannah silently left the room.

My wife and I were now alone with Dr. Bunke, although I knew for sure that the room was bugged. Éva's fierce maternal instinct came to the fore as she laid into the slippery adversary sitting before her.

"Where's Schneider?" she asked. "I want to offer my congratulations for his sterling performance the other day. He's certainly a better actor than you, Keller."

"He's away in Austria to…"

"Shut up! It was a rhetorical question. I know he's still here at this killing centre. I expect he's already listening in to this wired conversation. He's doubtless also fucking that blonde slut of a doctor who's just left us. Did she do it? Was she the cloaked assassin? Was it her hands that murdered my son? And what did she use? Poison? A pillow perhaps? Or did she strangle him with one of her cheap black stockings?"

Bunke looked bemused and flustered. He glanced over to me for assistance, but I was rather enjoying my wife's liberating rant.

"Don't look to him for help!" she continued. "József Sárkány is no more than an impotent little half-Jew that only looks out for himself: and to think that he's actually been working here – my own husband and father of my children – practising his so-called 'medicine' at this specialist centre of institutionalised infanticide."

"Now please listen to me, Mrs. Sárkány. You're clearly upset and not thinking straight. We did everything we could for your son, but sometimes everything isn't enough. We made his final moments as comfortable as possible. He felt no pain. He drifted away peacefully in his sleep. I am very sorry for your loss, and…"

"Enough! Just tell me the truth. Did you kill my son?"

"Certainly not, Mrs. Sárkány. We are a hospital. Our doctors and nurses…"

"And what about the destruction of life unworthy of living?"

Bunke hesitated and glanced over to me again. I detected a slight sneer on his face. He removed his spectacles and began to polish them on a pocket handkerchief. But there was no respite as Éva continued her verbal assault:

"I too have read the papers of Heinze, Hoche and Binding that fill my husband's study at home. Did my idiot little boy tick all the right boxes? Did my Jewish baby monster require putting down? Yes, of course he did, didn't he! What's wrong with flushing a useless lump of flesh down the drain? Well, everything except his brain, of course. You butchers will be certain to preserve his brain for future research into his mother's Jewish degeneracy. Did you gas him to death? My God, you did, didn't you?"

"Doctors Heinze and Hoche are both brilliant psychiatrists," said Bunke, playing for time.

"And what of Karl Binding? Is he also one of your heroes?"

Bunke looked at Éva and grinned. He finally seemed to be enjoying their *tête-à-tête*:

"You are right, Mrs. Sárkány. Hoche and Binding jointly advocate euthanising all those who are intellectually dead. For they are no more than useless mouths, contributing nothing to society, but taking much succour from it in order to perpetuate their own futile survival. If killing such an aberration in infancy means that healthy lives are ultimately saved, then this would seem to me to be entirely justifiable."

"But those who you may perceive as mentally dead may in fact be capable of so much more. How can you quantify a person's ability to imagine, to dream, to love and to live? Before casting them aside as worthless ballast, must you not first consult with their family, friends and carers?"

"We must not cloud our clinical judgment with sentimentality. Such lives weigh heavily on the national burden, especially during a time of war. And perhaps one day soon, society will come to realise that the elimination of the mentally defunct is neither criminally or morally at fault, but is, in fact, an exceedingly beneficial act. As both judge and executioner, the modern doctor must have the conviction to hang and the stomach to endure the decay."

"And what of my poor son who lies decaying on some slab in your mortuary?"

"Think of it more as emancipation. Time heals, and whilst the death of your crippled boy is still raw and difficult to bear, I resolutely believe that you will thank us in the long run."

"Murderer! Who are you, really?"

"My name is Dr. Keller. I am assistant deputy to Dr. Schneider. And now, I really must take my leave. Good day to you both. And once again, I am sorry for your loss."

~

Heidelberg, Hanukkah I

Éva has for a long time suffered terrible pains in her pelvis and lower belly, no doubt secondary to all that birth trauma.

Tonight, I heard her crying in the bath when all her scars were on full display to her. These wounds will never truly heal. They are a constant reminder of *Kristallnacht* and the short, tragic life of her only son.

Heidelberg, Hanukkah II

I'm currently sleeping on the living room sofa.

I heard noises in the early hours and put on the lights. Éva tiptoed downstairs, mumbling to herself. She was sleepwalking; eyes wide open, clutching the scarred hollow that was once the sacred seat of her Jewish womb. I jotted down her words on paper. They might prove useful if she ever agreed to see a psychiatrist:

"Can't taste or smell or even feel the sun on my face. Satan has ripped out my womb, my womanhood, my soul. He has murdered my only son. O *Adonai!* Why? Why me? I have been reduced to a living corpse; a naked Jewess, barren and desolate. I scream out to Zion, but Zion does not reply. Oh Israel, where are you?"

These cries for God and Israel failed to move me. If anything, they excoriated the itch in me to leave her once and for all.

But I'm a coward, so I prefer to carry on the pretense for the time being.

Heidelberg, Hanukkah III

Éva's sleepwalking continued again tonight. One part of her mundane mumbling intrigued me more than the rest:

"How can such a genteel Jewess hold so much blood? I can smell it, taste in on my lips, and even feel it ebbing in the barren backdrop of my belly. But the blood of a Jewess is foul and tainted. Aryans balk at the thought of it adulterating their people with the stink of Jezebel, impervious even to the balms of even Cologne and Grasse."

With these words, I perceived her Jewish guilt oozing out of her like pus from some corrupted boil. Did I feel pity? Perhaps... a little – maybe. But my dominant sentiment was that of peculiar satisfaction, almost smugness. Yes, I must confess to having enjoyed her pain: it felt like providential justice in return for all the suffering and loss I'd been through on her behalf.

Heidelberg, Hanukkah IV

I lost my job at Bernburg today. I'd been stabbed in the back by Hannah Fischer who's only interest in me was a handicapped son that she couldn't wait to get her murderous hands on. I thought about appealing to Eberl, but realised that it was all too late.

I ruminated over the news all evening, sulking with my wife and growing ever more bitter. I began to feel that my redundancy was again all Éva's fault. She was so rude to Hannah and Irmfried, and made no effort to be civilised to them on my behalf.

Yes, my Jewess wife continues to blight my life.

Heidelberg, Hanukkah V

This evening is the fifth in the Festival of Lights.

Éva burst into tears after dinner and seemed to have some sort of hysterical seizure. Her womanhood, her maternal instinct, her very essence writhed and contorted in a lament of indescribable agony. Finally, she calmed a little, composed herself, and stopped pulling at her hair. Her cries became contracted into a weak and thready voice; her eyes fixed and emotionless. She finally recited a verse from Jeremiah:

"A voice was heard in Ramah, lamentation and bitter weeping; Rachel weeping for her children, refusing to be comforted because they are no more."

I must admit to finding the whole episode rather sensational and affected. I almost wanted to slap her round the face and tell her to get a grip of herself.

Heidelberg, Hanukkah VI

During the obligatory lighting of the sixth *Hanukkah* candle, Éva began what I can only describe as her great psychological purge. I determined to take the verbal assault on the chin, and remained passive, cold and silent:

"What kind of a father are you? The twins hardly know you. You never remember their birthday and haven't attended one of their parties since they were toddlers. They recently asked me whether I thought their Daddy loved them. You take no interest in their school work. Emilia has a real flair for art, but not once have you commented upon the pictures she puts up around the kitchen, hoping to gain your attention. Olivia loves music. Her pianoforte has really progressed over the past few months. She played a beautiful piece on her *Bat Mitzvah* last September. But you missed it all of course because Daddy was far too busy with more important matters at work.

"And then there's little András. Did you really know what they were going to do to him? Were you even a part of it? O God, please tell me that you knew nothing about it. *Adonai!* Help me!"

I did nothing to calm her. I didn't even embrace her or attempt to hold her hand. I actually feared her more than anything else, as her escalating doubts and suspicions had made her increasingly agitated and violent towards me.

I put laudanum in her wine. The opium acted quickly, and soon pacified her before she dozed off on the sofa. It was then that I noticed fresh razorblade cuts and cigarette burns over her forearms: these stigmata of internal turmoil and self-harm were all too familiar to me.

Heidelberg, Hanukkah VIII

Éva attained her catharsis tonight after dinner. The twins were staying out with friends, and were thankfully spared the verbal onslaught that was directed at their father:

"What kind of a Jew are you? You make me feel guilty every single day for my own culture and heritage. I am ashamed of duping you – a salvageable *Mischling* – into my life of subhuman taint… I know that you regret marrying me. I'm aware that your Jewish daughters are a great disappointment to you. And I can't even begin to imagine what you thought of your handicapped son and *Untermensch*. For here was a baby human that you'd been reading and writing about for so long. He exemplified your own definition of a useless eater, and was a perfect example of Jewish degeneracy, whose best hope in life was nothing more than a merciful death.

"What kind of a doctor are you? What sort of man trains for six years only to end up desecrating corpses for a living? And what kind of doctor shuns the living in preference for the dead? All that clinical training, prescribing, bedside manner, caring – all wasted on the dead!

"What kind of a man are you? You glide and wriggle in an oily matrix of obsequious falsehoods and broken oaths. You have no real friends. You use and abuse people to suit your own selfish means. You barge and tussle for another slippery rung up that never-ending ladder, pointlessly promoting your self-importance and vainglory.

"What kind of a husband are you? You treat me as your domestic slave. And at the same time, you expect me to be your wife, your mother… your lover. I can't remember the last time you kissed me on the lips and actually meant it. You show me no love, no intimacy. I've tried, yes, I've tried… The fact that I managed to conceive András at all is a bloody miracle! I remember the single occasion well. You were drunk and upset about some trivial matter at work. Lena was away for a week visiting friends, and you'd obviously been missing her carnal attentions. So your obedient wife did her duty; tolerating the fumbling gropes and handful of feeble thrusts… But you're far more interested in the au pair, aren't you? Does Lena give you what Éva clearly can't? I bet she does… all those lunchtime meetings and overnight conferences when you're both coincidently away from the house at the same time. Well, I've had enough of the charade. I want that Polish slut gone by New Year!"

Again, I just let her rant. She was clearly unwell and needed specialist help. Nevertheless, her barbed words hooked deeply into my flesh and began to erode my cool exterior and patient indifference.

Finally, I exploded in a pique of rage. There was no shouting, no quarrel. I simply struck her round the face with my fist. She immediately fell unconscious to the floor. I blew out the *Hanukkah* candles and closed the dining-room door behind me.

~

Diary of Dr. József Sárkány, 1941

<u>**Heidelberg, Sabbath 26th July**</u>

Time ticks by, the days blur into weeks, the weeks condense into months, seasons pass, weather changes – and all summers must eventually lead to snow. The ribbed ice of National Socialism begins to bite and sting.

We are not wanted here. We are not safe. I have finally

come to realise that the Sárkány family can no longer avoid the talons of the black SS crows. We must flee back to Hungary, to the safety of Munkács and the Carpathian Mountains.

Munkács, Hungary, Monday 1ˢᵗ September

The move itself was a sombre affair, although we were all glad to be departing from the ever-increasing hardships of Nazi Germany. We travelled ahead of the delivery lorry on the long trip east to Munkács. I divided the car journey over two days, stopping overnight in Budapest.

The final 300 miles to Subcarpathian Rus took us just over six hours, and we arrived at Éva's parents' house in the mid-afternoon sunshine. They live in a large thatched cottage with four good-sized bedrooms and several acres of land that backs onto an adjoining cherry orchard. This will be our temporary abode until we're able to find a new home of our own. Munkács is a vibrant community, with a population of around 15,000 Jews and thirty synagogues.

Éva's parents looked tired and strained when we pulled into the gravelled double driveway. They are both retired teachers and respectable members of the Hasidic community. They taught at the Hebrew gymnasium, my wife's *alma mater*, and soon to be our daughters' new school.

We exchanged kisses and embraces. Mrs. Székely was preparing her specialty roast for supper, which included a selection of choice vegetables picked fresh from the garden. The old-fashioned cottage was warm and welcoming, with a blazing log-fire in the living room and the comforting aromas of dark mahogany infused with roast chicken.

I suppose that this change of environment will help my wife overcome her melancholic demons, especially with the extra love and support she'll get from her mother. She grieves for András every waking moment. I occasionally remind her that time is a great healer.

With her mother's permission, she carefully reassembled

his shrine on a side-table in the living room. The urn stood next to an immaculately polished silver *Menorah*, together with a small framed photograph and personal prayer called *Éva's Kaddish*. The old *Steiff* bear sat on top of the urn, guarding the ashes. My wife had made a new outfit for him from a selection of our son's clothes, complete with his very own black *kippah*. A glass teardrop was sewn under one eye.

Éva was weary and retired early to bed with the twins after dinner. Mr. Székely looked over at his wife. She gestured to the crumbling fossil of a man with her fierce Hebrew eyes, and he made his excuses to leave the table.

Mrs. Székely looked straight at me and sighed. We were alone, God help me. There followed a brief silence before the old battle-axe began to speak:

"Listen, and don't talk. I want you to hear what I have to say. I want none of your weasel words, excuses and lies. This is about Éva, not you. For it's always been about you, ever since you sullied her finger with that fake gold band all those years ago.

"Why my daughter remains loyal to you is disappointing for my husband and I, but not surprising. For you have married the purest, most loyal and loving woman you could ever possibly meet. Fortunate doesn't even come close to describing how incredibly blessed you are: for you are the luckiest of men, although you fail to see it that way.

"Éva is a wonderful woman because she is kind. Apart from her fierce loyalty and incredible sense of empathy, she lives her life for others, never for herself. After the loss of her brother to scarlet fever, she henceforth vowed to help others less fortunate than herself. She planned to dedicate her life to charity and nursing.

"She loved her brother dearly. I gave her his old toy bear which she has treasured ever since. She wept by his bedside for six months, lighting a candle every night. She even composed her own prayer for the dead which she recited every Sabbath. This *Kaddish* for her brother now sits next to your son's ashes. The inspiring words are well known to me.

34

And above everything else, they offer hope:

'The Lord will rebuild each body anew; for we are all unique temples in which the *Shekhinah* dwells. He will mend your skin and glue your bones. O hear me Israel, the Lord is one. He shall revive the dead and deliver new life. His holy breath with fill your lungs afresh. His radiance will reignite your eyes in holy fire, and you will gaze eternal upon His redeeming light, until the coming of His *Moshiach* and the rebirth of Zion'.

"But O, how you've ground that poor woman down! Through years of neglect and disregard, you have trampled my daughter's body into the dust. You have rejected her love, her Hasidic heritage, her very Jewish core: and for what? What could be more important than the love of a woman? For Éva's love is the purest and most quintessential love that any man could wish for.

"She was such a bright little girl. She shone at school and matriculated with honours. She was set for a place at Budapest's greatest Nursing College when a dashing Hungarian doctor from Szilágysomlyó entered her life and swept her off her feet. She gave up everything for you and your all-consuming career. She abandoned her family, her friends and her sublime Jewishness – all for you. She sacrificed her own aspirations and dreams. Your happiness was paramount to her. So, she followed you to Germany, into the beating heart of the wolf's lair.

"She has of course written to me during the years of her Babylonian Captivity. But the death of my only Grandson has been the most difficult period in my life. She mourns him still, perhaps forever. But she can heal with your help. Return to her, József! Be a husband and father again. Give back to her some of the love and kindness that she has poured into you over the years. She may even forgive you. Rediscover your Jewish heart. Pray to God. He will listen."

ÉVA SÁRKÁNY

Letter to Mrs. Ágnes Székely, Munkács, Hungary, Friday 23rd October 1942

Dear Mama,

I pray this letter finds you well and in good spirits. Your house must feel very different since our departure. At least you can enjoy a good deal more peace and quiet, and not have to worry quite so much about feeding four extra mouths every dinner time.

How is dear Papa? I hope his rheumatism isn't giving him too much grief during this current bout of damp weather. József has been suffering from headaches and joint pains recently. He puts it down to stress, but I do wonder whether he's hiding some more sinister illness from me.

Anyway, I just wanted to formally write to say a huge thank you for having us lodge at your home for all those months. We really couldn't have left Germany like we did without your enormous support and influence. You ensured that the Munkács community welcomed us all with open arms. Not only did you secure highly sought-after places for Emilia and Lily at the local school, but you also played an important role in helping József secure that teaching post.

We've been at our new home for just over a fortnight. The move went relatively smoothly as most of our furniture and larger items like the piano were in storage anyway. Despite its relatively small size, the house is really quite comfortable, and I've already started to put the Éva stamp on it. The three upstairs bedrooms mean that the twins can enjoy the privacy of their own personal spaces, whilst the master bedroom is big enough to accommodate the old double-bed from Heidelberg.

The plan over the next few months is for me to decorate the house. I'm more than happy to get out the paintbrushes and put up wallpaper, although József would prefer to have me making curtains and darning his socks.

The girls are fully engrossed in their studies, and have worked incredibly hard to catch up with all those months of missed schooling in Germany. They have set the bar high for their further education, and are already talking about university.

Both twins miss their Grandma's cooking by the way, especially the Sunday roasts:

"Why can't you get your roast potatoes crispy on the outside like Grandma's? And why doesn't the gravy taste as good?"

József seems to like his new teaching position, although he finds the balance of classroom and bureaucracy quite challenging. He enjoys teaching Chemistry to the twins, although I still get the impression that he sees them more as homemakers and mothers. His old-fashioned values have been a bugbear of mine for a while now, and there's not a week that goes by without me calling him a chauvinist at least once. He rarely talks of Medicine, although several locals have got wind that he's a doctor, and have suggested that he might do some private consultations or home visits in the evenings. We'll see...

Well, that's all I've really got to say for now. I hope to see you and Papa in the next fortnight or so, and perhaps have a proper catch up in my new home over afternoon tea.

With all my love,

Éva.

Letter (abstract) to Mrs. Ágnes Székely, Munkács, Hungary, Friday 30th July 1943

Dearest Mama,

I hope you and dear Papa are keeping well, and enjoying the late summer sunshine. I expect you're both as busy as ever in the garden, and no doubt enjoying the first homegrown fruits of your labours.

Where is this year going? I can't believe it will be August on Sunday. *Pesach* now seems like a world away, and it won't be long now until *Yom Kippur* and *Sukkot*.

My days are pretty much occupied with voluntary work at the hospital. I love caring for the sick, and take great comfort from it. József seems happier now that he's working as a doctor again. He still acts as a cover-teacher, but is gradually building up his own little practice of patients. He's now begun to perform some minor operations, and has been busy whipping out tonsils and adenoids this week. He still misses being a pathologist, but there are no opportunities currently available in this field, unless we all relocate to Budapest.

The twins continue to grow up fast. Olivia has become a highly accomplished pianist and is already talking about her application the *Liszt Ferenc* Academy of Music. She adores Beethoven, especially his piano concerto number 5, although we've recently been hearing a lot of Mozart and Chopin. Emilia on the other hand has little interest in music. She prefers the solitude of a bohemian artist, and has continued to expand her portfolio in preparation for her application to the University of Fine Arts in Budapest.

But you know all of this, of course. So why am I writing to you? Well, it's about me I suppose. I often find it much easier to express my feelings on paper than in conversation, especially if other people are listening in.

I'm so glad *Bubby* András isn't here anymore. How would he have managed? How would I have coped? I have come to see that his premature death was a blessing from

God after all. Although death must one day visit us all, there are certainly good and bad ways to die, just as there are good and bad times to die. Death must have surely liberated my little man, transforming his redundant arms and legs into the animated wings of an angel.

I am slowly getting over the grief, Mama, I really am. I am no longer Rachel weeping for her children. It is funny how time heals, how the brain comes to terms with the unimaginable, and how the soul makes peace with the present. I still hurt; I cry every day, but I'm beginning to be able to breathe again; no longer suffocating under a mantle of guilt and regret. The shroud of sorrow has been a heavy cloth to bear. Shedding it, bit by bit, has made me brighter, happier and more exposed to the warmth and light of the living present. I can once again smell the spring flowers and taste the summer honey on my lips. The autumnal birds are singing not cawing, and the winter wine is mellow once more.

My obsidian heart is softening. Even my knotted scars and contractures are fading. The niggling, gnawing pains of an eternal midnight are diminishing. I want no more numbing, dulling down; no more tranquillisers. I shall never harm my precious skin again with cold steel or hot ember.

My blood is ripe and red and beginning to pulse and flow anew. It nourishes my flesh and bone, and gives vibrant colour to my skin. It is pure blood, Jewish blood; clean and purifying – and untainted by Aryan National Socialism.

The vibrant and youthful Éva Székely is breaking out of her cocoon in a second birth and metamorphosis. She will mature into the *pillangó* of a new Éva Sárkány; liberated once more and free to spread her wings.

Here's to a new beginning!

With all my love – always, forever and eternally,

Éva.

PERSECUTION

Diary of Dr. József Sárkány, Munkács, Hungary, 1944

Wednesday 1st March

I often think about those women of my past. I miss Lena very much. She didn't love me like Éva, but I wanted more than matrimonial love back then. At times, I longed to visit Sodom and Gomorrah. I wanted a woman who was immoral, shameful and dangerous. Lena and Hannah fulfilled these roles. I could do things with them that I could never do with my wife. These adulterous acts were beyond the dignity and righteousness of the Hassidic marital bed. They were dark, sinful... wonderful.

Tuesday 7th March

I am reluctantly spending a little more time with my wife and daughters. Despite the escalating hardships and talk of imminent Nazi invasion, the family bond appears to be quite strong at present. But I remain uncomfortable with the concept of sharing life together in a wholly unselfish way. I am still clouded by hubris and forever distracted by my inferior position in the current medical hierarchy. I continue to reflect upon powerful doctors like Irmfried Eberl and Karl Brandt with a sense of awe and envy. And although I have prostituted myself in ways that were no different to the carnal devices adopted by Hannah Fischer, I will happily continue to develop these methods in furthering my career.

Monday 13th March

My relationship with Lily and Emilia is probably as good as it's ever going to get. I pretend to acknowledge my past failings and apologise quite convincingly for all the important life events that I missed or neglected during the course of their childhoods. Unfortunately, the twins want to recreate these times with me so that I can at least experience them retrospectively. They reminisce about birthday parties, *Bat Mitzvahs*, first teeth lost, learning to ride a bicycle, parent's evenings, trips to the theatre, piano lessons, artwork, even adolescent crushes. I vow to never miss another one of these momentous lifetime events. I even pledge to walk them down the aisle, and to be a far better grandfather than father. What a tremendous liar I am.

Thursday 16th March

Éva has asked me to erect a permanent indoor shrine to our first and only son. She wants her old *Steiff* bear professionally restored, and the glass teardrop replaced by a diamond. She has already arranged for a calligrapher to transcribe her *Kaddish* onto parchment before having it lavishly mounted and framed. The original urn and ashes are to remain untouched, although I've often yearned to smash it to pieces and erase all traces of that fake grey dust.

Monday 20th March

The Nazis are coming! I peer out of my bedroom window onto a deserted street below. An eerie silence has fallen over Munkács as the evening sun begins to bleed into the west. We're all inside, locked in, paralysed with fear. Shopkeepers have shut up early. The usual bustle of people has been supplanted by a quiet stillness that permeates the air.

And then I hear them, these soldiers of the *Wehrmacht*, marching inexorably towards our peaceful community in the midst of the Carpathian Mountains.

But the army doesn't worry me, no not really. It is the black-clad spectres that lurk in the shadows that are the real enemy. They are the Secret State Police, the Criminal Police, the Thought Police – these subtle interrogators, double agents and clandestine spies. But worst of all, they are SS men, vicious anti-Semites; the elite imperial Protection

Squad of Hitler's Third Reich. They are the grim reapers of death, no – more than death – of extermination… of genocide: a holocaust, a *Shoah* – upon the ruined bloody plains of *Tel Megiddo*.

As night fell, the fear in our house was now palpable; I could taste it, smell it in the air. We lit candles and sat in the gloom. Nobody spoke. Even the act of breathing felt too loud, too vulnerable. For what seemed like an eternity, we sat, still and silent – waiting, waiting for a bang on the door or a brick through the window. But nothing; nobody came.

The foreboding, the menace, slowly began to melt into the chimes of midnight. Éva whispered to the twins. They nodded. She turned to me and asked if I was hungry. I also nodded and accompanied her to the kitchen. Whilst she attended to the sandwiches, I boiled a kettle on the gas stove and made a pot of tea. There was a growing sense of calm, not relief – that would be too strong a word – but a definite feeling of temporary reprieve that soon turned to comfort as we ate our cold supper.

We all turned in just after one in the morning. I tentatively peered through a gap in the closed bedroom curtains. The pale yellow glow of street lights bathed the empty avenue. The wolf was in his den and the sheep could hopefully pass a peaceful night in safety.

Tuesday 21st March

Bad news came this afternoon. In a meeting held at the *Hevra Kadisha* building, teachers were informed that the Hebrew School was to be converted into a military hospital for the occupying Germans. My daughters were crushed by the news as they'd both planned to apply for university. The heads of year and school governors eventually decided to hold the matriculation examinations early and thereby expedite the academic year by the end of the week.

Wednesday 22ⁿᵈ March

Some of our Christian friends have become informers and willing collaborators. The non-Jewish population looks on apathetically as we are made to register and henceforth wear a ten-centimetre yellow circle to mark us out as fair game for the Hungarian gendarmes. It seems to me that many locals take pleasure in our humiliation and plight. This is partially driven by ignorance and indifference, but I also fear a mounting sense of anti-Semitic animosity.

Thursday 23ʳᵈ March

We are now labelled as Jews. Many homes have already fallen victim to night-time police raids. The houses are ransacked and pillaged. There is a particularly cruel gendarme called Mihály Nagy who delights in terrorising the Orthodox community and their children. His brutality and greed know no bounds as he rips earrings out of little girls' earlobes and pulls gold fillings from their parents' mouths.

I later heard that an Orthodox Jew was shot dead outside the main synagogue this afternoon. He attempted to flee whilst being made to destroy the Holy Ark.

Friday 24ᵗʰ March

The black fangs of the Nazi police state begin to pierce our feeble armour and inject their toxins. The shadowy forms of undercover spies and informers – SS, SD, SiPo and Gestapo – weave their sticky threads that cocoon and immobilise. There is no escape from Arachne's lair.

I feel utterly defenseless and vulnerable. The Nazi virus has no vaccine, and nobody is immune from its virulent and relentless onslaught. I'm frightened for my family. We're all sleeping in the master bedroom at the moment. I'm even contemplating some kind of nighttime watch, especially as neither Éva nor I are sleeping much anyway.

Sabbath 25th March

Like the ancient Israelites in Egyptian bondage, the captive Jews of Munkács are subject to a most pernicious form of human slavery. Hundreds of able-bodied men are rounded up daily into penal labour squads – surfacing roads, paving streets and digging ditches. Others are compelled to toil farther afield in armaments factories, saw mills, stone quarries and copper mines.

We have become slaves of the pharaoh. But who will deliver us from this vile servitude?

Thankfully, I'm now too old for this kind of heavy manual labour. My daughters, though young and fit, are also considered unsuitable; although I'm afraid that even they will be ultimately drawn into the ravenous maw of the Nazi war machine.

Sunday 26th March

Desperate Jews are paying enormous sums to acquire the right to work. So ingrained in the human psyche is the survival instinct that some are literally begging for what they perceive to be life-saving work permits. In my opinion, it's a futile exercise that may possibly give them a temporary reprieve, but ultimately, they'll be deported like the rest of us.

Monday 27th March

Many are still trying to acquire some sort of work permit, using any means at their disposal. Others consider going undercover and escaping to the capital, but these efforts are complicated by tight travelling regulations. Convinced it will spare them from being transported, some families choose to convert and join the Reformed Church.

Escalating hopelessness is tragically driving some folk to take their own lives. The hushed talk of suicide pacts permeates the city.

Tuesday 28th March

Éva's mental health is extremely fragile at the moment. Her chronic insomnia is taking its toll on her careworn mind and body. As well as feeling their mother's pain, Lily and Emilia are also struggling to come to terms with their new lives of prejudice and subjugation.

My God! Is this really happening to us? In the post-Trianon world of Hungarian society, have the Jews not been loyal citizens? Where are the conservatives and liberal thinkers?

And what is Miklós Horthy doing to protect us? Nothing! So much for our Regent... now we know where his true loyalty lies, and it's certainly not with the law-abiding Jews of Carpathian Ruthenia.

Wednesday 29th March

The Jewish intelligentsia is beginning to be lost in the night and fog. Bewildered families lose loved ones as they disappear under the smokescreen of Protective Custody. Thankfully, my own private and professional life has maintained a safe distance from the dissenting philosophical debates of these marginalised literati. That said; no Jew or even half-Jew is immune from slander in this current political climate. Against the countless informants and Nazi secret police, one really has no redress.

Thursday 30th March

I'm once again living in a land of regulation, restriction, exclusion and segregation: a world of pogroms, *Mischling* tests, broken glass, broken oaths, and broken lives. We can no longer practise medicine, law, engineering, science or midwifery. We cannot teach. Our children are barred from public schools and universities. We are banned from the theatres, the cinemas, the concert halls and public parks. We can no longer ritually slaughter our animals. We are devoid of economic, political, legal and civil rights. Are we even human at all?

From Berlin to Bucharest and from Prague to Paris – where are we supposed to go?

<u>**Friday 31st March**</u>

An absurd rumour has been circulating that preys on the desperate and the vulnerable. Jews who are able to prove their foreign citizenship are to be considered for emigration to a new *kibbutz* in Palestine. These lucky few have to pay an extortionate fee to a certain Adolf Eichmann in order to gain passage on this Ark to Freedom. Many are busy organising false documents in order to qualify. Are people really so naïve?

<u>**Sabbath 1st April**</u>

The twins were in a terrible state after returning from a walk into town. My wife wasn't happy to let them go due to the Sabbath, but the girls insisted upon getting out of the house and taking some exercise. Acting as adjudicator, I eventually agreed to their mounting adolescent protests.

They returned in floods of tears. Éva gradually calmed them and Emilia began to tell us what happened. Wandering down a small backroad, they had stumbled across two teenage girls lying half-naked on the pavement. The house behind them had been ransacked, with windows broken and a door hanging loosely open from one hinge.

Having composed herself, Olivia interrupted her sister. She explained that both girls had been molested and beaten. One of them looked up at her and attempted to speak:

"Hello Lily, it's me, Becky Kratz. We went to school together, remember? This is my younger sister, Ilona. Is she dead? You must leave this place; it's not safe. They're coming back. Go!"

Emilia began to sob again. "She had such lovely red hair…"

"Had?" I asked. "What happened to it?"

I learned that Rebecca's hair had been coarsely chopped, and an inverted crucifix shaved into the back of her head. Ilona, who was only semi-conscious, had also been shaved. The twins suspected that she must have put up a greater fight because her injuries were more severe: a large letter 'J' had been cut deeply into her bleeding forehead.

Éva inquired where the girls were now, and insisted that she must attend to their wounds and bring them something to eat and drink. But it was thankfully now dark. Lily and Emilia couldn't even remember where they were at the time, let alone the name of the road. The girls eventually said a prayer for them before bedding down for the night.

Sunday 2nd April

Rumours abound concerning torture chambers, shooting pits, deportations and death camps in Poland. The Orthodox Elders utterly reject the idea of extermination and believe that the Jews are vital to the German economy. They dismiss all such rumours as hysteria and scaremongering.

They are wrong of course. I know the Germans, no one better. I have also read *Mein Kampf*. Their fanatical anti-Semitism and ideas of racial purity are far stronger than any secondary sense of national economic concern. Hitler and Himmler want to purge Europe of its Jews, and there are enough submissive henchmen around to make this nightmare an absolute reality.

Monday 3rd April

Some locals behaved shamefully towards my wife and daughters as they went for an afternoon stroll in search of Rebecca and Ilona Kratz. Unable to walk much further than a couple of hundred yards, they were jeered at, spat upon, and told to leave for good.

And so it goes on…

Tuesday 4th April

Some of my Orthodox acquaintances became a source of spiteful entertainment this morning, being made to hop about and dance whilst reciting prayers and singing songs. After the morning sport was over, the Hungarian gendarmes cut their sidelocks and shaved their heads with razors lubricated in bacon fat.

Wednesday 5th April

Today we were forbidden from using public transport without a special permit. We were also prohibited from using the telephone and receiving regular mail. Furthermore, we were not permitted to leave our homes after nightfall.

Thursday 6th April

The yellow circle has now been replaced by the Star of David. Thank you, *Herr Eichmann*.

Friday 7th April

It is *Erev Pesach*, the eve of Passover.

A new *Judenrat* was established today, headed by Dr. Sándor Eisenstätter who replaced Dr. Peter Steiner. Other prominent council members included Oszkár Zoltán and Mendel Morvai.

Sabbath 8th April

Today marks the fifteenth day of *Nisan* and the first day of our Jewish Passover.

My family gathered to celebrate the *Seder*: a ritual feast of unleavened bread, bitter herbs and wine. The house had been purged of all leaven and we managed to obtain two *matzos* from the *Judenrat*. Unfortunately, the occupying Germans had stolen all our wine. I therefore began to recite the *Kiddush* and proclaimed, "Let us bless this tea."

Sunday 9th April

Eichmann's Gestapo agents are already beginning to infiltrate the *Judenrat;* the predictable conclusion being a Jewish governing body that is in the pocket of the secret state police.

Monday 10th April

Many more locals are now cooperating with the authorities on so-called ideological grounds. In fact, it is more to do with avarice and the confident expectation of material rewards confiscated from us. But how can we resist? Passivity and inertia seem to be our only choices right now.

Tuesday 11th April

Rumours now abound that the ghetto is imminent. In a perverse form of *nouveau riche*, the local gentiles are more than willing to take advantage of this freely available wealth. I hear that the housing office has been inundated with letters and telephone enquiries. Everyone wants their piece of Jewish pie as the gravy-train sweeps across Hungary.

Covetous neighbours quarrel in the streets over luxury apartments that will soon become available. The more substantial properties are to be handed over to important military personnel and politicians. I'm sure that Eichmann and his cronies will do very well out of this.

And so, the master plan finally uncloaks itself. Generations of Jewish homes, Jewish memories and Jewish toil are to be surrendered up to the avaricious Gentile State. I think about our lovely family home in Heidelberg that is no longer ours. I ponder over my in-law's beautiful cottage and our own modest house in Hungary. For these buildings are not only bricks and mortar: they are precious family heirlooms for the generations to follow.

But will there even be a next generation? I pray that my daughters will have some sort of future in Europe as citizens. And I hope, more than ever, to see Hitler's Third Reich utterly crushed!

Wednesday 12th April

Éva's mental health disturbs me. Her punctuated bouts of depression and euphoria continue to cycle in a frenzy of contradictory thoughts and incongruous actions. Her initial optimism has succumbed to the battery of physical and mental assaults, leaving her subdued and fearful. The following exchange occurred this evening:

"Just look at me, József! Look upon your wife! My hair is lice-infested. My clothes are ragged and filthy. My body stinks to high heaven because there's no running water. There's nothing to eat. I can't go on like this."

"Look, let's not argue. The Elders of the *Judenrat* confidently inform me that everybody will find local work in the factories and in agricultural labour. We have to trust them. Their sources must surely be more reliable than the idle gossipers and alarmists."

"Oh, come on! You know as well as I do that the *Judenrat* is in the pocket of Adolf Eichmann."

I had no response to this. She was right, as usual. I knew this fact all too well.

Thursday 13th April

Five teenage boys were shot whilst attempting to escape through the sewers. I was informed that their blood-soaked bodies were displayed outside the town hall, propped up on chairs with eyes wide open.

I know it isn't funny, but I confess to being somewhat amused when I paid them a visit this evening; chiefly out of morbid curiosity. A sign posted above their heads read: 'We're back!'

Friday 14th April

Having spent the last few days drinking ditchwater, our reckless next-door neighbours have all developed raging dysentery. This is unlikely to save them from the ghetto.

I was later called to see their two-year-old daughter. I could do nothing. She was too far gone, and any attempts at rehydration would have ultimately proved futile, as well as depriving my own household of precious water.

Sabbath 15th April

Today was the last day of Passover.

Flyers were posted through letterboxes, confirming our worst fears. Tomorrow will be ghettoisation day. We are allowed to take only a few items with us: two sets of clothing, blankets, pots and pans, food, and a further load of up to fifty kilos. I am ordered to lock up the house tomorrow morning and put the keys into an envelope bearing my name and old address. This envelope must then be handed to a member of the *Judenrat* who will collect it upon my arrival at the ghetto entrance.

There is a strict time limit of ten hours for relocation, commencing at 04:30 tomorrow morning and ending at 14:30 hours. I wonder how soon it will be before our house is plundered and defiled by the locals.

My greatest concern about the ghetto is lack of sustenance. Supplies are to be restricted to that which is deemed surplus to outside requirements. Smuggling of provisions from the outside will probably be the only way to avoid mass starvation.

So this is our lot! We are the lost generation: Jews in the ghetto – concentrated, shut in and shut out. Like incarcerated shades, we must stalk in the shadows, cut off and forgotten. We are the hunted, the quarry, and the doomed: for the Jewish *diaspora* has no future in the grandiose scheme of European National Socialism.

THE GHETTO

Diary of Dr. József Sárkány, Munkács, Hungary, 1944

<u>Sunday 16th April</u>

Today we were finally uprooted. Dispossessed of almost everything, we scraped together a few items of food and clothing, and made our weary way towards the fetid maws of the Munkács Ghetto.

Following Passover, the house was still bereft of all leaven, so we had very little provender to take with us. Éva had carefully wrapped the urn in dirty blankets, together with the *Menorah* and *Steiff* bear. I also smuggled in a handful of old diaries in the false bottom of my doctor's bag.

It was still dark when we left the house. We had barely locked the front door when several loitering individuals with torches began to bicker and brawl over who was going to get the fine furniture and curtains. Éva recognised a woman whom she had previously looked after at the local hospital. She quietly informed me that she had suffered a stroke last year, and how she'd been totally dependent on her nursing care during the months of rehabilitation. My wife smiled and acknowledged her with a gentle bow of her head. The woman glared, but made no response. If eyes could kill, then mine became instant murderers.

Olivia was crying because she'd had to leave her piano and sheet music behind. I did briefly consider taking some of her music books, but ruled in favour of my diaries. Éva tried to comfort her by saying that Beethoven's immortal notes were already tattooed on her brain.

Emilia, the quieter of the two twins, had begged me to take her artwork into the ghetto, but I refused on practical grounds. Many of her paintings were also infused with political satire, and would have undoubtedly caused offence to the Nazis if they were ever to have seized them.

There were strict instructions for the townsfolk not to have any form of contact with the incarcerated Jewish community. According to the *Judenrat*, this was to be punishable by death. Jews themselves were to be prohibited from leaving the ghetto without a specially authorised work permit and triple-stamped identity card.

The journey on foot was a little under a mile. Rain began to spit as the four of us fell into line behind a solemn procession of star-clad families carrying bundles and suitcases. But this was no Exodus to freedom. We were Munkács evacuees, snaking our way through the damp gloomy streets on the road to captivity and bondage.

The rain began to hammer down as the human column approached the brilliant floodlights of the ghetto's gateway. A dozen or more SS guards formed patrols either side of the entrance. Under the cover of two makeshift sentry huts, members of the *Judenrat* stood sheepishly before us with clipboards; ticking us off, family by family, Jew by Jew, and taking possession of soggy envelopes containing house-keys, car-keys, and any other key that might open up a box of untold treasures.

As I waited in line with my wife and daughters, I stared up at the illuminated enclosure before me. The perimeter was surrounded by a high wooden fence, topped with dense rolls of barbed wire. Several prefabricated buildings had been erected to one side of the gateway. These appeared to be temporary barracks for the SS guards. I also caught sight of a dozen kennels, no doubt the future abodes of ferocious guard dogs.

A series of commands were barked out by the Hungarian gendarmes. The queue was ordered to split into two files; men and children on one side, women and girls over fourteen on the other. My wife and daughters had to be pulled away from my grasp before they were shuttled to the back of a line of women. At the same moment, I caught sight of an SS officer exiting from one of the barracks. A German guard immediately rushed over with an umbrella and shielded him from the downpour. Cold rainwater streamed down my face and into my eyes. I heard the umbrella man address the officer as Lieutenant Colonel Eichmann, the architect of all our misery.

Eichmann asked if there was a doctor amongst us. I immediately stepped forward without thinking. He half-grinned and took me into the wooden building. Inside were four makeshift examination couches, complete with surgical lamps, metal specula, and an assortment of probes and forceps. Eichmann introduced me to his four 'midwives' and told me to be on hand to assist them if required. Our womenfolk were then led inside in groups of twelve. Four were made to immediately lie on the couches whilst the other eight awaited their turn in a shadowed corner. They all turned away from the examination couches in discomfiture and shame.

Eichmann was in attendance during these humiliating internal examinations, casually smoking his Davidoff's through a cocktail-length cigarette holder. The first eight were cleared and escorted back outside amidst desperate sobs.

During the next search, an excited midwife removed a muslin gauze bundle from a middle-aged woman. Inside the wrapping were five diamond rings looped through the chain of a golden necklace. I was ordered to perform a further sweep and then pass a speculum. Sat in the patulous opening of her cervix was a cluster of three pearls which I was able to extract with forceps.

My wife and daughters were at the back of the next group of twelve. When it came to their turn, a distraught pregnant woman in front refused to be violated. Eichmann coolly approached her, drew deeply on his cigarette, and blew tobacco smoke straight into her face. She coughed violently and screwed up her eyes. With the flick of his hand, he signalled to two SS men who dragged her to the nearest couch and held her down. The lieutenant-colonel finished his cigarette before calmly removing his calf-leather gloves.

He then proceeded to fondle and probe his pinioned victim amidst whimpers and muffled pleas to stop. Deeper, deeper he delved – faster and faster, frantic and frenzied. Then suddenly it was over. Blood engorged his face, flushed and contorted; barely able to hide the rush of euphoria.

The entire spectacle was upsetting, but at the same time, perversely arousing – even for a doctor.

Calling for his chilled Beluga vodka, Eichmann rinsed his hands as a guard poured the spirit liberally from a bottle. After drying off, he took the half-empty bottle and splashed vodka all over the woman's exposed pelvis. He lit another cigarette and hovered over her with the naked flame that still burned from his Dupont lighter. I was paralysed by both horror and inquisitiveness, unable to even turn my head away. The woman begged for mercy and for the life of her unborn child. Eichmann gazed at her, completely still, silent, flame burning, drinking in every exquisite moment. At last, he broke his stare, raised the lighter to his face – and with an air of finesse – blew out the flame.

Monday 17th April

The ghetto is terribly overcrowded. I estimate that there are some 7000 souls crammed into the rickety tenements spread over five miserable streets. We're completely sealed off. The recently occupied and renovated apartments are exclusively reserved for a few dozen privileged Jews. What remains is a hotchpotch assortment of derelict houses, boarded up shops, an abandoned nursery and a convalescent home.

The living space allotted to my family consists of a single bedroom in a dilapidated residential building on Latorica Street; devoid of carpets, furniture, heating and running water. The communal pump is half a mile away and the sanitary conditions are dire. There is no bedding of course. We make ourselves as comfortable as possible. It is not long before the urn, bear and *Menorah* are carefully hidden under the rough wooden floorboards, along with my diaries.

The walls are damp and mildewed, with a nasty looking patch of mould growing in one corner. There is no view from the window as the cracked glass panes have been crudely whitewashed to prevent any communication with the outside. A single lightbulb hangs precariously from the ceiling, with a multitude of coloured wires dangling out from either side. Its only function would appear to be decorative as there is no electricity in the building.

We share the room with two teenage girls, Becky and Ilona Kratz. They were abruptly made orphans last month following a surprise Gestapo visit to their family home. Their parents were taken away for questioning and haven't been heard of since. Although the sisters escaped arrest, they were both beaten and one of them repeatedly raped.

With the help of the twins, Éva had eventually managed to locate their house on Kupelna Street. During her daily visits, she brought a flask of hot soup, often accompanied by some bread and jam. She nursed and counselled the girls for over a week. They had no idea why their parents should have been targets of a Gestapo raid. They were also ignorant of my undercover role as an SS informant.

Ilona's forehead scar was slow to heal and kept breaking down. She was also suffering from agonising pelvic pains and a malodourous discharge. After much cajoling, Éva eventually forced me to accompany her on a visit. Rebecca Kratz was doing fine. I remembered this attractive girl from my teaching days. Her once vibrant locks of fiery red hair had been reduced to ugly stubble, although her face was still pretty and alluring.

Ilona was altogether worse off. I bathed her infected scar in a tincture of iodine, and also managed to debride some of the dead tissue. And after some additional counselling from Éva, Ilona allowed me to perform a limited pelvic examination. Her entire perineum was inflamed and sore – with grazes, tears and bruising in various stages of healing. This was complicated by a purulent vaginal discharge that could only be gonorrhoea. Although reluctant to relinquish

my limited medical supplies, I prescribed her a course of
Prontosil at the insistence of my wife.

Quite how the Kratz girls have ended up sharing a room
with us in the ghetto is a mystery to me, although I suspect
that my wife and daughters have played a part in it.

The twins quickly got chatting to them. They were all
still deeply upset after yesterday's tribulation at the ghetto
entrance. Éva had forbidden me to mention it, although I
overheard the four teenagers whispering about the shameful
ordeal in a corner of the room.

Our roommates were desperately hungry but we had
nothing substantial to offer them from our own limited
rations. They told us later that they'd decided to leave the
ghetto via the sewers, and promised to return with bread
and water. I tried to dissuade them, and warned them that
the SS men and Hungarian gendarmes would surely be
guarding every manhole and drain. They heeded my advice,
for the time being at least.

Tuesday 18th April

Rumour has it that *Judenrat* members are living comfortably
with their families in a special quarter of the ghetto, where
the food reserves and makeshift infirmary are located. Most
had been prominent and honest pillars of the community
before the occupation. But power corrupts; as does a rotten
apple in a healthy fruit bowl, where its black veins of mould
infiltrate and intoxicate. I should know.

Wednesday 19th April

As a doctor, I am still permitted to leave the ghetto each day
and visit my dwindling non-Jewish patients in their own
homes, although increasing numbers are now refusing to
answer the front door. I notice signs in the windows, saying
things like 'Jews not wanted!' or 'This family has nothing to
do with the Jews!' Nevertheless, due to inadequate numbers
of other healthcare workers, the prohibitions are generally

relaxed and sometimes disregarded altogether.

The ghetto is therefore more permeable and less restrictive to the Jewish medical fraternity. Only those who practise outside have the opportunity to smuggle in food. But even this is difficult due to stringent searches upon entering and leaving.

House Commanders – in charge of orderliness, cleanliness and discipline – were elected in the ghetto this evening. My wife was chosen to be in charge of our residential block. She even gave a little address to the hundred or so people in the backyard; stressing the importance of compassion, cooperation and teamwork.

Éva's bountiful kindness is a constant source of surprise to me. Her new position as House Commander also fills me with a degree of envy and resentment. I am now technically below her, a woman, in status. She will surely come to relish her little bit of power over me in the ghetto, knowing full well how much I've already lost on her behalf.

Thursday 20th April

A People's Kitchen opened for business today. Most of the poorer folk were unable to afford the hyperinflated prices set by the corrupted *Judenrat*, leaving the wealthy elite to eat their fill. Today's culinary offering was a mouthwatering vegetable soup, served with wholemeal bread and fried onions. It was delicious.

Friday 21st April

There is a curious rupture of identity going on. Especially affected are the middle-class professionals, some of whom now regard themselves as agnostics and not truly Jewish. Perhaps I fall into this category? Others call themselves first-generation Christian converts and vigorously disown any affiliation with the Hebrew faith or culture. They bicker amongst themselves about how un-Jewish they really are, and how successful they've been in integrating into secular

Hungarian society. These gullible fools assume that their incarceration is some sort of misunderstanding; a bureaucratic blip that will soon be rectified once the German authorities realise how important they are.

The *Judenrat* had organised a gathering in the new People's Kitchen this evening before sunset. But its conservative members had also stipulated the separation of men and women. Many felt that in our current situation, the community must endeavour to make the best out of the situation and pray together as one. However, the Orthodox men amongst us stormed out of the room on the grounds that Jewish commandments were absolute and finite, and must be strictly adhered to, regardless of circumstance. Even cooking together led to disagreements. The Orthodox families refused to use the communal amenities because they just weren't *kosher* enough.

For those who chose to stay, a growing unease pervaded the event as Jews of different social backgrounds were thrust together into the communal melting pot of ghetto life. Many bemoaned the fact that the *Judenrat* and other professional classes had better accommodation, better facilities and even access to the best food rations. This was true of course; even for its unofficial members, spies and informers – like me.

After an entertaining quarrel between a farmhand and pharmacist, the former punched his opponent and bloodied his nose. It was all because his Yellow Star was perceived to be slightly larger and cut from a finer cloth.

Sabbath 22nd April

Today was Black Saturday.

On the first *Shabbat* in the ghetto, I was forced to join one of twenty dismantling squads who were ordered to destroy the last remains of the city's synagogues. Why I should have been selected for such a task was a mystery to me, although it was probably due to the heated argument that I had last night with an influential *Judenrat* Elder.

Laden with pickaxes, spades and mattocks, my working party of fifty was directed to the largest synagogue in Munkács. Our journey was at running pace in the form of a column of twenty-five pairs, all chanting Jewish prayers. We were accompanied by ten SS guards who bawled at us incessantly, striking out at anybody not keeping up.

One flagging man about five rows ahead of me was struck violently in the face with a rifle butt. He staggered and fell to the ground. The column opened up to pass him and then rapidly closed back in to resume its tight formation. I dared not stop, nor even turn around to see how he was. Nevertheless, my curiosity was soon answered by the sudden burst of gunfire from behind.

Upon arrival, we were hurried inside the derelict synagogue and commanded to begin destroying the furniture and seating of the *Beth Midrash*. A distinguished intellectual, a 50-year-old Rabbi called István Mayer, foolishly dared to challenge one of the guards. He was severely beaten and his bleeding body left in full sight of the rest of us. After three hours of twitching and groans, he thankfully remained still and silent.

And so the torture continued throughout the morning. After a long lunch and several bottles of alcohol, the SS men returned to their sport and urinated all over the synagogue floor. We were then forced to mop up the fluid with our own clothes, *tallits* and *kippahs*.

As afternoon faded into dusk, the demolition work was nearing completion. We had systematically smashed up centuries of our culture and heritage – furniture, seating, doors and windows. Finally, a huge pile of debris was made in the outside courtyard, supplemented by books, scrolls and exquisitely embroidered tallit bags. The Nazis then set the whole thing ablaze and ordered us to dance around the bonfire, reciting Solomonic prayers of lamentation.

Eichmann arrived just in time to witness the humiliating finale to this blackest of days.

Sunday 23rd April

I have had a day of much-needed rest and respite. I was utterly exhausted after yesterday's ordeal, and Éva attended to my cuts and bruises as best she could. The twins looked on in disbelief as I turned onto my back to reveal the red stripes of Nazi whip lashes. Lily started to cry, followed by Emilia, then Éva.

The Kratz sisters inquired about food. There was none. We were all famished. Éva looked dreadfully gaunt, and I knew for sure that she'd been sacrificing her own meagre rations to supplement those of the twins. Becky and Ilona began to sob with the others. I pretended to join them.

Monday 24th April

The ghetto is completely cut off from the outside world. No food is allowed in; rubbish and waste are not collected, while dead bodies begin to litter the streets. The allocated tenements are so overcrowded that outbreaks of dysentery and typhoid fever now ravage the community.

This most desperate of public health situations is further exacerbated by a complete lack of medicines and nursing facilities. I must confess to having a somewhat limited supply of essentials, but prefer to keep these hidden away for a time of personal need.

Tuesday 25th April

We're all starving. I feel like a caged animal, but even captive animals are fed. We currently rely on the good will and generosity of those rural Jews who are better supplied with their own vegetables. But even their provisions are wearing thin, and our daily ration of turnip soup grows ever closer to resembling dirty dish water. My own additional covert rations from the *Judenrat* have ceased since my quarrel with Oszkár Zoltán last Friday evening.

Wednesday 26th April

The ghetto is beginning to suffocate me. We live as swine amidst the filth and deprivation of a gigantic pigsty. I've learned that the electrical generators and water supply have been deliberately sabotaged. My clothes are now filthy and lice-infested, and I appear to be suffering from the dreaded scabies mite.

Thursday 27th April

I was introduced to the Munkács Mint this afternoon.

The Gestapo suspected me of smuggling food and medical supplies into the ghetto during my outside visits. This rumour was no doubt instigated by my new adversary in the *Judenrat* who clearly wanted me dead.

I was picked up at the gate by the sadistic Gusztáv Órendi. He escorted me to The Mint in handcuffs. The building was within the ghetto itself and I recognised it as the old rubber factory. To my horror, Éva and the girls were already there.

The room was in shadow except for a brightly lit wooden chair in the centre. The air was filled with the pungent odour of singed flesh. Eichmann, that ubiquitous phantom of the night, was once again in attendance.

I was ordered to strip naked and then beaten on the testicles with a short rubber hose. The twins began to howl. Éva covered their faces and begged them to stop.

I really can't remember much more, needless to say that I was slapped repeatedly about the face and rendered unconscious. I have a vague recollection of cold water or urine being thrown over me and then an intense searing pain on the soles of my feet. They still ache terribly and are covered in raw welts from being struck with some sort of wire cable.

Fortunately for me, I was unable to procure any contraband for myself this morning, and after a thorough search of my clothes and bodily orifices, I was sent hobbling on my way, accompanied by my unscathed but mentally traumatised family.

On the journey back to our residence, Éva related how they were earlier compelled to witness the torture of a young woman who was caught smuggling in a bar of soap. Eichmann inserted electrodes into her mouth and vagina. Turning the dial on some sort of battery device, the woman was then subjected to a series of excruciating electric shocks.

Whether she survived the ordeal, my wife didn't know, or chose not to remember. However, the girl's name was known to me. We had actually met outside the ghetto where she accepted my soapy offering in return for carnal favours. However, she reneged on our bargain and fled with my last bar of precious soap. I had reported her to the *Judenrat* that morning, hoping to curry favour once more with Oszkár Zoltán. The plan backfired badly for me, but at least Krisztina got the shock of her life.

Friday 28th April

Today was Red Friday.

Eichmann's SS men unleashed an unprecedented killing spree throughout the streets and houses. As the sun set and the *Shabbat* began, at least a hundred souls, mainly women and children, were herded into the remains of a communal hall and locked in.

I can't even begin to imagine the horrors that must have followed, needless to say that all perished horribly as the building was set ablaze.

Rebecca and Ilona Katz were amongst the victims. They were just too dangerous to me and my family. And at least they're now reunited with their parents...

Sabbath 29th April

We are the damned – shut out, alienated, stigmatised and murdered. And why? Are we not valued members of society? Many of us are teachers, engineers, lawyers and doctors. Yes, we are all Jews, but why should that matter? Do we not belong anymore? Are we really so despised that we need to be segregated, isolated... annihilated? We are civilised human beings, just like everybody else.

Sunday 30th April

Our women and children are being forced to perform meaningless work, simply to keep them occupied and to entertain the Hungarian guards. Beatings are now a daily occurrence and have evolved into a kind of perverse theatre. The perpetrators enter the ghetto whenever they feel like a bash, often after a heavy drinking spree.

Monday 1st May

The death toll increases day by day. Swathes of people, mad with hunger, stalk the streets and pillage what they can from the dead and dying. Unburied corpses lie rotting on the pavements and roads. The stench of death is everywhere within this Godforsaken ghetto. The public kitchens have no food and the makeshift hospital has no medicines. A small Jewish police force tries in vain to maintain law and order, but anarchy now runs rife and looting is endemic.

Tuesday 2nd May

My hunger is all-consuming. We are worse than prisoners, far worse. For with a custodial sentence comes the likely prospect of survival. For us Jews, there is no such vision. Slow and lingering, or swift and brutal, our fate must surely end in death.

Wednesday 3rd May

The elderly folk are dying in droves. Outbreaks of diphtheria, measles, scarlet fever and whooping cough blight our children. There are stillbirths and miscarriages.

Women die in childbirth or succumb to puerperal fever. Many are ravished by scabies, lice and impetigo. Others take their own lives, or simply give in to exhaustion and despair.

Thursday 4th May

Liquidation seems imminent. On Garibaldi Street, several houses are being prepared as storage facilities in which the last of the plundered property can be sorted. All cellar entrances have been whitewashed so that the Germans can quickly find hidden Jews.

Friday 5th May

Today I visited the ghetto infirmary. The dozen or so patients were in a pitiful state of existence, strewn haphazardly upon the concrete floor in pools of urine and excrement. There was no nurse or doctor in sight. These people were the abandoned vestiges of neglect and deprivation.

I did nothing but look, then wiped my shoes – and shut the door behind me.

Sabbath 6th May

We are soon to be herded as cattle to the slaughterhouse. The question of resistance torments us all, but there is no solution to it. Everybody knows that the death of just one Nazi will have terrible reprisals, and may even result in the massacre of our entire community. But is mass slaughter what's in store for us anyway?

Sunday 7th May

We begin to hear dreadful rumours about an annihilation factory in Poland. After plundering the last of our earthly possessions, the rapacious Nazi war machine will even rip the very clothes from our backs. But even that is not enough for these profiteering monsters. Our mortal remains must first be ransacked and defiled – hair shorn, teeth pulled, body cavities opened, skin flayed and fat processed – and so it goes on and on. And only then – when there's nothing left but desiccated sinew and bone – only then will we find peace in the industrial incinerator.

Monday 8th May

House raids began today. Either through chance or providence, the urn, bear, *Menorah* and diaries went undiscovered.

Some families are committing mass suicide to avoid the inevitable. It is like Masada all over again.

Tuesday 9th May

At four o'clock this morning, a posse of eight SS men banged on our front door and forced entry. Cursing and yelling, they stormed through the building and chased everybody outside into the pouring rain. Mothers clung desperately onto their children who were crying with fright and confusion. Anyone unable to move at a lightning pace was beaten until they either started running or fell. Once down, these poor languishers never got up. Moshe Horpács from the room next door was catapulted down the flight of stairs. A heavy boot then crunched down on his ribcage and he breathed no more.

There were now over a hundred people outside our block, most still wearing their sodden night attire and drenched to the bone. Giggling and clumsily gesturing with her hands, walked a disturbed young girl of about fourteen; hair shorn, eyes blackened with running mascara. She paced barefoot in a crumpled nightgown that bore the rusted stains of menstruation.

Across the street sat an old blind man in dark goggles. His name was Alter Szabó. He had lost his sight to chlorine at the Somme, fighting for Kaiser and country. He wore a yellow armband with three black circles to signify his blindness. Pinned proudly on his chest was the Iron Cross. For a split moment, I believed that this may have some resonance with the Germans. My delusion was shattered however as a well-aimed bullet thumped into his heart.

We were herded into line and harried along out of the ghetto. After a forced march in the driving rain, we eventually arrived at an abandoned brick factory on the edge of town. Many hundreds of evacuated families soon joined us. A cold wind was blowing and the forsaken factory building didn't even have proper walls.

Éva was beside herself when she realised that we had left our son's ashes behind. I did my best to reassure her that the urn was well hidden under the floorboards and unlikely to be disturbed. I solemnly vowed that once this infernal war was over, we would both return to the house and recover the last mortal remains of baby András. She wept, but appeared to be comforted by my empty promise.

Wednesday 10th May

The past two days have been pure misery. There is no shelter from the elements, and we all sleep huddled together under sheets of tarpaulin. We did manage to get hold of some straw, but this is damp and does little to ease. There's no sanitation, no running water, no heating… no food.

In what feels like an irretrievable state of total disintegration – corporeal, psychological and spiritual – death now seems like a release. I crave the ecstasy of nothingness.

CAT & MOUSE

Transcript of secret recording (unknown source) in the office of Rudolf Höss, Auschwitz, Poland, dated Tuesday 9th May 1944

Höss: Good morning Kramer. What time is *Herr Eichmann* joining us?

Kramer: *Guten Morgen, Herr Kommander.* Eichmann is expected at ten o'clock.

Höss: He's sure to be punctual; the man's a machine.

Kramer: He's complaining as usual about the transport quotas not being fulfilled.

Höss: Tell me about it! I'm sure to get a lecture on the intricacies of his railway timetables, right down to the last bloody Jew!

Kramer: But what an achievement if he pulls it off.

Höss: You mean if *we* pull it off! Don't forget that the swine will arrive here very much alive – well most of them. What Eichmann fails to see is the logistics of disposal. It's all very well getting them here, that bit is relatively easy; even the killing really isn't too much hassle: but when it comes to incineration, now that's when things get really hot under the collar!

Kramer: I guess you'll need to dig more pits.

Höss: Yes, I'll need at least five trenches just to keep on top of things. And we'll probably have to reopen the White House. I'm going to bring back Moll.

Kramer: Manic Moll! The man's a fucking lunatic! He'll keep down the gas bill though.

Höss: What do you mean?

Kramer: Well, one look at that mad throbbing face, well – all the Yids will die of fright!

Höss: Quite so – that's very good Josef.

Eichmann:	Welcome back to hell's kitchen, Rudolf! Or should I say *SS-Standortältester Höss,* the mighty Commander of the Garrison?
Höss:	Hello Eichmann. Höss is just fine.
Eichmann:	How are we doing with our little city of Jews?
Höss:	Not too bad. The burning produces the aroma of suckling pig that permeates throughout the camp. As Jews are unfamiliar with the smell of pork, our new arrivals think that we're roasting chickens here – on an industrial scale. The crematoria are working flat out though. I'm not sure if we'll have the capacity to deal with all your Hungarian chicken.
Eichmann:	Don't blame me – I'm only the train man! Just give me data. I only require two columns of figures: the number of arrivals on the ramp and the number of departures through the chimneys.
Höss:	Birkenau really hasn't been easy: it's basically a Polish swamp. I've invested a huge amount of manpower in the levelling and draining of its marshy terrain. I estimate that we lost around 18,000 Soviet PoWs between March '41 and the beginning of '42.
Eichmann:	What's a few ruskies at the end of the day?
Höss:	Well, the main graft is done. The women's section has been expanding since Ravensbrück began its purge of Poles and Slovaks.
Kramer:	Argh! I hate all these 'owskis and 'ováks. These fucking easterners are really doing my head in! Give me Müllers and Mayers any day – good Aryan names.
Höss:	Thank you for that, Kramer. That will be all: you may leave us.
Kramer:	Right away, *mein Standortältester!*
Eichmann:	How many prisoners does each barracks currently hold?

Höss:	It depends on supply and demand, but there are around a thousand per hut. Each roost holds ten to twelve inmates, which is about the size of a coffin.
Eichmann:	Sounds cosy! Well at least they'll keep each other warm, providing they don't snuff it in the night. How is the industrial plant at Buna?
Höss:	The tedious little men from *IG Farben* seem happy with the workforce we supply. It certainly brings in substantial revenue.
Eichmann:	And it undoubtedly fills the coffers of *Lindenfycht* and *Carinhall*.
Höss:	Schwartz, however, is forever moaning about the constant lack of manpower.
Eichmann:	Well, you know my position on the matter. I'm now glad to be free of such issues. My duty is one of transportation, not slave labour. Anyway, I'm sure these industrialists are quite interesting if you get to know them. I'd happily eat schnitzels with any German, just so long as it's not Martin fucking Bormann!
Höss:	Anyway, shall we get down to business? I'm a very busy man.
Eichmann:	Busy? Ha! You don't know the meaning of the word! Your production line, my dear Höss, is only as good as my transports. Just remember this when sipping your cognac and smoking your cigars: you're nothing without Eichmann!
Höss:	How is your great conquest of Hungary?
Eichmann:	The authorities are eager to drink up their Jews. But I want their flesh! I am the bloodhound of the secret police that craves the meat of Abraham and the blood of Isaac. Yes, a mechanical bloodhound: an efficient machine – like Heydrich. He must surely be smiling down on me from Valhalla as his vision of the Final Solution comes to fruition.

Höss: We must continue to fight the Jewish bacillus that suppurates in the lungs of Europe. This is not about ideology; it is a matter of hygiene.

Eichmann: The Jewesses – like swarming blowflies – continue to disgorge their larvae all over Hungary. Like creeping mould or poisonous mushrooms – they fester and fungate in the damp darkness of the *shtetl*.

Höss: You put it so poetically.

Eichmann: Perhaps… How are my bunkers doing? Are they still operational?

Höss: Both have been mothballed since the crematoria became fully operational. We still use the undressing rooms to deal with occasional bottlenecks.

Eichmann: Anyhow, let's return to the matter at hand: Hungarian Jewry. 800,000 are scheduled for resettlement. I'll round them up from the ghettos and send them straight your way for Yahweh's big spring harvest. Ah, what a spectacular achievement this will be for us both! Just think of the glory, the honour… Make sure your photographer is ready to record the event for posterity.

Höss: You mean Hoffman in registration.

Eichmann: Yes, Ernst – he'll do a first-class job. We'll make a compilation album of his best work and dedicate it to the memory of Heydrich. Your ravenous sorting-huts will soon be overflowing with the riches of Budapest.

Höss: Everything of value goes to the WVHA.

Eichmann: Everything? Come now. Let's not play these puerile games. I know exactly what goes on in your *Kanada* section.

Höss: The *Effektenlager* is about storage, sorting, packaging and dispatching.

Eichmann: And what about *organising*? I too have some

	knowledge of camp parlance.
Höss:	Yes, I know… We'll need plenty of SS doctors for the selection process.
Eichmann:	Really? Is that so? I personally think that such selections are pointless at this stage of the resettlement program. Why take the risk of another typhus epidemic when all can be purified within a few hours of arrival?
Höss:	Buna wants its fresh labourers and the doctors covet their research material.
Eichmann:	Ah, yes! Mengele must have his twins and mutants! Alright, fine. You can have your share of my Hungarian Jews… all of my Jews. Come unto me, O ye children of Israel. The sacrificial temple at Auschwitz awaits you all, and will soon be incensed with your burning flesh. I am the Pied Piper and your *kinder* are my rodents. The only difference is that my rats drown in gas, not water.
Höss:	What a great achievement this will be for you.
Eichmann:	Yes, indeed! I have systematically combed the map of Europe for the Jew. Catching them is an empirical skill, learned through years of observation and experience. I am the Master Fisher of Jews. Europe is my Sea of Galilea, and I've learned precisely which hooks to apply. The result – a new Dead Sea!
Höss:	And if the tables are turned and you become the fish?
Eichmann:	Then I hope that all of them follow me down into that abyss they call Gehenna. Ha! I'll gladly leap into my grave with the blissful satisfaction of knowing that I have millions of dead Hebrews on my conscience.
Höss:	But what will happen at the end of all this transporting and processing?

Eichmann: All will be silenced. The ghettos, synagogues, prayer books – all gone! They'll be no more spewing babes, no more *Bar Mitzvahs*, and no more nuptial *chuppahs* in the *Judenfrei-* mountains of Carpathian Ruthenia... But we mustn't be too sentimental about it all. The Jews are just numbers on a page that get turned into cargos and transports and smoke. And when the final victory is mine, the Führer will surely appoint me World Commissar of the Jews. *Ich bin Obersturmbannführer Eichmann!*

THE PIT

Diary of Dr. József Sárkány, Munkács, Hungary, 1944

<u>Thursday 11th May</u>

The first deportation took place this afternoon. Some 3000 souls were put on trains, my wife and daughters included – destination unknown.

We arrived at the railway platform just after midday. A row of endless cattle cars awaited us, stretching down the track as far as the eye could see. An immaculately dressed Hungarian gendarme stood on top of a podium and addressed us all with the aid of a microphone connected to several loudspeakers:

"Good Jews! Loyal Jews! My name is László Ferenczy. I am delighted to inform you that you will soon be re-accommodated in a brand-new work camp in Poland. There you will no longer go hungry, but reap the benefits of honest work and good living. This enterprise has the full backing of your wise Council of Elders.

"Ladies and gentlemen, sisters and brothers, I therefore stretch out my hands and politely entreat you all to board the train in an orderly fashion. May I wish you all a pleasant journey, and I hope that your new lives are both happy and long-lived."

Slowly, the front column of people began to spill onto the platform where dozens of Hungarian guards organised the crowd into boarding parties. As I stood in line with my family, I overheard two German guards in casual conversation nearby. I managed to catch their names – Klaus and Günter – amidst their cryptic and disturbing remarks:

Klaus: There they go, two by two – these beasts of
            Noah's ark.
Günter: *Auf Wiedersehen Juden! Alyah!* Don't forget to

74

	send us postcards!
Klaus:	The Chosen People will soon be departing for the Promised Land. Will there be milk and honey in Zion, I wonder?
Günter:	They'll be lucky to get water. Or perhaps their Hebrew God will send down manna from heaven.
Klaus:	No, I think *Adonai* has truly abandoned them!
Günter:	Look at their fat luggage; suitcases packed to bursting! They'll be rich pickings when this stuff hits the *Kanada*.
Klaus:	Plenty for the bonfires too. All those yellow stars will be burning bright!
Günter:	As will the gold fillings…

Finally, I moved along the queue, glad to be out of earshot. If these two were the Master Race, then humanity was dead.

Éva fumbled for my hand and clasped tightly onto it:

"József, I'm scared. Where are they taking us? What shall I say to the girls? They keep asking me if they're going to die."

I gently squeezed her hand, but could find no words of solace. Lily clasped on to my right hand, whilst Emilia took her mother's left. I desperately tried to think of us as one united family, one inseparable unit – one miserable faith.

Just ahead we caught sight of Éva's parents. My wife gave a cry of joy and called out to them. The last time we had seen the Székelys was before ghetto lockdown, and I could see the immense relief on everyone's faces. I tried to feign happiness, but my weak smile betrayed me.

"Look, András! It's Éva and the girls. They're alive!"

I noticed that I wasn't mentioned, but perhaps I didn't really count as family in the eyes of Ágnes. Anyway, there was no opportunity to talk or even embrace, even if I'd wanted to. The twins blew their grandparents kisses whilst Éva vainly attempted to get closer to them in the queue.

It was getting hot. The cattle cars were jam-packed to

capacity. Heaving swathes of people were crammed in tightly, arms flailing amidst cries for air.

Éva, her mother and the twins were the last to be taken onto the platform in a group of a hundred or so. I desperately tried to join them, but it was too late. I watched helplessly as they were bundled inside the last carriage with the others. Quite what had happened to Mr. Székely was not immediately apparent to me. I suspected that he was dragged aside to enable more women and children to board.

Guards now tried to close the doors, but were prevented by the bulging mass of heads, torsos and limbs. Several shots were fired. My own queue jolted forward and people began to scream. The amplified voice of László Ferenczy once again boomed out from the loudspeakers:

"Please move right down inside the carriages, ladies and gentleman. Use all available space. Your journey is a brief one, and you will soon be able to re-join your families."

Order was quickly established. The last doors were slammed shut and secured with bolts and latches. The Hungarian guards finally boarded in a separate carriage, a loud whistle blew and the great steam locomotive began to pull away. As the thirty wagons creaked and rattled on by, I tried in vain to catch a glimpse of my wife and daughters. Where were they going? Would I ever see them again?

I looked around to survey the situation. I was among a group of about 400 Jews that remained on the platform. With me was Éva's doddery father who suddenly appeared from nowhere. He was disorientated and evidently having trouble getting his breath in the stifling heat.

Everybody was silent. What would happen next? Was there another transport coming to take us too?

Shouting orders in German, the SS guards began to separate the remaining crowd into two groups. I immediately noticed that the elderly and sick were segregated off with the women and children. My father-in-law appeared dazed and confused. Whilst my back was momentarily turned, he wandered away from the throng.

When I realised what had happened, I frantically tried to pull him back, but it was too late. He approached one of the guards and bowed his head in a gesture of courtesy:

"Please sir. There must be some mistake. We are law-abiding peaceful Jews…"

Before he could finish his sentence, the SS thug smote him round the face. He fell into the mud and was dealt another blow; this time a boot below the ribcage. I ran over to help him and soon realised that we were both in the wrong group of around 250 people. The guards now surrounded us and steered us further to one side with the gesturing movements of their rifles. We eventually formed a long column, arranged in files of five abreast. Éva's father stood bent over to my left. He was wheezing and in obvious pain. But I was helpless, always impotent.

Ordered to remain calm and silent, we marched away. Our luggage, we were told, would follow separately, but we were no fools. There was a palpable fear in the air. Mothers carried children in their arms and whispered empty words of comfort. Husbands and wives held hands, perhaps for the last time. The column moved on.

It began to rain. The water on my face was refreshing and I eagerly opened my parched mouth to catch a few enticing drops that comforted but did not quench. The scenery began to change as we passed the final few tenements of the city. The sun broke through the rainclouds and I beheld a rainbow on the distant horizon. The rain stopped. We carried on.

We walked for over an hour. Arriving at a small clearing of trees on the edge of a shallow ravine, the guards ordered us all to undress. My heart sank. This was surely the end. I helped my father-in-law to disrobe. He was such a proud man and I felt sickened that he'd been reduced to this. A guard pulled me out of the crowd with three other men. We were all still fully dressed.

I gazed around and saw groups of women and children. There was no dignity, no decency. They huddled together like naked apes and tried their hardest to hide their nudity, their shame. The guards jeered at the women, blowing kisses and wolf-whistling. One girl caught the eye of an inebriated SS man. Tall and thin, she had dark eyes, long braided hair and flawless white skin. The German stared at her searchingly and then called out to her:

"Come here, *Fräulein*! Come to *Onkel Moritz*."

The girl was stunned and bemused. Her trembling hands tried desperately to cover her breasts and sprawling pubic hair. She did not move.

"Hey, don't you want to live? You're so beautiful *mein Schatz*! I tell you again to step forward and come!"

Seeing his beckoning gesture, the girl tentatively approached. He caressed her cheeks and then gently removed the hand that was covering her pudendum.

"O what a beautiful thatch you have, my love. I would like to explore it further if I had a little more time. But then again, you're a filthy Jewess, aren't you? Yes you fucking are, you little bitch! You've put me under your evil Jewish spell!"

Not understanding his German but sensing his anger, the girl misconstrued the situation and removed her other hand to expose her ample bosom, thinking this would placate him. The guard glared at her breasts for a moment as if transfixed. He unholstered his pistol and pushed her over. A single shot to the head ended her suffering.

"*Juden* whore!" he muttered. The other guards laughed. He then parted her thighs and inserted the barrel of his revolver inside her.

"You want something German inside you – then try this!" He pulled his trigger for the second time.

Incredibly, another woman dared to approach the same guard, more out of desperation than logic. She clutched a tiny baby in her arms.

"What do you want from me?" she asked. "I'm just a poor housewife and mother! Please, don't hurt my baby girl. Please! I beg you! What harm have we ever done to you?"

Unable to understand her Hungarian, the SS man

laughed and spat in her face. He began to pummel her with his rifle butt before grabbing her by the hair and yanking her to the ground. She managed to sink her teeth into his leg. He cried out in pain and kicked her in the face, dislodging several teeth and breaking her nose. A torrent of blood flowed. The woman momentarily lost consciousness and relaxed the vice-like grip she had on her infant daughter.

The naked baby tumbled out of her arms and rolled onto the earth – delicate, exposed and vulnerable. Then to my horror, this German – this noble ancestor of Mann, Goethe, Leibniz, Gauss, Kepler and Händel – swept the child up by one leg and suspended her upside down in the air.

Coming out of her swoon, the woman beheld her baby dangling high before her. She screamed and pleaded for mercy. But our heroic German was in such a rage that he tossed the infant high in the air and into the pit below.

The distraught mother was now hysterical. He stood over her imperiously, like a colossus, enjoying this moment of prolonged maternal suffering; of power over life and death. He lit a cigarette and took a deep, satisfying drag. As the smoke escaped from his nostrils, he finally raised a muddy boot and stamped it down hard on the woman's head. The skull audibly cracked. Death was immediate.

Now the Germans rounded up the first hundred or so people and ordered them to assemble themselves in a long line at the edge of the trench. Women were permitted to hold onto their babies and young children. Four SS guards formed two pairs, with each couple hurrying to opposite ends of the line. One of the soldiers carried ammunition, the other a revolver.

Then it began. Shots were fired from either end of the line. As each person collapsed forward into the pit, the guard moved methodically on to the next victim. Screams of terror and disbelief filled the air around me.

I saw innocent people – women and children – shot in the back of the neck. Babies were spared the bullets but fell forwards in their mothers' arms. Others crashed to the ground and were tossed into the ravine like pieces of rubbish. Round after round of shots were fired; volley after volley, systematically and without care or compassion. The second guard exchanged the spent revolver for a freshly loaded one. Finally, both shooting parties met in the middle and a hundred bodies lie strewn on the ground.

Along with three other men, I was ordered to climb down into the pit and pile the people up in orderly rows at the bottom. We dragged the bodies off the embankment. Some were still alive and trying to lift their heads, with blood and spinal fluid oozing from their bullet wounds. The babies were either crushed or suffocated, but several still gasped and cried. There were no mercy shots, no *coup de grace* to end their suffering.

The sickly metallic odour of fresh blood overpowered me. I staggered and almost fainted. But before I realised what was happening, the next battery of gunshots resounded and more people flopped before me. A scarlet geyser spurted violently from one victim whilst another writhed and grabbed hold of my ankle. I wanted to finish them off, I really did. But I couldn't. I felt utterly powerless.

I lost all sense of time as I frantically dashed from one body to another; dragging, pulling and arranging them neatly in rows of five deep. I looked up momentarily and quickly averted my gaze as an SS man stood behind my father-in-law and pointed a pistol to the back of his head. I braced myself. I heard the gunshot crack. Then I shuddered upon hearing the pitiful dull thud before me in the pit. I rushed over to him. He wasn't breathing. I was unable to feel a pulse. He must have died instantaneously as the bullet pierced his brainstem. A wave of relief filled me and I shouted to a colleague to help move his body. I mumbled a prayer and closed his eyes. But many were less fortunate.

Finally, the butchers finished their grisly work; but what about the four of us in the pit? One of my companions made a run for it. A guard ordered him to stop, but he kept going. I heard a shot. He stumbled and limped on. Another shot. He fell. Then there was another shot, then another. I was the only prisoner still standing.

I raised my hands in submission and cried out in German, "*Arzt!* I am a doctor!"

The SS man lowered his rifle and stared at me long and hard. He signalled for me to join him. I staggered out of the trench. A senior guard approached and began to question me. He seemed to be impressed by my fluent German. I explained my role as a Gestapo informer and added that I would be very useful in a military hospital.

"*Vielleicht, ja.* You shall go to see *der Todesengel.* I'm sure he'll find something useful for you to do."

What did he mean, Angel of Death? I nodded. He laughed and pointed to a pile of sand and gravel. I was ordered to shovel this over the bodies whilst another guard applied a thin dusting of quicklime.

Limbs and torsos jutted jaggedly out of the white dust, twitching and convulsing. An occasional submerged groan was discernible from the zigzagged heap of heaving flesh. The sand soon developed gruesome red streaks which expanded like a crimson cancer and coalesced into enormous geographic blotches.

One girl, choking and asphyxiating, tried desperately to scramble up to the top of the pile – to breathe and gulp in mouthfuls of revitalising air. This had a horrible rousing effect on the other dying people, who began to judder and shake. They all began to lash out, biting and scratching. Fingernails clawed and dug into her arms and legs; pulling her down, down, downward into the pit. The helpless girl was once again sucked under, and this time she did not re-emerge from the open grave.

So here they all lie, amidst the grume and milky brain splashes, children crying, all dying; in their last throes of suffering; naked, shot – but not dead. Red eyes glared upward. Blood bubbled out of necks.

My mouth filled with thin saliva as the colour drained from my clammy face. I bent over, slobbered, heaved – but had nothing to bring up. Euthanasia be damned!

Seemingly oblivious to the suffering before them, the SS guards casually debated the need for cremation, deciding to return once the deportations were nearing completion.

I was eventually escorted back to the brick factory where I joined a new party scheduled for transportation in the morning. Visibly shaken and bloodstained, curious people approached me and asked what had happened. I didn't have the strength nor the inclination to tell them the truth, and tried my best to allay their fears.

I thankfully managed to track down my Gladstone bag that had been left by the railway platform earlier on. I was comforted to find that my journal was still inside. For it was my duty to record everything – every crime, every horror.

After a meagre supper of stale bread and rainwater, I settled under one of the tarpaulin shelters and recorded the horrific events of this afternoon in my diary.

Sleep does not come as I ruminate about my family, crammed into that suffocating cattle car. I just pray that they have arrived safely and are all bedded down with warm blankets and full bellies. I doze for perhaps two hours. The night is cold and damp, but at least it's not winter.

THE TRAIN

Diary of Dr. József Sárkány, 1944

Friday 12th May

I see oceans of red corpuscles, platelets and plasma – all flooding my senses in a trinity of blood. I can smell it, even taste the iron on my tongue. Is this a premonition of things to come?

Aroused from my sanguineous musings by the wail of a baby girl, I perceived her hunger and malnourishment amidst the pitiful cries that embodied the most primeval form of lamentation.

I tried to focus on Éva and the girls. I had vivid flashbacks of yesterday, and yearned to hug my family once more. I felt naked and exposed without Éva; only half a person, defenceless, almost paralysed with fear of the unavoidable troubles ahead of me.

Eichmann's black devils arrived at the brick factory shortly after seven this morning. They blew whistles and began to herd us together into rows. They barked repetitive commands in German – always the same:

"Out! Come on! Hurry! That's it! We've organised special trains for you."

Trucks were loaded with the elderly and infirm, whilst the pedestrian cohort was marched towards the station. Upon arrival, we were greeted by more whistles as the all too familiar chaos ensued. A long chain of brown boxcars was waiting for us to board. There was no possibility of escape. The SS were omnipresent, and sentry guards with fierce Alsatians were posted at every possible exit.

Ferenczy's oily tones were once again broadcast over the loudspeakers that hissed and crackled. The same old reassuring lies were told to optimise the packaging of his Jewish livestock.

I noticed three young women standing in front of an SS

guard. They were all wearing red lipstick and mascara. One fell to her knees and implored him with outstretched hands:

"We're still so young! We all want to work! We'll do anything – *anything*, you understand."

They spoke in fluent German, but it might as well have been Hungarian. Their pleas fell on deaf ears.

And so, I finally boarded my freight car. Like cattle off to the slaughterhouse, we were impacted together like pieces of meat – nameless, just random numbers. My ultimate destination was unknown, but I suspected some heinous human abattoir in central Poland.

The door finally slid shut and we were enveloped in an eerie gloom. The sound of bolt and latch informed us that we were now locked in. To be categorically certain, the rattle of a padlock and chain followed shortly after. The interior was dark and claustrophobic. The tiny excuse for a window was festooned in corroded barbed wire: a kind of metallic brown ivy that throttled us all.

The thin air hovered over us in a stymied pocket. The ventilation grill was stubbornly rusted in a permanent state of semi-occlusion. We managed to dislodge the dust and dirt, and a barely perceivable draft of air appeared to circulate. Those fortunate enough to be standing next to the window greedily took in gulps of air. They looked peculiar, like fish out of water, but nobody cared.

A whistle blew and the great steam locomotive finally pulled us away from the station. The German guards smiled and waved incongruously as cattle-car after cattle-car creaked and shuddered past them in the May sunshine of late morning.

My profession was well known to most. Several women immediately begged me for tranquillisers, but I had none to spare. A cacophony of wheezes and brittle gasps for air soon joined the monotonous dissonance of clanking metal.

The first two hours passed incredibly slowly. People were forced to elevate arms above their heads in order to manoeuvre through the tangle of packed bodies. I tentatively suggested that we try to rearrange ourselves in order to optimise all available space. There was a general consensus, and we decided to stack all suitcases at one end of the carriage. Some were reluctant to part with their possessions, but eventually conceded. The suitcases were stacked from floor to ceiling. There wasn't the room to open them. The softer baggage containing clothes and blankets we used as cushions for the elderly, sick and pregnant women to perch on. The rest of us had to stand. We decided to rotate round intermittently in an attempt to let everyone get a bit of fresh air from the window and vent.

Another problem was the lack of water. None of us were quite sure how long the journey would last, but we guessed that Warsaw was at least 350 miles north of Munkács. Depending on the speed of the train and the number of station-stops, I suggested that the journey would be spread over two days. Knowing how difficult it was to pack us all in, I was certain that we'd be stuck inside this boxcar for the duration of the journey. This didn't go down well.

The only bucket of water provided currently held about twelve litres. This was important, and I got several separate estimates that ranged between eleven and fourteen litres. I performed a quick headcount. Incredibly, there were 105 bodies crammed into this enclosed space. I didn't quite believe it at first, but it was soon independently verified by several other passengers in different parts of the carriage.

There appeared to be a greater number of women, at least sixty: four of these were heavily pregnant and two were in the second trimester. The remaining forty-five included twenty children, of which three were babies, and about twenty-five men. Half of all the adults were at least fifty years or older.

For everyone to get an equal share of water, I calculated that each should receive about 120 millilitres. An elderly man stood up and passed me a pewter hip flask from his jacket pocket. Long empty, he said that it held four fluid ounces, which I estimated to be around 120ml. So, it was agreed that we would all have one flask of water, beginning with the pregnant women and children.

The solitary privy bucket was our next problem, particularly in attempting to maintain a degree of privacy and dignity. The easiest option was to have two volunteers hold up a bedsheet at either end, creating a temporary screen when the latrine was in use. This laborious manual draping was quickly improved upon by permanent attachments to elevated suitcase handles. Many desperately tried to hold on for as long as possible. Some, I'm sure, preferred to soil themselves with sporadic trickles, whilst others ran the gauntlet and braved the humiliation of the bucket. Several women were suffering from cystitis, which added its own pastiche to the already fetid air.

Tensions now ran rife as people succumbed to frustration, discomfort and fatigue. Various arguments erupted across the carriage. A heated exchange took place directly behind me as I waited in line to use the communal bucket. It was as much a clash of classes as anything else, and involved a middle-aged banker and a young bohemian artist. The argument ran something like this:

Banker: Excuse us please; my mother needs to use the bathroom.

Artist: Bathroom indeed! Who do think you are? You, with your tailored black suit: there's a queue here, and you're at the end of it!

Banker: All I ask is that you show some consideration for my mother please. We may be herded like animals, but let's still maintain some decorum.

Artist: Too late! Mama's had a little accident.

Banker: O my dear God! How awful! Please don't cry, Mother.

Artist: It won't be long before we'll all be standing ankle-deep in our own filth!

Banker: We have to stand together – as one; united in solidarity against the common enemy. We

	have to remain decent humans.
Artist:	What are you talking about? The Germans plan to dehumanise us even more. We'll end up like wild animals: feral and vicious. It'll be about our primitive instincts, survival of the fittest. We'll become obsessed with self-preservation – dog-eat-dog! We'll bite, scratch, tear, kick, thieve and grovel in the dirt – just so that miserable bit of bread comes our way.
Banker:	I disagree, young man. We're civilised human beings with a set of moral codes and ethics.
Artist:	*Ach!* Don't you get it? Civilisation for us Jews is over. We'll soon be scurrying like rodents in the grime. We must become savage, selfish, bestial and barbaric. Morals and ethics are nothing but dangerous anachronisms. Just give me a place to eat, sleep and shit! You can leave morality to the intellectual dreamers and the Godforsaken piles of cultivated dead!
Banker:	We're valuable workers for the German war effort.
Artist:	Wake up Joseph and stop your multicoloured dreaming! We've been flushed down the latrine with all the other excrement! We're on a collision course with chaos, anarchy and ultraviolence. The ghetto's been nothing but child's play up 'til now. Just wait and see what's waiting to bite you at the end of this infernal railway line! The conquering boot of National Socialism will smash into all of our faces and beat us down into the dust from which we came. Anyway, enough! Just shut up and go wipe the piss off your Mama's shoes.

We arrived at Košice in the late afternoon. I guessed that we'd travelled some ninety miles from Munkács. The vast and bustling railway station was heavy with smoke that drifted away westward in silent black plumes. The Hungarian gendarmes alighted from the train. They flamboyantly waved goodbye to us, laughing at our misfortune and cracking jokes.

We were now in the unkind claws of Eichmann's *Schutzstaffel*. Dozens of them spilled onto the railway platform, carrying tantalising jugs of iced water. They taunted us with these thirst-quenching vessels of *aqua vitae*, trying ever so unconvincingly to squeeze them through the gaps in the barbed wire. Feigning sadness, they eventually proceeded to pour out the water onto the hot tarmac floor.

Hundreds of people across thirty carriages surged forward, perversely trying to imbibe the evaporating fluid with their eyes. It was a pathetic and puerile torture, designed to humiliate us even more. Their dogs greedily lapped up the puddles. I glimpsed shattered chunks of ice and imagined them sliding meltingly around my mouth.

This was the final straw. Like wild animals before dying, we all began to bash and beat our hands on the freight cars, crying out for help:

"Please give us some water. PLEASE! *Oy vey!* We are dying of suffocation and thirst! PLEASE somebody help us! We are good Jews. We have done nothing wrong!"

There followed a rattle of machine-gun fire, and order was once again restored to this warped travelling circus. No, we were worse than animals: we were Jews…

The train eventually began to move again, monotonously, mile after mile. The Carpathians were well behind us now. We prayed for rain so as to at least moisten our mouths, but God had truly abandoned us.

It was dark when we arrived at our next stop; a railway-siding in Tarnów. The guards exited the train with overnight bags, so it looked as if we'd be staying here until tomorrow. Again, there was no water, no food… no hope.

It's hard to describe the misery around me as I had my turn to perch and put pen to paper in the shadows. All this collective wretchedness must of course be amplified thirty times or more. As my mind wandered, I tried desperately not to ruminate on my family, but the emotions soon overwhelmed me and I wept without tears in silence. Sleep eventually came, but was rudely interrupted when I had to surrender my seat to the next weary passenger.

I observed a young mother and baby during the long night. She desperately tried to suckle her infant, but her milk had dried up. Dozing and drifting in and out of consciousness, my head slumped forward momentarily. The man in front nudged me sharply backward and I came around with a start. The soothing voice of the mother drew my attention:

"Shlomo, wake up little *schmeckle!* Come on sweet *bubbeleh!* Mama's got some lovely warm milk for you."

I focused on the small bundle in her arms and saw a perfectly still baby; eyes half shut, mouth open, lips blue. He was dead.

I engaged with the woman, explaining that I was a doctor and gently asking to examine her child. She was reluctant to accept. She surely knew that he was no longer breathing but wanted to pretend, at least for a little while longer. After an hour or so, I bent down to address the woman at eye level:

"I'm so sorry. But your baby... your baby has gone. You have to let him go."

"What? *Feh!* You're a liar! Shame on you! Call yourself a doctor. Your word isn't worth *bubkes!* He's sleeping, that's all. The journey's worn him out. Look! He's still warm."

Sabbath 13th May

It was perhaps three hours since the light of dawn when the steam locomotive finally began to pull away from Tarnów station. The lingering stale odour of a hundred humans was oppressive. The bucket was now filled to the brim and began to slosh its vile contents onto the floorboards. We decided to siphon off the liquid with a shallow bowl and poured it through the window where it trickled down the outside. The remaining sludge was scooped out and hurled at the barbed wire mesh where it dripped in gloopy lumps down both sides of the carriage door. This primitive form of sewage control must surely be happening along the entire convoy of moving cattle-cars.

When it was finally my turn to get some water, I greedily guzzled it down. I used the last few delicious drops to moisten a morsel of bread stashed in my pocket. Then I opened up a seam in my suit jacket and removed Éva's wedding ring. Pushing it gently into the damp bread, I rolled the doughy mass into a ball and swallowed it whole. There was a slight scraping sensation as the bread came away in my gullet, but the band eventually found its way into the hidden depths of my empty stomach.

On seeing me do this successfully and with apparent ease, an elderly woman removed a handful of *Fillérs* from the lining of her coat. When she eventually received her share of water, she began to swallow the coins one after the other. She had one coin left to get down, but the hip flask was now dry. The man next in line snatched it from her and filled his own ration from the bucket. The woman stared at the coin. Several people nearby warned her not to attempt to swallow it, but she ignored their advice, tilted her head back and put it in her mouth. She swallowed and immediately began to choke.

I barged my way through the crowd who obligingly raised their arms to create more space. The panic-stricken woman was now gagging and drooling as the coin remained lodged in her throat, occluding her airway and suffocating her. I smacked her sharply on the back – once, twice, three times, again and again. She spluttered and gasped and gagged once more – but nothing came up. I felt helpless as a raucous stridor now ensued and saliva poured copiously out of her mouth. Her eyes began to bulge as her engorged tongue protruded forward through purple lips. The last moments were the worst for me as her fight for life slowly ebbed away. Her eyes glazed over and half-closed; her complexion changed to a slate-grey, breathing shallow and episodic. Finally, there was a prolonged wheeze as she collapsed to the floor. Then she breathed no more.

I asked for her name but nobody seemed to know her. We then realised that her husband was one of the six casualties that failed to make it through the night. Her demise now brought the death toll up to eight: three women, four men and one baby boy.

We continued northward and travelled for about four hours before halting once again at the imposing station of Kraków. The pungent odours of stale sweat and halitosis now formed an unholy alliance with the mordant fumes of cystitis and dysentery. And from one corner there began to emanate the pervasive reek of putrefaction.

The noxious atmosphere inside our human crate was both maddening and stupefying. The initial bickering for space, air, light and water was now replaced by protracted bouts of silence, punctuated by moans and prayers.

After another change of guard and several tortuous hours of more waiting around, our train journey continued for forty miles or so before grinding to a halt once more. An antique sign in quaint gothic lettering declared the name of the station to be *Oświęcim*. I had never heard of it, but the rustic surroundings looked benign enough and certainly put my mind at ease. After some noisy shunting, it was not long before we were off again.

What can there really be left for us at the end of the line? Noah had his rainbow after the deluge. What has God got in store for us? For this is no Ark of Salvation. Ours is a grotesque convoy of carnage: a perverse serpent of wooden crates that snakes and rattles forever on. Thirty decrepit wagons crammed to bursting – people panting, suffocating, squatting, soiling. How pathetic are we? Locked up, shut in, like meat left to hang in the larder; penned in like pigs, we squeal in the dark. But our muffled moans for deliverance fade into nothingness.

Nobody listens. Nobody cares…

Part II

Into the Crematorium

WELCOME TO
AUSCHWITZ-BIRKENAU

Diary of Dr. József Sárkány, Auschwitz, Poland, 1944

Sabbath 13th May

We began to slow. I was right up against the window and had a view outside. Several signs contained the word *Brzezinka*, so I assumed that this would be our next stop. The train was shunted onto another sidetrack and began to roll slowly onward. We passed under an enormous brick archway before finally grinding to a halt. People started to weep. A sense of unease and fear permeated the carriage. The sound of dogs barking could be heard through the closed doors. The great steam engine blew a piercing whistle. We had arrived at our destination.

A chorus of shouting erupted as people begged for air, water, bread… life. A violent surge forward pressed me up tight against the door. I peered outside and attempted to take in the scene before me.

There was a great coming and going of men in striped uniforms, rushing about frantically. They were being shouted at and harassed by SS guards carrying whips and truncheons. I caught a glimpse of ferocious Alsatians pulling at their chains and snarling. They appeared agitated and excited by our arrival, due no doubt to their keen sense of smell.

A volley of machine-gun fire erupted out of nowhere. Despite the heat and suffocating claustrophobia inside our carriage, everybody froze in terror. There was a momentary pause in the pushing and heaving and moaning and sobbing. We remained still and silent, wondering what kind of hell now awaited us outside.

A guard halted in front of our boxcar window and sniggered. He ran a finger across his clammy throat and stuck out his tongue, pointing at me. He then mimicked a noose around his neck, feigning hanging. This grisly piece of mime appeared to amuse him. Finally, he approached the elevated window and stared up at my shadowed outline. Warm spittle struck my face. It reeked of alcohol and tobacco. He laughed before moving on to the next window.

A group of three prisoners in striped apparel assembled outside our carriage, waiting in line for the doors to slide open. Their faces were flushed and damp with sweat. They seemed impervious to our cries for air and water, but instead stood perfectly still; their faces emotionless.

The guards blew synchronised whistles. One of the prisoners dashed to our door with a stepladder. He climbed up and removed the double-padlocked chain. He waited for another whistle to blow before yanking on the door bolts that ground open with a brain-curdling screech. An interpreter outside then spoke to us in Hungarian, explaining that the doors would shortly be opened and that we must all stay in our carriage until instructed to leave.

The prisoner waited for yet another whistle before sliding open the door. He immediately gagged, then retreated back down the steps and filed back into line. His face was oddly familiar.

"Get out! Everybody down! Leave your heavy luggage behind!"

I was first to exit, holding on tightly to my Gladstone bag. The sunshine dazzled my eyes and took me by surprise after two long days of darkness. I gradually adjusted to the vista that surrounded me, and peered around through scrunched-up eyes.

From the elevated door I beheld a gargantuan ramp of sun-bleached earth and yellowish gravel that was rapidly filling with people from the adjacent boxcars. All around was an arid flat terrain that was punctuated by row upon row of wooden huts, windowless and terrifying in their number and geometric precision. These hundreds of rickety old barracks had the appearance of horse stables, covered in flaking tarpaper roofs, painted green.

Then it hit me. The entire landscape was fenced in and compartmentalised by endless palisades of curved concrete pillars, along which were strung lines of taut barbed wire. White ceramic insulators indicated that the fence was electrified under high tension. Unambiguous placards warned: 'Attention! High voltage! Risk of death!'

Directly ahead were the imposing outlines of two enormous chimneys. Each seemed to be square in form and constructed of red bricks. They suggested the presence of two great crematoria, situated either side of the railway ramp. A gentle breeze conveyed the acrid fumes of scorched flesh and singed hair. I recognised the smell: any forensic pathologist worth his salt would. It was the pungent odour of burning human viscera, fat, sinew and bone; a sickly, cloying aroma akin to candles made from carrion tallow.

Beyond the ramp I saw long streets of dried mud. Occasional trucks, including a Red Cross van, travelled past on the bumpy camp highway. The latter was comforting to see and temporarily lifted my spirits, before my eyes then fixed upon the files of emaciated men in faded striped pyjamas, scurrying along the network of pedestrian thoroughfares in all directions. One group carried shovels and picks on their muddied shoulders, whilst another was weighed down by rough-sawn planks. Along the barbwire perimeter, at a distance of eighty to ninety metres from each other, elevated watchtowers housed SS sentries in greyish green uniforms. With a rifle over one shoulder, each guard was manning a machine gun, mounted on a tripod.

I looked around at my decimated travel companions, alighting from the wagon after me. We had lost a total of twelve on the journey. These included the infant, Shlomo Gellér, and two children under two. The remaining nine fatalities included the woman who choked to death, and her husband who predeceased her. The others were all elderly men and women, whose weakened constitutions and tired hearts could no longer cope with the struggle for life. I counted 92 people off our wagon after me.

Utterly exhausted and traumatised by our two-day odyssey, the elderly stared soporifically into the empty skies. Many of the younger faces showed signs of terror as they were growled at by an array of canine fangs.

A prisoner whispered in Yiddish to the younger teenage boys: "You're eighteen, you're a carpenter. You're nineteen, and you're a bricklayer. You're eighteen, you're a roofer," and so on.

To the teenage girls, another prisoner whispered: "You are twenty and a seamstress. You're nineteen and a nurse. You are eighteen and a cook."

After being told that he was a forty-year-old scaffolder, I heard a former member of the *Judenrat* loudly protest:

"No sir, I am fifty-three and a Professor of History. And besides, we're all lucky Jews today. I just overheard two SS men saying that most of our transport will be given *Special Treatment*."

"Then you're a dead professor of history!" came the laconic reply.

Once emptied of the living, two striped prisoners entered our carriage and began unloading; passing down trunks and suitcases in rapid succession to their associate outside who stacked them haphazardly on either side of the door.

More orders were yelled out in German as we were pushed and pulled into line:

"Men here, and women here!"

The noise of sand crunching under heavy boots grew ever louder as a tall SS officer strolled casually past us. He was wearing a long white doctor's coat over his green uniform. His face was shadowed by the black visor of his cap, above which glistened the ominous insignia of a deaths-head skull. His hands were gloved in delicate pale-grey velvet, and he gently fanned himself with a leatherbound notebook. After reaching the end of the line, he paused momentarily to light a cigarette. Then casually he strolled

96

back down the long queue of people. He paused before a fourteen-year-old girl called Ilona Temes. His voice was oddly familiar, but I was unable to fully see his face and couldn't quite place him:

"How old are you Sarah?"

"I am nineteen years old, *Herr Doktor.*"

"And do you have an occupation, my dear?"

"Yes, sir – I am a seamstress."

"That's very good, *Meine Liebste.*"

Two rows were formed; men on one side, and women and children on the other. My eyes once again turned to the smokeless chimneys on the horizon.

But the second phase of selection was already underway. The line of men now paraded in single file before the SS doctor who perched on top of a stepladder. He scarcely looked up and seemed more interested in the cut of his gloves. After a nonchalant flick of his hand, his assistant bellowed out either 'left!' or 'right!'

So, following a barely perceptible hand gesture, we found ourselves in two new groups. I was on the left-hand side, accompanied by middle-aged men and youths. Next was the turn of the women and children, many of whom ended up in the right-hand column.

The doctor wanted to separate a mother from her young boy of around seven or eight. She was a nurse, and begged not to be separated from her son. Her drawn and beleaguered face betrayed all the deprivation and hardship she'd had to endure over the past few months:

"Please, *Herr Doktor* – I must stay with my son. He's very frightened and also suffers from diabetes."

"Please don't concern yourself, my dear Jewish mother. You'll be back together sooner than you think. I can guarantee that you'll be enjoying a hot meal together in no time at all. But first you need to have a nice hot shower and change of clothes."

A high-pitched screech suddenly resounded along the ramp before an amplified Hungarian voice emanated from a series of loudspeakers:

"Good afternoon, ladies and gentlemen. Welcome to Auschwitz-Birkenau. I recognise that your journey has been a lengthy and arduous one. I can only apologise for the inexcusable travelling conditions. Please be reassured that this is an isolated incident, and we will be contacting the appropriate Hungarian authorities in order to rectify this temporary mishap. However, I appreciate that some of you have lost loved ones en route, both young and old. Please accept our sincere condolences for this deplorable loss of life, and take heart that their mortal remains will be treated with the utmost dignity and respect. There is a Jewish cemetery just north of this work-camp in which your dearly departed will be laid to rest and given the full *Kaddish*.

"Now, I will not keep you much longer as you must be in dire need of sustenance and rest. It is however camp policy that every new arrival is subject to our strict rules of hygiene and quarantine. You have therefore been temporarily divided into two groups for separate shower-baths and disinfection in our brand new, state-of-the-art sanitation facility – the Central Sauna. For the sake of your own modesty, men and women will take separate showers. We clearly do not wish to separate mothers from their young children, and we also find that the elderly gentlefolk are a great source of comfort and wisdom to the nervous youngsters. They also provide an invaluable extra pair of hands in the undressing and shower rooms.

"So without further ado, may I once again welcome you all to your new home in Poland. Sanitation Party 1 will be escorted on foot to the Central Sauna building. Transports have been provided for Sanitation Party 2, so please make your way to a nearby truck in an orderly fashion when prompted to do so. I can guarantee that you'll soon be reunited with your loved ones. After a refreshing shower and change of clothes, you can finally all sit down to a delicious bowl of hot broth and buttered bread. And please do not concern yourselves about your left luggage. All baggage will be conveyed directly to quarantine and arranged according to your carriage number. All of your possessions will therefore be ready for pickup upon your arrival."

Portable wooden stepladders were brought to a waiting Red Cross truck. The SS doctor sat dispassionately nearby as it began to fill with the elderly, frail and infirm. He beckoned to one of the prisoners who immediately ran up, removed his cap, and stood rigidly to attention with head bowed. The doctor extracted a cloth from his coat pocket and casually pointed to his glossy black boots. The prisoner fell to his knees, received the cloth and began to buff up the leather to a luxuriant shine. Meanwhile, the doctor fingered a golden *caduceus* badge on his left lapel, completely indifferent to the swelling crowds around him.

Two men chatted quietly next to me whilst we watched the trucks being filled:

First man:	Clearly, *Herr Doktor* is a very important man. He's in charge around here, for sure.
Second man:	I'm not entirely familiar with the SS ranks, but I overheard one of the guards address him as Captain.
First man:	Excuse me (addressing a striped prisoner). Who is that gentleman sitting in the shade over there?
Prisoner:	That is *Hauptsturmführer, Doktor Mengele* – a senior physician of great importance! He is present on the ramp at the arrival of every transport where he takes a particular interest in the selections.
Second man:	What do you mean by *selections*?
Prisoner:	Never mind, comrade! Now move on quickly before *Kapo* Kinski beats us both to a pulp!

Mengele? I thought for a moment. Then the penny finally dropped. Mengele! Yes, of course – I knew his partly obscured face looked oddly familiar. It was surely Josef! I hadn't seen him for several years, ever since he stitched me up on *Kristallnacht*. He'd kept to his word and joined the SS. Well, he'd certainly done well for himself. I wondered if he'd remember me. Perhaps he knew where my wife and daughters were. Yes, this was surely a piece of luck that had finally come my way!

As the final lorry-loads of people departed from the ramp, I was amongst the bewildered pedestrians left behind. We were quickly assembled into lines of four abreast and I found myself right at the back.

As the long human chain began to move forward, an SS officer counted us off the ramp, row by row. When he got to the end, he finally called out, *"Einhundertfünfzig!"* I then realised that our group was some six-hundred strong.

We trudged through a heavily guarded gate and made our way along a road running perpendicular to the ramp. The broken outlines of four chimneys grew ever nearer as we passed through a sentry post to enter a wooded enclosure. Through the branches to our left, we could make out a small sub-camp of some thirty barracks in which several bonfires were burning outside.

We finally reached the entrance to an enormous brick building. A German guard approached and shouted out: "Welcome to the *Zentralsauna* at *KZ* Auschwitz!"

~

We entered the Sauna building through an east-facing door. The first thing we had to do was remove all our clothes. At the far end of this anteroom were two SS doctors in long white coats. They watched us like hawks as we paraded naked in front of them. A few of the skinnier men with protruding ribs were examined close up.

Mr. Bródy the greengrocer began to cough. I could see

that he'd desperately tried to hold it in, but it eventually burst out in a fruity expectoration. His face was flushed. He swallowed the phlegm that had clearly filled his mouth. One of the doctors asked him to step forward. He examined his teeth before going on to percuss his chest. Finally, he placed his stethoscope over both lung bases and asked him to breathe deeply, in and out. My heart sank as I heard coarse wheezes and crackles, followed by another fit of coughing.

"Spit it out!" commanded the doctor. Mr. Bródy reluctantly transferred the sputum into the cupped palm of his hand. The gloopy mass looked rusty green.

"Very good," said the doctor, evidently pleased. "You can stand over there."

The greengrocer looked devastated. His eyes welled up and he slowly shuffled to one side to join five other men.

"You six will be taken directly to the camp hospital," said the second doctor. "The rest of you can now proceed to the showers. Just follow the corridor ahead."

Our party headed up the corridor before entering a large room. There were ten barbers inside, all male prisoners in striped uniforms. Nobody said a word. They seemed to be in an enormous hurry and were also under constant scrutiny. After a preliminary cut with cropping scissors, the dull razor blade began to scrape over the contours of my scalp. There was no lubricating soap and the blade chafed my skin. An occasional sharp pang indicated a deeper abrasion, and I suspected that my head must be bleeding.

The barber now told me to raise my arms. Again, he scraped and scratched in the recesses of my armpits. A quick rinse in a bloodstained jar and he proceeded to shave my arms, legs, chest, back and pubic hair. I winced several times as the razor nicked my groin and then grazed the thin skin over my shins.

I joined the back of another queue, this time in front of an examination room. When it was my turn, I was hurriedly made to open my mouth and lift up my scrotum. An SS doctor wearing a light on his forehead now ordered me to bend over. He parted my buttocks widely and inspected the area for any hidden items. I was then told to get onto the couch, turn on one side and bend up my knees. A probing gloved finger proceeded to ferret around in my rectum. No contraband was found.

I quickly moved on to the shower-room where I was first dunked in a bathtub of *Lysol*. The chlorinated green solution stung my eyes and irritated my razor cuts. Still rubbing my eyes, I was finally shoved towards the communal showers.

We all huddled together under the fifty or so shower heads and waited for the water to fall. A guard controlled the taps and made vulgar remarks while we stood naked and shivered, covered in bloodstains and drenched in disinfectant. A fierce jet of water then hit us. We all smarted and jumped about. It was icy-cold and made me catch my breath. The guard howled with laughter. The water temperature abruptly changed to scalding-hot. We cried out and instinctively moved out of the way. Amidst the great clouds of steam, another guard lunged forward with a truncheon. He beat us savagely and ordered us to get back under the water. We all moved back into the blistering torrent, gritting our teeth. There followed several alternating bursts of cold and hot jets. The guards found this hilarious.

Finally, the torture was over and we were harried into yet another room to drip-dry.

A dozen tattooists sat along one side of the room. Upon a long wooden table in front of them were various jars, ink bottles, needles and pieces of paper. Like a factory line of naked dripping dolls, we awaited our turn to be tattooed. I eventually sat down opposite a young Jewish prisoner who took my left arm and laid it supine on the table. He removed a long sharp stylus from a jamjar filled with murky water: a mixture of blood and ink. A greasy film of hair and scum floated on the surface. He dipped the pointed end into a bottle of black ink and then proceeded to make rapid shallow punctures into the sensitive skin of my forearm. The stuttering pricks began to form throbbing and bloody

102

hieroglyphs. With every unhygienic penetration, I prayed that the raw area would not get infected.

Upon completion, I waited around for the others to receive their numerical marks of bondage. I immediately got to work in dabbing the tattoo site with my own saliva, and began rubbing the area to dull the throbbing. Wiping away the puddles of blood and gullies of ink, I finally beheld my new identity.

I was no longer Dr. József Sárkány. I had been processed and transformed into Prisoner A-7938.

Still drip-drying, our party was now hurried along another lengthy corridor until we arrived at a large room in the south wing. Prisoners were stationed at one end, busily sorting through bundles of clothes for us to receive. There was no attempt to assess individual sizes, and my pile looked distinctly shabby and frayed. I received a striped hessian jacket, trousers and cap. With these were one pair of threadbare socks, shoes and a single pair of underpants. The shoes were tatty and had a small hole in the left sole.

We all began to try on our new prison garb. My trousers were too long and my jacket too tight. However, we were all in the same boat, and after a bit of frantic swapping with the other men, I managed to acquire a slightly better overall fit. Some unlucky prisoners ended up with a pair of coarse wooden clogs. They looked horribly uncomfortable and would no doubt excoriate the skin and cause infected ulcers.

After four hours in the Birkenau Central Sauna, we eventually filed out of the building through double doors. It was dark outside and there was an odour of charred flesh in the air. I thought about my wife and daughters, and wondered if they'd been subjected to the same dehumanising induction process. I shuddered to think of them without their hair, tattooed and wearing a mishmash of tattered rags. Where were they? They must surely be housed somewhere in this vast metropolis of concrete and barbed wire. And what of Éva's elderly mother? I wondered whether she'd even made it off the train.

We were escorted back onto the main camp road. Hundreds of arc lamps now blanketed the surroundings in a spectral artificial light. The illuminated watch towers and ominous hum of the high-tension barbwire added to our sense of oppressive incarceration and helplessness. We entered through a sentry gate into the vast men's camp of Auschwitz-Birkenau.

~

Accompanied by an SS guard, I was segregated from the other prisoners before entering into my new abode. Once I got over the stench, I quickly surveyed the squalid interior décor. What I beheld was truly staggering; like some distorted nightmare that defied the laws of physics – the very laws of humanity. But no, my eyes did not deceive me.

I estimated at least a thousand prisoners crammed into this single wooden barracks. From within their cage-like boxes they formed a grotesque pulsating mass of entwined limbs. They were arranged haphazardly, some eight to ten to a pallet, sharing a single coarse blanket. I saw row upon row of muddy boots and clogs beneath each bunk. The ulcerated feet of one prisoner oozed onto the face of another, whose wide eyes and vacuous expression indicated that he was dead. Others scratched, pinched, bit and kicked in a vain attempt to gain a little bit more space – a little more comfort. Their shaven heads lay lengthwise and crosswise and back-to-front. Deprived of all humanity, these dying animals clung on to the final embers of their pitiful lives.

A man peered from behind a makeshift curtain and hobbled towards us. He stood to attention and accepted my registration card from the guard who departed with due haste, telling us not to loiter.

Before me stood a short, thin man of some fifty years. Vinegar-bottle lenses massively amplified his blue eyes. His face and neck were flushed. His breath was rank, and I noted a mouth full of brown teeth. We shook hands. He glanced at my registration card and duly noted that I was a doctor. His hands were trembling and arthritic:

"Welcome, Dr. Sárkány, to Hospital Barracks 12. My name is Dr. Arndt Krömer. You've been spared the façade of quarantine and sent directly to me instead."

He spoke to me in German. The civility overwhelmed me for a moment and I caught my breath.

"Thank you," I eventually stammered.

He beckoned me to follow him and we sat down together on a small bench in a cubicle off the main hall. He drew his curtain and lit a candle. A few moments later the electric lights cut out, and we huddled next to each other in the flickering gloom. He offered me a cigarette which I gladly accepted. He then swigged from a rusty tin. It smelled of rubbing-alcohol and I politely declined a nip.

"Suit yourself," he whispered. "You'll be begging me for the stuff by the end of the week."

His tremor improved greatly after a couple more glugs, before he finally drained the tin:

"Christ! That's better! Now let me fill you in on this hellhole they call Birkenau. Ah, but just one moment. Yes, I almost forgot in all the excitement. I've got a little present for you: call it a welcoming gift of sorts."

He produced my Gladstone bag from under his bed and proudly handed it over. Without thinking, I quickly looked inside and grabbed my last piece of emergency bread ration. Cramming it into my mouth, I chewed it ravenously. Krömer smiled and handed me a cup of water. I drained it in one satisfying guzzle. I'd never tasted bread so sweet nor water so quenching.

With supper over, I turned my attention to the rest of the bag's contents. Things had evidently been disturbed, but I was heartened to see that nothing appeared to be missing: various work permits, passport, doctor's licence, ink bottle, pens, and glasses – yes, it was all there.

I surreptitiously checked beneath the false bottom and was equally relieved to find my private journal securely wrapped up in an old pillow case.

"It seems you've got a secret admirer," said Krömer. "I'm not sure *who* precisely, but I suspect it's one of the SS doctors: any ideas?"

"No – not really," I replied, rather unconvincingly. Mengele! It had to be Josef – yes of course! He must have become aware of my arrival following registration.

"Anyhow, I'm happy for you," said Krömer. "You'll need all the help you can get in this place!"

After a protracted sigh, this polite and civilised German doctor began to unload his life story upon me, as all veteran prisoners invariably did, I supposed.

"Where do I begin? Well, I was born in Bochum in 1896. I commenced my medical studies at the University of Tübingen in 1914. The outbreak of war meant conscription, but I never saw action due to a crippling form of juvenile arthritis that had only recently flared up. I lost my father at Ypres in 1915 and my mother was killed in a French air raid the following year. After the war, I managed to complete my medical studies, but had become hopelessly addicted to morphine, which I was injecting regularly for pain relief. My arthritis seemed to abate and burn itself out, but the addiction remained.

"I eventually found a position in a small hospital in Munich where I developed an interest in psychiatry. It was here that I witnessed Hitler's rise to power and the failed *Putsch* of '23. After the Röhm Purge, I decided to leave Munich and settled in Stuttgart. I began to work with a range of handicapped patients and to explore the diverse range of mental health issues associated with their disabilities. After a chance meeting with an old acquaintance, Dr. Karl Brandt, at a medical conference in 1939, he managed to secure me a senior position at the Samaritan's Asylum in Grafenfck. I knew him through my long childhood friendship with his wife, Anni Rehborn.

"All was well until the autumn of that year. I had heard rumours that the hospital was to be converted into some kind of killing centre for disabled people. I made some enquiries and when my worst fears were confirmed, I managed to organise the evacuation of 120 patients to a monastery in Switzerland. When my actions were discovered, I was sent to Berlin and interrogated. I'm pretty sure I would have been executed if it had not been for Dr. Brandt who commuted my sentence to life imprisonment in Sachsenhausen. From there, I was finally transferred to Auschwitz-Birkenau in the spring of last year. Why, I'm not sure, but I've been rotting here ever since.

"Although the concentration camp system got me off the morphine, I'm now wracked with all sorts of ailments due to months of deprivation. My only comfort now is alcohol. I'm not fussy about what form it comes in: just as long as it settles my nerves and stops the shakes. My liver is shot of course; and my eyesight is rapidly failing. I've perhaps got a few more months before I can no longer see, and then it is liberty at last – well, through the chimney."

Stitched onto the left breast of his striped shirt, Krömer wore an inverted green triangle. The colour was faded and the edges worn and threadbare. I asked him what it meant and he told me that it was his emblem of shame, advertising to everyone that he was a convicted criminal.

"Will I be given a badge?" I asked.

"Oh yes: you'll soon be reunited with your Jewish Star. I'll sort this out for you after morning roll call. As a practising camp doctor, you'll also need a black ribbon."

It was getting late as we continued to converse in muffled whispers. My anxiety and curiosity kept fatigue at bay. I inquired about the armband he wore.

"This beautiful piece of cloth I have earned. It is the mark of a Block Leader, and with it I am able to acquire certain privileges, including a bed of my own and extra rations. I'm in charge of this particular barracks, and ensure that the camp regulations are strictly adhered to. My subordinates include a man who is in charge of cleaning and a clerk who keeps a written record of all inmates."

Krömer explained to me the complex organisation of the camp, with its precarious hierarchy of prisoners. He rattled off the names of innumerable SS guards in every sector and enlightened me about the prominent camp prisoners who wielded power and position.

"Each working party or *Kommando* is under the Chief *Kapo* and his supervising foreman. They're generally sadistic individuals and literally have the power of life and death over prisoners. Their reign of terror begins at roll call and ends, if you're lucky, at lights out. But you must understand that these *Kapos* have to be cruel: that's part of their job description. I heard rumours of one particularly brutal Chief going soft on his long-suffering men after a head injury. Seeing this sudden change in personality as a threat to their own authority, the SS were quick to strip him of his armband, his status and his privileges. Forced once again to share a communal bunk with his fellow inmates, they wasted no time in tearing him to pieces!"

I discovered that Birkenau was the largest extermination complex of the Third Reich. Krömer also spoke of the selections which took place every week in the hospitals and barracks.

"As soon as you arrive through Birkenau's archway, you're in essence a dead man! You will either die immediately in one of the gas chambers or slowly as a registered camp prisoner. The latter is by far the worse of the two evils: for you'll first have to suffer. You've only got to look around you in this place. The squalor and overcrowding of these lice-ridden stables will kill many in the first few weeks. And whilst the Nazis have their God-given *Führer*, in Birkenau – Typhus is king!

"Another lethal barrier to life is the lack of food and water. The Germans provide us with just enough calories to exist, but not enough to live. Starvation inexorably takes hold and results in a complete physical and mental collapse. If you're unable to organise extra rations then you'll eventually end up as a *Muselmann* – a living skeleton, soon to become a corpse. These apathetic wretches are the walking dead. Starved down to about thirty kilos, these emaciated caricatures of humanity patiently wait their turn for the Special Treatment. Then with a quick and callous chalk mark upon the timber frame of their bunk, the death sentence is pronounced by an SS doctor on his ward round. And so, twice a day, the Red Cross trucks pick up these camp lepers and bear them to the gas.

"And then there's the next obstacle – work. If you're fortunate or have friends in high places, this may be something indoors, away from the outside elements. Heavy labour outdoors is a death sentence that lasts perhaps a month at most. The body is assaulted in every possible way, from the relentless beatings, the back-breaking toil and the starvation rations. I've seen many drop dead from sheer physical exhaustion; others from heart failure, shock and internal bleeding. A few desperate souls go to the wire, or are shot to pieces in the infamous Death Zone."

Krömer sighed once more and rifled under his straw mattress for an unopened bottle of surgical spirit. He took a long swig.

"Are you sure you don't want some of this? No? Well, that's fair enough I suppose. This stuff takes the phrase 'blind drunk' too literally. Anyway, I'm feeling generous so you can share my bed tonight – just tonight mind; then we'll have to find you a berth you can call your own. That shouldn't be too difficult in this place as there's usually a dozen or so deaths every night. Roll call is in five hours so I suggest you get some sleep."

Krömer drained his bottle and crashed down on the bed. He immediately began to snore and I decided that it would be an opportune time to put pen to paper.

As I sat writing in my journal, a dreadful whining sound came from a nearby bunk. Krömer was oblivious to the noise and continued to snore. I tentatively peered through the curtain and looked down the rickety rows of wooden bunks with the light of the candle. The moans were originating from a decrepit figure, withered to the bone. He was hovering out of his bunk as two neighbouring prisoners continued to shove him over the edge

"You dirty bastard!" one of them muttered. "You've shat all over the blanket again – well, not for much longer!"

The hapless victim eventually tumbled backward, hitting the floor with a squelch and immediately evacuating his bowels. He writhed for a moment in his own faeces. His dysenteric innards gurgled and sloshed, implacably gripped by paroxysms of diarrhoea. Then his sunken eyes met mine. He stared vacantly through me, halfway between this world and the next. His skull-like face was ghastly and ghoulish in the candlelight. His skin was stretched and almost transparent. His desiccated tongue thrashed aimlessly back and forth, too swollen to fully retract. Another wave gushed down his legs, themselves a festering morass of sores.

Ecce homo! Behold the Man of Hitler's new world order: A Renaissance Man – an Auschwitz *Muselmann!*

ANOTHER AFTERNOON
ON THE RAMP

Journal of Michał Kowalsky, Auschwitz, Poland, 1944

<u>Saturday 13th May</u>

Why I'm still writing in this pointless journal is beyond me. Nothing's really changed in the past year. The Nazis continue to kill and the rest of us continue to die, some quicker than others. But why am I still here? Why haven't I been consumed like the rest of the Polish chaff? How have I avoided being gulped down whole and breathed out as chimney smoke? I know why. It's hatred that keeps me going. Yes, I'll get my revenge one day! The SS scum won't know what's hit em when Michał Kowalsky gets out of this Godforsaken shithole. I'll hunt them down and send them back to hell, all these psychopaths and homicidal maniacs.

But the Auschwitz doctors – these oath breakers, hypocrites and traitors – well, they're on another level of evil. And Mengele, you're mine! You'll eternally freeze in deepest Dis with the other Hippocratic backstabbers, but only after I've made you hurt up here first. And don't expect a quick bullet in the brain, my dark Angel of Death. God no! You'll live for years in paranoia and inconsequence before I'll finally put ye down like the beast you are!

Anyway, stop daydreaming Michał. Get back to the present. Exorcise your rage into this page. Let the ink bleed into the paper and be a permanent testimony to the thousands upon thousands upon thousands…

The new unloading ramp was seething this afternoon. The SS were buzzing round everywhere; these half-tight blond thugs with semiautomatics and ferocious fucking hellhounds that were even more racist than them.

It was sizzling hot, even for us nobodies in our piss-stained pyjamas. But for the Nazis it must have been bloody unbearable. They were already sweating bullets in the fierce noon sunshine, devoid of cloud or shade. I managed to bribe one of the older guards who let me swig from his canteen. It tasted like warm piss, usually only reserved for the insane or the Musulman. I could have killed for a nice fat lollipop. I'd have crunched the stick of course; there's surely a few good calories in a piece of sugar-soaked wood.

I was really after some paper money this afternoon. It was worthless as camp currency, but enough of it made damn fine toilet paper.

I dug around my pocket and pulled out a piece of fishy black bread. I organised a bit of herring juice from the SS canteen yesterday and had the bread marinating in my bowl all night. It tasted delicious, and I savoured the oily flavours and textures on my tongue. I was actually pretty good at organising stuff in camp. But one had to first acquire a list of bribable guards which was no mean feat.

Ear-piercing R75s suddenly pulled up and revved, delivering SS officers to the imminent freak show. These pathetic excuses for men were all drenched in medals and adorned with shiny brass buttons. They particularly loved themselves in their tailored Hugo Boss uniforms, especially when sporting their polished leather boots and riding crops. Some even wore leather coats – in this heat!

I caught sight of Psycho Moll. His fair-skinned face was shiny and red; his spiteful features contorted in the sunlight, lips thin and right eye twitching furiously. He held a long thin whip – like some fucking circus ringleader – as he muttered an order to one of his boys who immediately passed him some water. He poured it straight over his cropped blond hair and down the back of his sunburnt neck.

Kramer strolled majestically onto the ramp; his enormous hands tucked behind his back. The silver squares on his collar glittered in the sunshine; the gravel crunched under his boots; his bamboo cane bent impatiently. Moll greeted him, Roman fashion.

Then all hell broke loose. Another Jewish transport from

Hungary was coming. Big bad Eichmann appeared form nowhere. All eyes turned in one direction. The black steam locomotive entered under the archway and the clattering convoy of brown cattle-cars began to roll in. In the tiny, barred windows appeared pale, wilted human faces; terror-stricken women with tangled hair, unshaven men. They gazed at the ramp in silence.

Suddenly, there was a stir inside the wagons and a frantic pounding against the wooden boards as wails of lament melted into synchronised cries for air and water.

These were heartrending cries, but not to me. My heart, my humanity, my Jewish soul had died long ago. Now I was just a pitiless worm: a maggoty gullet that ate and shat and existed best he could. I laughed incongruously, but why? I didn't feel pity, but it wasn't funny. Perhaps it was a nervous laugh, an excited laugh, who knows… who the fuck cares.

Contorted faces now crammed up against the windows, squashed against the barbed wire; skin oozing through the bars, mouths gaping and gasping for air. The moans grew louder.

I side-glanced at Moll. His eye was now twitching magnificently, his taut lips quivering, his fat face full of spite. He became restless and irritated. It had probably been a good hour since he'd brutalised someone and he was clearly getting withdrawal symptoms.

Kramer drew deeply on his cigarillo, flicked the smoldering butt onto the ground and signalled to one of the sentry towers. The guard engaged with his mounted automatic and fired a stuttering hail of bullets along the carriages. All was momentarily quiet. Meanwhile, several pickup trucks and Red Cross vans had arrived.

The first whistle was blown. I collected a portable stepladder and joined my unloading work detail. The three of us stood in an orderly queue, ready at our designated position outside the door of Number 17. On Moll's second whistle, I positioned the stepladder and climbed up to unbolt the door. My key unlocked the two padlocks and I pulled off the great chain.

Waiting for the final whistle, I turned around and saw Kramer joined by Höss, Eichmann and Mengele. The suave and scented doctor was wearing his white coat and carried a thin attaché briefcase. A woman had also joined the throng, whip in one hand and hound in the other. Bony and flat-chested, her greasy thin hair was streaked with shots of skunk-white. Her name was *Frau* Bormann. Weasel-like, haggard looking, perhaps a little over five foot tall, this repulsive specimen of German womanhood, of Aryan purity, turned my empty stomach. She detested feminine beauty with the hatred of a woman who was herself repulsive, and fucking knew it!

Kramer gestured to a now fidgeting Moll who shouted out: "Are you scumbags ready?"

"*Jawohl mein Hauptscharführer!*" we all cried. The hundred men of the *Kanada* Squad were primed and raring to go.

"Then begin!" shouted Moll, blowing his whistle for the third and final time.

The bolt creaked; the door slid open. A great stench and fine mist erupted from inside the carriage, causing many SS men to cover their noses and mouths. But I was oblivious to it. No, maybe I gagged today. It all depended on the state of the cargo. A wave of fresh air rushed inside the dank interior. I beheld human beings, people, Jews – crammed together and now half-buried under incredible heaps of suitcases, trunks, packages, crates, and bundles of every description. Hideously squeezed together, they had fainted from heat, suffocated, and crushed one another. Now they spilt towards the opened door in a great heaving surge.

"Get out Jews! Everybody down!" I hollered.

The first to exit was a middle-aged bespectacled man. His expensive suit was badly crumpled and he wore a battered fedora hat. Clutched tightly to his chest was a Gladstone bag – a doctor, I guessed. Yes, I recognised him! He was Dr. Sárkány, the renowned pathologist. I was his mortuary assistant for a time at Heidelberg. We exchanged

BROKEN OATHS

glances but he didn't recognise me. Why would he?

The doctor was suddenly blinded by the sunlight and stood bewildered for a few moments before I helped him down the steps onto the ramp. There followed a number of women and children next, together with a mixture of the old and the young. Some of the sprightlier teenage boys jumped down from the carriage, bypassing the stepladder altogether.

The unloading was both slow and laborious, taking a good twenty minutes to get the hundred or so people out of the boxcar and onto the platform below. Endless questions were fired at me and my colleagues whilst the dazed and disorientated Jews alighted from the train.

"Please kind sir, where are we? What's going to happen to us? Where are you people from? Why do you wear those funny striped uniforms? Look! Our cracked lips are bleeding and our parched mouths all crusted. Water! Please, sir – when can we have some water?"

"You'll be fine," said one of the Hungarian translators. "Good food and drink await you after you've had a nice refreshing shower in our brand-new sauna."

It was camp law: people going to their death had to be deceived right up to the very end. This was the only form of charity in Auschwitz-Birkenau!

A young Jewess caught my eye. Delicious-looking and intoxicating, I drank her in with my eyes. Her silky black hair bounced on her shoulders. Her curvaceous figure was the essence of unbridled femininity, wrapped in a light cotton blouse. Why tarnish and destroy such perfection? Why shave that beautiful hair? Why tattoo that flawless skin? Why replace that lovely soft blouse with coarse hessian? Why dump this perfect feminine form into a stinking pigsty of lice-infested filth? Why subject her to animal hunger, inhuman labour, disease and destitution? Fuck knows!

Heaps of luggage slowly piled up on the ramp as I began to empty the carriage. There were suitcases, trunks, bundles and bags. Some spilt open to reveal clothes, blankets, photographs, perfumes, makeup and lots of pill bottles. The odd bundle contained food rations – bread, butter, pies, sausages, marmalade and jam. I glared covetously at all this mouthwatering nosh. My aching belly cried out for provender, gurgling with delight and anticipation. I really couldn't wait for these poor people to leave so that I could swoop down and stuff my face.

A flustered woman walked briskly past me, weaving and dodging in and out of people from side to side as if hurrying away from somebody. A toddler in pigtails ran after her, unable to keep up, stretching out her little arms and crying. She knew. Somehow, this mother's intuition had clocked onto the deception. She understood her immediate peril.

Stunned by her cowardice, I grabbed hold of the woman. She squirmed in my arms.

"Pick up your child!" I demanded

"It's not mine! Please sir, not mine I tell you!"

She shouted hysterically and covered her face with her grimy hands. She wanted to hide, disappear and dissolve into the crowd.

But the little girl pursued her, wailing, "Mama – don't leave me!"

"It's not mine, not mine! No, not my child!" protested the woman.

Witnessing all the commotion, Moll stormed over and grabbed hold of the woman. His eyes were glassy from vodka and heat. He shoved her to the ground then yanked her up by the hair. She winced and begged him to let her go. His beefy red face twitched with excitement.

"You spineless bitch! So, you're running away from your little runt to save your own worthless skin. Well, I'll show you – you debauched Jewish slut!"

Moll's sweaty hands fastened round her throat, choking her. He lifted her off the ground. Her congested face started to turn blue as her legs pumped furiously in the air. She was finally thrown on to one of the death-trucks like a worthless bag of cement.

"Here! And take this little brat with you!" Moll tossed

the child at her feet.

There was no time to even catch my breath as I scurried towards the Red Cross vans, frantically shoving the old and the sick up the wooden steps, packing them in tightly, fifty per vehicle. They would soon be off to join the other truckloads at the four crematoria.

An elderly Jewess wandered around in a circle. Her head bobbed up and down repetitively, waving her arms in the air and whining. She was one of many whose already fragile mind had succumbed to the horrors of the train journey.

Two prisoners were carrying a redheaded little girl with only one leg. I hurried over and adjusted her dress to cover her underwear. But why Michał? Was this compassion?

"Bit young for you, Kowalsky!" joked one of the men. He held her by the arms, the other man by the leg. Tears ran down her flushed face and she murmured faintly:

"Please nice sirs, it hurts."

I told them to be gentler, but they ignored my request and chucked her roughly inside the truck. Upon hearing the thud, I hesitated, but quickly regained my composure. Then we all turned away – job done!

The freight train was now emptied of its live cargo.

A scrawny SS guard peered inside my unit's assigned boxcar. Recoiling in disgust and covering his pockmarked face, he motioned to the three of us, pointing at the door and shaking his head:

"Hey, you lazy bastards – get over here! Clean all this shit up! At the double! I want no traces of fucking Jew!"

We braced ourselves and climbed up inside the carriage. The dark interior was rancid and repellent, though all too familiar. Along each of the thirty boxcars you would find pretty much identical pictures of prolonged captivity, coupled with lack of ventilation, sanitation, nutrition and space. But even so, it was impossible to get used to such a site, to take it in your stride.

The enclosed space was like something out of hell, or worse. It immediately attacked the senses and caused a peculiar kind of paralysis. Every fibre of your body said 'get the fuck out of here'! But you knew you had to push forward, mind and body in violent conflict, leading to momentary inertia.

In the corner of the dank chamber before me was the trampled remains of a baby boy; a naked little travesty of humankind. I picked up the poor little mite by the legs, like a chicken. My instinct was to toss him out the door like a piece of rubbish, but an ever so tiny bit of humanity pricked my dull conscience. I found myself cradling the infant, climbing down out of the carriage and placing him gently on the ground.

The skinny SS guard saw what I was doing. He snarled and yelled out:

"Get a move on, you worthless piece of Polish shit! I haven't got all fucking night! Just throw out the bodies for now. You can dump them on the corpse-cart later."

I climbed back up into my boxcar and dragged out more bodies from the mounds of meat. Everywhere vomit and excrement: a necropolis of bodily humours, tinged orange by the afternoon sun. Some people were horribly swollen, others trampled, smothered. Some were still breathing but unconscious. If not quite dead, they soon would be – thank God!

And so, another sunny afternoon in Birkenau drew to an end. Tadeusz, that greedy bastard, had just devoured a full jar of Hungarian marmalade. Pig! He'll definitely get the shits with all that sugar flooding his withered guts.

The brilliant sunlight of late afternoon now bathed the dusty ramp. The empty cattle-cars at last stood silent. Heaps of luggage and bundles of clothes were sprawled across the platform. The shimmering heat warmed the tan leather suitcases. There was a humming in my ears and my sunburnt head began to pound. I really wanted to puke – to purge myself of all this corruption.

My seething body dripped with sweat. I could feel clinging moisture on my sticky eyelids. My eyes were sore and heavy. The toil was nearly over for another afternoon. Then we'd do it all over again this evening; then the next day, and the next – until there were no Jews left in the whole wide world.

~

It was still hot for many hours after my afternoon on the ramp. I'd got a few precious hours to cool off and rest until the next transport of Hungarian salami arrived for smoking. My libido was rampant. I yearned to spend the evening with a ripe bint in The Puff of Block 24. What a reward that would be! I'd have happily gone without rations for a week for just half an hour in the Doll's House. But the brothel was strictly reserved for the prison elite, and certainly not scumbag Jews like me.

I'd heard how each punter had to be examined before gaining entry. I guessed they were looking for telltale signs of syphilis and clap. Each lucky customer then got fifteen minutes with his lady, and the entire performance was watched by an SS guard through a peephole in the door. This was under some ridiculous pretext that the missionary position had to be strictly adhered to, but the guards surely got off on it.

You had to feel sorry for the women though, even if they were working inside and privy to extra rations. Apart from being forcibly sterilised, some of those big bald *Kapos* were absolute animals. And to have endured up to eight of the pigs in one evening – well, I'd rather have gone to the gas!

If I ever did manage to lay my grubby hands on a brothel token, I'd probably end up with some fat blonde *Frau* with bad breath and gallstones! Polish girls are so much prettier – dark, thin and lusciously sophisticated.

I eventually went outside and peered across at the bald-headed beauties in the women's camp. I imagined these sweat-drenched girls of the *FKL* lying naked on their bunks, packed in eights, nines, even tens – stinking to high heaven.

Mmm – yes! There's meat here lads. Bit streaky and green round the gills, but flesh all the same.

Hang on! Who are you kidding? They're the cause of all this typhus for sure. Absolutely filthy they are. They're stinking out the entire camp with their non-existent feminine hygiene. Sugar and spice and all things nice – bollocks! More like crabs and lice and a life of vice. No, come on Michał, you're being a misogynistic fuck! Men smell just as bad, circumcised or not.

The heat continued and the hours were endless. My libido wilted away.

A dishevelled old Rabbi was among the lowly bottom bunkers in my hut; his head covered with a piece of old rag that failed to muffle the wailing prayers that spouted from his mouth.

Could somebody shut him up? He'd been raving all fucking afternoon! Oh, let him rant. They'll be taking him to the gas that much sooner: better for me, even better for him!

"Hey Rabbi! You can't seriously believe that there's a Jewish God?"

He stopped his infernal chanting and poked his head out of the bunk like some demented old tortoise:

"It is true that the Lord has temporarily forsaken His Chosen people, just as He did with the Egyptians, Babylonians and Romans before. But we shall all rise again from the ashes of Auschwitz and sing psalms of praise from the mountaintops of Zion!"

"This place is my Zion!" I replied. "*Kanada*, my *Kanada* – my sweet haven of sausages, onions and marmalade. *Kanada* is my salvation, my *Arcadia*. We have access to all the perishables of the gassed; intrinsically worthless to the Nazis, but belly quenching and delicious to a load of half-starved Jews. We tuck into succulent white loaves with real butter, jam and honey. These life succouring calories are gifts from the dead, brought wholesale from Hungary and baked in the *shtetl* ovens just days before."

MENGELE'S MORTICIAN

Journal of Michał Kowalsky, Monowitz, Poland, 1944

<u>Friday 2ⁿᵈ June</u>

Michał, you bloody idiot! You've really pissed your life up the wall this time. After months on the Birkenau ramp, fortune has finally fucked you over. No more perks, no more extra rations, no more organising – and no more *Kanada*.

A surprise inspection from the SS finally uncovered my hidden stash of gold and jewellery; not to mention the two kilos of marmalade and pile of pornographic postcards. As punishment, I've been transferred to a Godforsaken work camp at Buna, some seven sodding miles or so from the Birkenau complex.

The Buna Works are owned by *I.G. Farbenindustrie*. They have a fraudulent financial arrangement with the SS to hire out camp inmates for slave labour in their chemical factories. They've even built a cosy little sub-camp for us all at Monowitz, bless them! The camp commandant is a stone-cold sadist called Schwarz and the camp director is another serious social deviant called Schöttl the Shit.

I would ideally like to join the infirmary at Monowitz. I've certainly got the right temperament for it, not to mention my detailed knowledge of anatomy and years of experience as a mortician at the University of Warsaw. I'm as equally dextrous with a scalpel as I am with a marmalade spoon or a bra strap!

But the bitching Buna Works are about punishment and fuck all else.

My heart sank into the stone this afternoon when I discovered that I'd been assigned to the infamous Concrete Squad, together with five other delinquents all caught with their proverbial pants down.

We stood in line on the parade ground before our new Block Senior. He was an evil-looking bastard with pockmarked face and eyepatch. His welcoming address, in the coarsest form of Low German, pulled no punches:

"My name is *Kapo* Osterloh. If any of you miserable pieces of shit have heard rumours about me before today, then I'm delighted to confirm them all in person. My nickname around here is *Shark*, and I'm one hell of a sadistic cunt! I like to strike out with my fists, my boots and this black baton. But if you bastards really piss me off, I will bite down on your flesh and rip it off!

"As our newest recruits, you're unfortunate enough to be in my 197th Concrete *Kommando*. You'll soon realise that Buna's no fucking holiday camp. There's no namby-pamby, kiss-my-arse quarantine here! No time to get settled in and pen pissing postcards to your Mamas back home in Jewland. You're here to work! Yes, my boys – you're Shark's toys now! I'll work your bodies to the bone and beat the crap out of you 'til you all croak in the concrete!

"Observe if you will the ground you're standing on. Imagine for a moment, buried deep within, the miles of cable laid with precision by your long-forgotten forbearers. And where are they now? Well, Shark knows exactly where they are – yes, he fucking well does! They're all under your feet, entombed in six feet of concrete! Ha! Just let your minds roam and picture their fossilised torsos immortalised in stone. Then multiply your vision by two hundred, and thank your lucky yellow stars that this isn't you – yet!"

Shark began to walk down the line. We all stood absolutely still, caps by our sides, looking forward. His inspection stopped abruptly in front of me. I continued to stare forward, avoiding eye contact at all cost.

"Show me your hands!" he barked. His breath smelled of paint stripper and rotten fish. "Sweet baby Jesus, you've got the fingers of a girl! Ah, just look at those soft little dainties. Well, not for long! Two days in Shark's *Kommando* and they'll be cracked and cut to fucking shreds! What were you – a bloody school teacher or some poxy retard of a librarian? Argh!! It makes me mad, all you Jewish intellectual types, full of fancy fucking titles and a string of letters after your names. Let me guess, you're Dr. Israel Cohen – yes? Well? Cat got your tongue?"

I was tempted to explain my three years at medical school before being expelled after almost killing a fellow student in a brawl. This would have surely impressed someone like Shark. I also wanted to tell him how my anatomical skills would be far better suited to the camp infirmary; treating wounds and assisting in operations. But I knew better. Complete silence was always preferable in such circumstances: I had learnt this lesson the hard way.

"That's right," murmured Shark. "You're a clever little Jew, aren't you? Knows when to keep his mouth shut, this one. Knows where to look, how to stand, how to shit – yes? Well, Shark's got his eye on you! Brains don't mean shit around here! The fascists don't want you Jews to think: they want you to work and die! Extermination through labour is the formal name. I call it sport! Now fuck off!"

Osterloh was a typical senior prisoner in the corrupt camp infrastructure. These privileged professional criminals – murderers, rapists, paedophiles and arsonists – the scum of humanity: Buna welcomed them all into her ample bosom. Most were so ultraviolent, so rapacious and corrupt that they were hated even more than the Nazis. I recently heard a story of one *Kapo* called Novák the Embalmer. He got typhoid fever and ended his days rotting in some hospital barracks. Rumour had it that one of the doctors shat in his mouth after he snuffed it. What a legend!

I finally got to enter my new barracks. Shark had a cordoned-off bedroom near the entrance. Opposite, another little room functioned as a dorm for the *Pipel* – a young boy of around twelve years who was at the *Kapo's* beck and call. Duties included making the bed, washing linen, polishing boots, running errands, and no doubt satisfying his carnal urges. Every barracks had its very own bum-boy, hand-picked at selection and used exclusively for the pleasure of the *Prominentia*. Our *Pipel* was called Jan, although Shark called him *Spoons*. He'd been in Buna since April and was no doubt fully broken in by now.

Saturday 3ʳᵈ June

It was a wet afternoon at the Buna Plant. The *Kapos* and SS guards took shelter from the elements and drank mugs of steaming hot coffee around glowing iron stoves: but not for us. Shark's 197th Concrete *Kommando* was ankle deep in clayey mud and torrential rainwater, shifting soggy bags of cement and slippery metal poles. The damp air clung to my clothes and penetrated to the bone. The grinding noise of a dozen concrete mixers churned on and on.

I was on cement-bag duty. It was backbreaking work and quickly sapped me of energy. I'd tucked a piece of reinforced paper under my shirt. Torn from a discarded concrete bag, it was a feeble attempt to protect my shoulder from abrasion and moisture.

Edek Steinfeld was chasing in thick electrical cables above my head. The driving rain pounded down on the scaffolding. He suddenly lost his balance and slipped off the platform. Falling about fifteen foot, he landed badly on his legs which crunched beneath him. The chasing grinder wasn't far behind and hungrily buzzed into his thigh. We tossed the contraption to one side and gently pulled him up out of the gloopy mud. He'd clearly broken both ankles; trimalleolar fractures to be sure. A jagged shard of shin bone projected through his sodden trousers. This poor sod needed morphine – and loads of it!

I quickly recalled my own biomechanical studies on high-impact fractures in cadavers, as well as the scientific papers of Pott and Charcot. I really wanted to use my skills and control the blood loss. The fracture dislocation deformities of both ankles also needed immediate reduction under anaesthesia, with proper fibular rotatory alignment and restoration of syndesmosis.

Only with prompt surgical intervention would Steinfeld be able to avoid amputation and keep his feet. If not, the vascular compromise would quickly lead to ischaemia and ultimately gangrene. Infection was another potential problem in the absence of timely sterile dressings and large doses of intravenous antibiotics. But we could do nothing!

Out of the rain, the imposing hulk of Shark suddenly materialised like Moby fucking Dick. He was accompanied by an SS guard, now dripping wet. The German looked angry and demanded to know why we'd all downed tools. I politely explained that our young Polish co-worker had fallen from the scaffolding and was in need of urgent medical attention. I even volunteered to attend to his injuries until backup arrived.

"Continue work!" was his terse command.

Shark glared at the casualty. "Drop him!" he ordered.

The two men supporting him duly obeyed. Steinfeld's body crashed once more to the ground. He moaned ever so slightly as consciousness and agony flooded his senses once more.

And so the hard and monotonous work continued; the helpless body of Steinfeld lying before us, in full view, hour after hour.

At last, it was time to pack up and return to base camp. Only then did Shark permit us to remove our injured companion and stretcher him back to the hospital at Monowitz. On many occasions appeals for assistance were futile, and were generally dependent on the popularity of the injured party. Less fortunate individuals could well be left to perish overnight. Those considered to be worth saving required carefully organised bribes, so that the hospital bed came at a heavy price to fellow inmates. As a rule of thumb, failure to recover after a convalescence period of two weeks meant a Red Cross escort back to the Birkenau gasmen.

After roll call and supper, we heard through the grapevine that poor Steinfeld hadn't made it. The doctor thought he had some sort of fat embolism. Poor bastard! Well, at least it was quick, I hope.

Shark was unmoved when he heard the news, but insisted that the ringleaders be punished for interrupting work and causing an SS man to get wet in the rain. As I was one of the six inmates involved in the incident, I had to endure twenty lashes.

Shark's instrument of choice was a piece of hard rubber hose that he kept under his bed. His strokes were made in slow succession and had to be counted out loud in German by the recipient. If the victim made a mistake or called out too late, then the punishment began all over again.

And so, with five others, I received my corporal ration. Apart from some nasty bruising, the skin was unbroken and would hopefully not get infected.

After Mengele, Shark was now second on my hit list.

Sunday 4th June

Buna is a shithole! It's a Godforsaken slice of Hitler's Reich, devoid of morality, marmalade and marzipan.

It was 3am. We all rose from our muddy bunks as Shark hurled abuse at us. Well, this wasn't entirely true: most of us arose. Some had croaked in the night or were too fucked to even sit up. The man on my lower bunk had given up. I had to endure his infernal moaning all bloody night. We told him to shut it, but the miserable noise droned on until reveille.

Anyway, we soon put him out of his misery. Waksmann quietly throttled him before breakfast. The man put up no fight. He was ready to die. We quickly surveyed his clothes which were stripped in seconds, like flesh in a bowl of piranhas. Four of us drew lots. I got the string vest and, in a flash, had it off. It stank to high heaven of course, but I really didn't give a shit. Waksmann took his shoes.

We left the poor cunt in his bunk and went outside for muster – the first torture of the new week.

Shark looked particularly sadistic this morning and had

a few hours to kill before the SS arrived. Lined up, rank upon rank, in neat rows of ten, we first performed the caps on, caps off drill; whipping them off and slapping them against our thighs with the flats of our hands. If done correctly and in complete synchronicity, the desired effect was a whip-cracking snap. Shark made us repeat it over and over and over again, at least a hundred times!

And so, the first hour limped by...

Next was the inspection. The smallest aberration meant punishment, often under the slightest pretext – a mild stoop, a sudden twitch, a cough or a sneeze. Shark aimed his blows to the back of the thighs, causing legs to buckle and the unfortunate victim to crumple and writhe in agony. But all this was just the warm up routine: a gentle prelude to the main event.

Ten contestants were chosen for the Sunday Games. Only one poor sod would survive. I was relieved to have escaped selection, although this was not entirely random and tended to reflect overall work performance during the previous week.

Shark ordered his prized athletes to start running around the parade ground, faster and faster. After two laps, the first competitor collapsed. It wasn't long before Shark was ready for the kill. He crouched over him. The man pleaded for mercy, but this was Buna, where no quarter was given – ever. The *Kapo* gripped either side of the prisoner's bald head and plunged his thumbs deep into his eye sockets. Right down went his thumbs, piercing through jelly and bone and brain.

"And then there were nine!" he cried, getting to his feet and wiping the gore from his hands. "Come on you lazy bastards! At the double! Run!"

And so the sport continued. One by one they fell, and one by one they died... horribly!

There were now only four remaining. Shark finally ordered these quarterfinalists to stop and they all crumpled over – gasping, panting and pouring with sweat.

"Right, let's go again! At the double! On your bellies! Crawl! Get up! Hop! Run! Jump! About turn! At the double! Run you miserable fuckers!"

Like startled quarry, the final four were harried, chased and beaten across the parade ground. The first to collapse had his nose bitten clean off. The second lost an ear, the third his tongue. All were bludgeoned after their savage mauling. The last man standing dropped to his knees. He was flushed, grazed, streaming with sweat – but alive!

Once the dead bodies were cleared away, Shark returned to the barracks with his *Pipel* in tow. We all stood still and silent. After perhaps twenty minutes, the two re-emerged from the building; Shark wearing a clean set of clothes under a wilting erection, whilst poor Jan looked pale and pained.

The SS officer finally arrived. It must have been precisely 7am. Shark made his report to the *Blockführer* who scrutinised the roll-call list and nodded in approval.

From amongst our ranks, I heard a man muttering to himself. He arrived yesterday under a Gestapo escort. He was a former Czech barrister by the name of Lowenstein.

"My God, this is intolerable," he continued. "What on earth is going on here?"

The rest of us kept *shtum*. What was this moron babbling about? Unbelievably, he then broke file and walked straight up to the *Blockführer*. We all cringed inside.

"*Mein Herr*, if I may have a frank word in your ear. As a human right's lawyer, I really must protest – in the strongest possible tones – about the unacceptable behaviour of *Kapo* Osterloh. You're no doubt unaware, but I'm pained to inform you that he has arbitrarily murdered several innocent men just before your arrival. The Czech authorities have formally vouched for my own personal safety, and I have various signed documents and affidavits to ratify my privileged political status. You may or may not be aware that Section 7, Paragraph 2b of the Geneva Convention categorically affirms…"

The *Blockführer* looked astonished. His face grew livid.

He interrupted the foolhardy lawyer in mid-sentence:

"*Kapo 212!* Get over here – now!"

"At once, *Herr Blockführer!*" Shark replied.

"Did you hear what this Yid's been blabbering about?"

"I did, *Herr Blockführer!*"

The German un-holstered his pistol and immediately shot the lawyer in the head.

"Welcome to Buna!" he said casually, then walked away.

Shark was visibly shaking with a mixture of anger and fear. He looked down at the bleeding corpse and proceeded to bury his boot into the man's face. We heard the vivid crack of bones as his skull was crushed to a pulp.

~

Shortly after roll call, the men of Shark's 197th Concrete *Kommando* stood in line behind the wooden tea vats. Our breakfast was an hour overdue and must now have been stone-cold. We waited patiently to be doled out a ladleful but, as it turned out, we were waiting in vain: for Shark had other ideas about our Sunday morning refreshments.

"You scum aren't entitled to a ladleful of my shit! I can't wait to see each one of you go up the chimney! Nice little stiffs, all dead, all burnt to a crisp – lovely dead Jews, reduced to smoke and ash!"

With parched mouths and craving eyes, we watched the beautiful black infusion drain away as Shark tipped it onto the dry ground. I was so thirsty. I craved luscious cold tea: this cooling, slippery fluid that would wet and quench and soothe the fire in my throat.

It was three hours to the noon soup ration, so I pulled myself away from the empty vat of tea and braved a visit to the latrines. But this would be no leisurely Sunday purge with newspaper, comfy seat and flushing water. I joined the end of a long queue all waiting to empty their withered innards into one of the thirty communal holes. Any more than a minute or so was considered excessive shitting time, and generally meant a shove or a kick from the next in line. Many of the sick had already relieved themselves in their bunks during the previous night, and it was always advisable to move these nocturnal secretors onto the bottom bunk unless you wanted a face full of dysentery.

We lived in shit! Our own, other people's, that of animals, lice… we were cocooned in excrement!

The next part of Sunday recreation was the weekly delousing. We were all plagued by the parasitic buggers. They crawled and swarmed all over our clothes, our bed pallets and blankets. For the next hour or so, I picked out the blighters from my clothes. The string vest I inherited was alive with vermin to the point where individual cotton fibres were moving. Many congregated in the seams where they gorged on dead skin cells, oils and dirt.

The lice shat all over us, spreading typhus and reaping fevers. We raked over our skin, opening scabs and creating new sores that festered. We were the filth! God only knows what we smelled like, but even basic hygiene – running water, soap, clean towels – were non-existent.

Delousing was followed by the weekly ordeal of a soapless cold-water shave with razors so blunt and rusted that the hairs on one's face were torn out rather than shaved off. The inevitable cuts could be potentially fatal if they got infected. The beard lichen was an affliction of nearly all of us. We ravenously drank the bloodstained water after the depilation was complete. We all drained our cups in one gulp - hairs, skin, lice and blood included in this thirst-quenching aperitif before Sunday lunch.

Noon – and it was time to eat. The aroma of the thin, bubbling soup in its steaming cauldron pervaded the yard. Ravenously we watched and sniffed the air, temporarily revived by the thought of sustenance. Harassment, torture and violent death – *adieu!* For now, we were to greedily bolt down the soup of the day. What in normal life would be inedible muck, the thought of this mangel-weed broth made our dry mouths ache in anticipation. This liquid nourishment of perhaps two hundred calories would at least partly rehydrate us and keep us alive for a few more hours: for we lived from hour to hour…

~

Jan paid me an awkward visit later this afternoon. It was the first time we'd spoken. The barracks was pretty much empty as the men were all outside in the sunshine. Our young *Pipel* was plainly uncomfortable and blushed with embarrassment. He told me that he'd heard many good things about my practical medical knowledge from the men. He looked suddenly terrified when I asked him to sit down beside me on the bench.

I eventually learned that Jan had a somewhat delicate problem. Further gentle questioning revealed that he'd got something stuck in his rectum. Unable to remove it manually himself, he had reluctantly come to me for help. He wasn't entirely sure what was up there, but he explained that Shark had been using some kind of metal implement during their intimate encounter earlier that morning.

I beckoned the boy over to the nearest vacant bottom bunk. I asked him to pull down his trousers and lay down on one side, with his knees bent upwards towards his belly. His ravaged anus was gaping and torn, with bloodstained mucus oozing from a deep fissure over a bruised perineum. Just visible was the edge of a metallic handle of some sort.

I asked Jan to take a few deep breaths before inserting my hand and getting a good grip on the object between index finger and thumb. Then with a firm but gentle pull, I managed to negotiate the handle out of the boy's arse. It glided out with reasonable ease until an abrupt stop. Then I realised that the other end was some kind of ladle! The spoon-shaped bowl clearly wasn't going to budge without a lot of tugging and some clever manual dexterity.

Thankfully, the contours were smooth, and I was therefore able to be fairly aggressive without ripping his delicate innards. He winced and whimpered, begging me to stop. Then, with one final and desperate yank, I managed to extract the 5-inch bowl on its side. There was an enormous – and immensely satisfying – sucking sound as I finally laid the glistening object on the bunk.

After a small rush of gas, I wiped Jan down and packed the area with some moistened newspaper. He sat up with tears streaming down his eyes. When I showed him the serving spoon, I began to laugh:

"You might want to wash this before returning it to the kitchen."

Monday 5th June

I was taken to the Monowitz hospital barracks this afternoon. My feet were as swollen as a bull's bollocks and I'd got a weeping sore on the inside of one ankle. I prayed that I hadn't developed diabetes. Thankfully, the quack said that it wasn't too bad and should hopefully heal up after a few days of bedrest. I sighed with relief. I honestly thought I was a goner!

And so, a corpsman – not a corpse-man – bathed my feet and smeared a mixture of salves on my wound. He then applied a light lint dressing. I was instructed to get as much bedrest as possible and to keep my feet elevated when sitting down. Thinking of my good fortune, I tucked into my extra ration of milk soup with grits, accompanied by a heavenly chunk of proper white bread.

Everything was going well. I was happily painting the pickle when I overheard Dr. Körner talking about an SS inspection planned for tomorrow evening. My cock shrivelled when I heard the name, *Doktor Mengele!* A sense of impending doom once again returned, and I erupted in an itchy heat rash.

Körner, a French physician from Nice, prescribed me some calamine lotion and told me about the visit tomorrow. Mengele was apparently looking for doctors and technicians to work in the new Birkenau crematoria. He had recently converted part of *Krema* I into a modern postmortem room and laboratory, with an anatomical museum planned for *Krema* II. Körner informed me that he'd already been selected to work as a *Sonderkommando* doctor in *Krema* II. Mengele's visit tomorrow was to seek out a technical assistant, preferably one with mortuary and autopsy experience, to assist his new pathologist, Dr. József Sárkány.

What luck! I couldn't bloody believe it. I began to laugh and muttered Yiddish gibberish in my excitement. Körner looked bemused and probably thought I was delirious. I regained my composure and explained that I was a fully qualified mortician with over ten years' experience at the University of Warsaw's Institute of Anatomy. The doctor congratulated me and shook my hand. He probably wouldn't have if he'd known where it had just been!

Tuesday 6th June

A tall SS officer entered the room, accompanied by two assistants. I recognised him instantly from my months on the *Judenrampe*. It was Mengele alright.

Complete silence followed. We all rose to attention, removed our caps and bowed our heads. Unnecessary eye contact with our Aryan superiors was strictly forbidden. Mengele told us to sit as he scanned the room. I was right at the front and perceived the slightest irritation on his face, no more than a momentary twitch and certainly falling short of a grimace. He nonchalantly dropped his glowing cigarette butt. A fawning assistant deftly stubbed it out with the tip of his boot. The doctor beckoned him nearer and whispered a few choice words. The assistant flushed and nodded his head. The dozen or so women amongst us were hurried out of the room.

Silence once again prevailed. Mengele lit another cigarette and inhaled deeply. He checked his watch then spoke:

"My name is Dr. Josef Mengele. I am here to personally hand-pick a select group of personnel for my pathological research. The successful candidates will be given preferential treatment in all aspects of camp life, including extra food rations, civilian clothing and many other privileges that are unheard of elsewhere in the Birkenau complex. But beware! I do not take kindly to purveyors of lies and mediocrity. Therefore, I preface this request with the following caveat: failure to comply with my prerequisites will result in a most *unfortunate* outcome!"

There followed a menacing gesture as one of his assistants drew a finger across his throat in a timely manner of rehearsed choreography. With a wry grin, Mengele continued:

"So, to business: I am looking for pathologists and morticians who have attained qualifications or experience at a reputable university or hospital. A mastery of the German language is also vital. They must also be thoroughly versed in postmortem techniques and morbid anatomy. Experience in the field of forensic pathology is also desired, but not essential. Step forward to the front if you fulfil these criteria."

Silence resumed. No one dared move. I glanced around to my left and right. Perhaps there were no pathologists here? Or perhaps none had the balls to admit it. Nobody got up from his chair to step forward. Fuck it! My own mind was made up. I arose from my seat and walked up to the front of the room. My feet were still bloody painful, but thankfully less swollen, and I managed not to hobble like some spent old prostitute. Mengele didn't even look up at me. He sensed my presence, smelled my fear.

I began to sweat. Had I made a massive mistake? Was this some sort of trap?

He nodded to one of his cronies and exited the room like the pompous prick that he was. Everybody else was ordered to leave. I stood there before Mengele's two sidekicks, nervously awaiting my fate. One of them approached. I looked up momentarily and caught his eye. He raised a clenched fist. I flinched, expecting the worst. They both laughed. The man lifted my chin up to regain eye contact whilst the other rolled up my sleeve and recorded my prison number in his notebook:

"*Herr Doktor* will call for you later. I recommend that you prepare yourself for some searching questions and close scrutiny of your qualifications. You may go."

It was past 10 o'clock when I finally got the summons from his fucking Lordship. I entered a small room and stood to attention before Mengele who was sitting behind a lamplit desk. His face was in shadow and engulfed in plumes of tobacco smoke.

The interview felt more like an interrogation as he grilled me on all aspects of my former work. He asked me where I had studied and with what professors. He probed me on dissection, how long I'd worked in that field, and my views on vivisection. He also inquired as to the particulars of my special autopsy techniques, how I eviscerated and what instruments I used. He finally grilled me about paediatric pathology, with particular reference to multiple births and twins.

After what seemed like an eternity, Mengele glanced down at his watch and gave off a subtle air of content. The precision of my answers and my fluent German appeared to have satisfied him as he lit a fifth cigarette, pausing momentarily to offer me one, but then thinking better of it. The monster now appeared to fully relax, lounging back and taking in long drags of smoke:

"As a pathologist's assistant, you will help in the drawing up of many autopsy and forensic medical reports. Together with blood, serum and tissue samples, you will then ship them to the Institute at Berlin-Dahlem. Their replies and correspondence will need to be carefully file indexed in a manner of my choosing."

My transfer from Monowitz was formally signed by *SS-Unterscharführer* Becker of the Medical Service. I was finally free of Shark's diabolical Concrete *Kommando* and the sprawling rubber factory of *I.G. Farben.*

At sunset, a metallic grey car pulled up outside the hospital barracks. To my surprise, Mengele was driving. Accompanied by two companions, Dr. Jecheskiel Körner and Dr. Dénes Görög, we all bundled into the back of his Opel Admiral convertible. The night was dry and warm, and Mengele had the roof down. The padded upholstery felt wonderfully comfortable and I tentatively stroked the soft cream leather with the tips of my fingers. Perhaps he wasn't so bad after all.

Darkness was beginning to fall. High above my head the stars were already twinkling; soon to be annihilated by the dazzling light of a thousand arc lamps in Birkenau's concrete necropolis. I gazed up at the firmament and longed to fly away into the sky. I studied the constellations and fixed upon *Ursa Major*, marvelling at the order of the cosmos. The cool air of the late evening breeze might have been refreshing, invigorating even; but as we fast approached the main camp, the air became tainted with the acrid fumes of bonfires.

"Hold on tight!" cried Mengele. "The camp roads are no *autobahn.*"

We drove through the vast complex of Birkenau. Mengele accelerated and we were tossed about like pancakes as the car traversed the bumpy ground, punctuated by potholes. The brilliant lamps atop concrete pylons dazzled and flashed speedily past us.

Mengele broke hard and we all jolted forward. We halted before a closed iron gate. He impatiently sounded his horn. A guard hurried from his sentry post and rushed to open the blockade for the all-too familiar car. We proceeded for another few hundred metres along the camp's main street, passing dozens of wooden barracks that flanked us on both sides.

The car came to a gradual stop outside an elegant brick building. Mengele got out. We all followed and hastily pursued the SS doctor through a heavy entrance door. We went inside. A bespectacled man in striped prison garb sat studiously behind a lamplit desk. He leapt to his feet and stood stiffly to attention, head bowed and twitching. I noticed a pustular eruption over his shorn scalp that oozed ever so slightly and glistened in the lamplight.

Mengele approached the desk and the two exchanged words. The three of us stood nearby, but were unable to catch what they were saying. The man nodded and proceeded to call me over before resuming his seat. He removed some small cards from a drawer and deftly entered my details in exquisitely neat calligraphy. He passed the completed data to Mengele with a flourish and gentle bow.

"You can forgo the social niceties, Sentkeller!"

Mengele seemed vexed by the glimmer of sophistication that my fellow prisoner projected.

"You may have neat handwriting but you've got the degenerate skin of a Jew! Your scalp is a bloody mess! See to it very soon or I'll be sending your head to Berlin-Dahlem as a pathological specimen!"

After my two companions were registered, we all left the camp office and made our way back to the car. After another bumpy ride, we finally arrived outside *Krema* I.

We were introduced to Dr. József Sárkány, my new boss and supervisor. I had met him before at a medical conference in Berlin, and we'd spent a little time together at Heidelberg University. I also remembered seeing him briefly on the ramp, and helping him down from the train. He did not appear to recognise me or even know my name.

The Doc had a pompous and arrogant demeanour, and delighted in subjecting us all to a detailed résumé of his training and expertise in forensic pathology. He had studied and worked under the supervision of Dr. Karl Reuter at the

University of Breslau. His doctoral dissertation was an analysis of female suicides in Breslau over a five-year period.

Later, I got the lowdown on Mengele from the *Sonderkommando* who lived in the attic. He had arrived here last year at his own request. Due to his previous military decorations, he commanded the general respect of the SS guards who both looked up to him and feared him. He first became the main SS doctor of the Gypsy camp, and rapidly obtained a research grant for experimental work from Berlin. Now he was one of the leading doctors in the men's hospital and Chief Medical Officer of Sectors B-IIa, b and d. He was shortly to be appointed principal doctor of the SS garrison hospital.

Thursday 8th June

Sárkány is acutely aware of his own medical acumen and feels entirely able to negotiate the contours of his new life in the crematorium. Moreover, he is deluded by the fact that his status as a Jew will somehow be overlooked by Mengele. He unwisely pictures himself above the other Jewish inmates, or at least only at the fringe of their turpitude.

In the dissection room, it is Sárkány who is the superior man – a Renaissance man and polymath – empowered by his knowledge of medicine and German. He appears to have shaken off his Jewishness like a snake sheds its skin. He has become Dr. József Sárkány, the renowned anatomical pathologist, expert in autopsies, and chief doctor of the Birkenau *Sonderkommando*. Medicine, he tells me, will assure his survival. He remarks candidly on the opportunities offered by the camp in providing medical research, not only with diverse human subjects but also with rare diseases. And apparently insensible of any ethical concerns, he boasts that his groundbreaking research on hereditary syphilis in Roma children will help develop new treatments for noma. This naturally involves a continuous supply of postmortem material, as well as *in vivo* experiments using antimalarial serum combined with a brand-new arsenical called Novarsenobenzol.

Sárkány is already Mengele's puppet. He holds court in the dissection hall and accompanies his master on his rounds to the various hospital barracks. I overhear him bragging about his research to the network of eminent inmate physicians – Krömer, Grósz and Lévy – to name but a few. After the morning dissections, several French doctors visit, asking him for instruction in the technique of lumbar puncture and epidural anaesthesia. That these are bodies of other Jews does not inhibit these doctors from wanting to practise and experiment on them. Sárkány is also more than happy to oblige, and I begin to see a blurring of ethical boundaries between victim and perpetrator.

FRIENDS IN HIGH PLACES

Diary of Dr. József Sárkány, Auschwitz, Poland, 1944

<u>Sunday 14th May</u>

My first day in camp began abruptly. For those who made it through the night, the 3am wake-up call took the dissonant form of shrill whistles and shouts:

"Out! Out! Everyone out! Get up! It's play time!"

We had no time to think as we were all driven towards the exit. I joined the stampede of men as they poured from the building like a herd of bewildered zebras, for nobody wanted to be late for roll call. An elbow in the face and a fist to the midriff greeted the unfortunate loiterers, too sick to be out of bed, let alone stand outside in the early hours. Nobody cared though. We were all too preoccupied with maintaining the linear geometry of our block formation.

An hour passed in the dark. We stood. And so the infernal roll call lingered on into its second hour. The grey light of dawn began to illuminate the now all too familiar sights of barbed wire, barracks and chimney. So it went on and on… A dozen times the roll was counted; this way then that way, forwards, backwards, sideways and diagonally along the rows. If a line wasn't straight, the entire block had to squat in the mud for half an hour. Soon everyone's legs were trembling with exhaustion. Those succumbing to cramp quickly had it kicked it out of them.

The arrival of the *SS-Blockführer* heralded the fourth hour of this unholiest of mornings. Washed and shaved and smelling of cologne, he struck a Napoleonic pose; hand buried inside a pristine jacket, freshly laundered and pressed. He began to inspect the ranks and files, scrutinising every man for the slightest anomaly. We waited with baited breath – nothing. Did he not detect a single aberration, the merest anomaly – anywhere?

He suddenly pounced on a man in the third row. He struck him round the face: but why? No one knew. Nobody even contemplated the rhyme or reason. For this was Auschwitz sport. There were no rules, no rubrics, and no codes of conduct. In a place devoid of morality and ethics, people perished daily at the slenderest of pretexts.

Next to be inspected were the cadavers: there were seven this morning, propped up on either side by pairs of weary prisoners; for even the dead had to be present and correct if the morning headcount was to tally. But not until they were carted away to the crematoria could they be finally scratched from the register. And when it occasionally happened that the Corpse *Kommando* was overwhelmed with work, these sorry shells of disintegrating flesh must continue to present themselves for inspection and counting.

With muster finally over, we returned to our barracks and waited for breakfast. The last of the corpses was removed and piled outside the doorway to await collection.

Krömer had found me a sleeping space on a middle tier near to the stove.

"This is the best I've got for the time being," he said. "It's actually a good position, and the straw mattresses were changed only last month."

He went on to explain that the top bunks were susceptible to drafts and even rainfall as the roof was not entirely waterproof, especially in a sudden downpour.

"You really don't want to get a wet mattress," he continued. "A small amount of urine is generally unavoidable in this place, but a deluge of rain is impossible to get dry again and will lead to mould and infestations."

"And the bottom bunks?" I inquired, although I guessed what the answer would be.

"These are by far the worse positions," he replied. "They're too near the insects and vermin on the floor, and in the direct line of fire from incontinent or lazy prisoners above. No, stay in the middle and you'll have a much easier ride when it comes to getting some rest… Ah, I nearly forgot: you'll need this."

Krömer handed me a metal mess tin from under his jacket.

"I managed to procure this for you this morning. It's the best I could find – not too rusty and relatively free of lichen. I'll try to organise a spoon, but such items are a rare luxury."

An SS guard entered, covering his nose. He approached Krömer and handed him a piece of folded paper. Looking around in disgust and disbelief, he hurried out again without saying a word.

Krömer opened the paper and smiled. "You're one lucky bugger!" he cried. Then he read the note out loud:

"Prisoner A-7938 is to have two days of protected rest and an extra ration of bread for a week. He will then commence his medical duties in Block 12 under the direct supervision of the Block Eldest. Failure to obey this order will incur a serious penalty: signed *SS-Hauptsturmführer* Dr. Josef Mengele."

Krömer stared at the note for a moment, hands trembling. Then his eyes lit up and he smiled:

"So, it's Mengele that got you out of quarantine. Yes, of course: it would have to come from high up the pecking order of SS doctors. Is he an old friend of yours?"

"We were at medical school together," I replied. "He treated me several years back for a scalp laceration, but I haven't seen him since. I certainly wouldn't call us friends, especially in the current political climate."

"Well, who would have believed it? The Angel of Death has become your very own Guardian Angel!"

"What do you mean, Angel of Death?" This was the second time I'd heard this remark.

"Never mind," replied Krömer, looking slightly uncomfortable. "Here, you'd better hold onto this, and make sure you keep it safe." He handed me the note. "Right then, I think it's high time for breakfast, don't you? We wouldn't want the scrambled eggs and mushrooms to get cold!"

The Birkenau breakfast consisted of a quarter-litre of tea: a black watery infusion of indefinable plant origin – nettles, weeds, linden leaves perhaps, who knows. There was muddy sediment at the bottom of my tin which I swallowed anyway. Coffee was served on alternate days. This, Krömer informed me, was a bitter brew of roasted acorns, dandelions and hops: unsweetened and wholly unpalatable.

After a lazy morning catching up with some sleep, I was served the noonday meal: a thin vegetable soup of dubious calorific value – devoid of salt, flour or seasoning. Evening finally brought the banquet ration of commissary bread, no more than perhaps thirty grams. I got two pieces as directed by Dr. Mengele, and had no intention of sharing it with anybody else.

This camp bread was of the very worst kind, baked with coarse chestnut flour and no doubt cut with sawdust. A tablespoon of margarine substitute that smelled of lignite was also distributed, together with a mouthful of watery salami. To wash this ration down, a half-litre of thin soup concocted from nettles, cabbage and a few beets: nothing proteinaceous, nothing fatty... nothing wholesome.

A DOCTOR'S LIFE

Diary of Dr. József Sárkány, Auschwitz, Poland, 1944

<u>Sabbath 27th May</u>

My new life is a toxic swill of vomit, excrement, urine, sweat, pus, mucus, blood and bile: all the horrible humours of humanity. The rancid breaths of the diphtheroid and the dropsical hover and hang around the febrile muddy banks of dribbling dysentery. Gut-shattering diarrhoea is everywhere; filling every dead hour of every dead day – draining, desiccating and devouring. And amongst all this filth lay row upon row of dilapidated skeletal structures, emaciated, not human but humanoid; an anti-race with glazed, staring eyes.

But these seemingly lifeless eyes are all-knowing, wise through experience; *Kaddish*-denying atheist eyes – waiting for death not deliverance: for there's a threshold to human degradation that, once exceeded, leads inexorably to psychosomatic breakdown and initiation of the death instinct. This self-destructive path at first proceeds sluggishly but soon gains momentum until the once charming and sophisticated father of four becomes the inglorious *Muselmann*: inert, docile and utterly indifferent.

I am in a place where it is tough to remain a man, but excruciating to be both man and doctor. There is supposed to be one male nurse for every twenty patients. Today our barracks contains 958 patients and there are just nineteen hospital attendants – so-called corpsmen.

Many of the bedridden soil themselves. Those lucky enough to get a bedpan have to wait for hours before it is removed. They frequently get chemical burns if exposed too long to the receptacle's uneven lining of caustic lime and moss.

Sleep is rarely undisturbed and almost never refreshing.

The nights are just a continuation of the day's torture, fraught with anxiety and misery. Apart from the cold, damp and incredibly cramped conditions, the constant coughs and moans of a thousand people bring very little peace and quiet. The cold also promotes diuresis, which only adds to the stress. The latrine bucket will inevitably become full and require emptying outside by the unlucky person who used it last. Others too weak to move invariably end up soiling themselves and everyone around them.

Food and drink are never served hot. It is lukewarm at best, but often stone-cold. The *Kapos* get the lion's share of the bread ration, leaving the stale and mouldier morsels for the rest, although even this has a pecking order. There is a very occasional sausage ration. This is largely fat of the poorest quality, and no doubt made from the offal of mangy horses... or worse. Very few prisoners have a spoon, and there is no opportunity to clean your hands or rinse out your mess tin. Indeed, this tin often serves as a receptacle for both food and faeces.

A handful of special prisoners receive much better treatment and hospital care. Krömer keeps a hidden inventory of drugs that are currently available on the camp's black market. The diverse list runs over two pages and includes: coumadin, uritone, butamirate, metamizole, quinine, combelin, transpulmin, gardenal, eubasina, sympatol, prontosil, novalgin and istizin.

Aseptic surgeries are also performed on privileged and senior inmates. The records indicate such procedures as: cholecystectomy, appendectomy, hernia and hydrocele operations, mastoidectomy, tonsillectomy, skin grafting, rotator cuff surgery and various orthopaedic interventions, including amputation. These surgeries are all performed under anaesthesia with ether, novocaine or chloroethyl. However, surgery for the average prisoner is confined to castration, sterilisation and incisional drainages of pus.

The protean forms of skin infection include abscesses, phlegmons, carbuncles, impetigo, erysipelas, sycosis barbae and cellulitis. In fact, dermatology is the only area where camp inmates get prudent medical care, presumably because it is quick and cheap, and does not interfere too much with productivity quotas.

Prisoner clothing neither keeps the body warm nor protects it from the common cold. Some bolster their threadbare socks with sawdust and wood shavings. Others manage to organise extra layers of insulating paper, although this does not last long and invariably gets eaten. Hand infections and whitlows are commonplace, as are an extraordinary number of ear infections.

But by far the most important item of clothing is footwear. A pair of good quality shoes and socks is so highly prized that many never take them off, even at night. Those unfortunate enough to be given wooden clogs are doomed to die after perhaps four to six weeks, especially in autumn and winter when the camp grounds become a disgusting morass of mud and excrement. These ill-equipped people can be seen to stagger about and fall, as their ill-fitting clogs sink into the foul and sticky mudbath. The constant abrasion causes blisters and sores, which rapidly get infected and suppurate. The ensuing abscesses and phlegmons begin to spread up the leg, making any sort of weight bearing nigh on impossible. Necrotising cellulitis, gangrene and septicaemia set in before the febrile body melts away into the damp straw bedding.

Wooden crossbeams in the roof display sardonic messages in German telling us to 'Be Calm!' and to 'Keep Order!' The long concrete channel running down the centre of the mud floor is supposed to warm the whole barracks, conveying heat in metal pipes from the two stoves at either end. These are never lit and are for the sake of appearance only. Black soot stains the brickwork of the stove in order to deceive potential camp inspectors. It is generally accepted that this was smeared on after the stoves were built. No soot deposits are seen in the flues or around the chimney tops.

OLD FRIENDS

Transcript of secret recording (unknown source) in Crematorium I, Auschwitz, Poland, dated Monday 29th May 1944

Muhsfeldt: There's a Yid outside. Apparently, you're expecting him.

Mengele: I assume he has a number.

Muhsfeldt: He says he's a doctor.

Mengele: Then treat him like a doctor! Bring him through.

Muhsfeldt: Prisoner A-7938.

Mengele: József! Oh dear, look at you!

Sárkány: My wife and daughters – are they safe?

Mengele: Ah, yes – I see. I shall of course make some enquiries. I'm sure they're fine. I… I was also sorry to hear about your son.

Sárkány: Thank you, *Hauptsturmführer.*

Mengele: Josef, please. Do you still cut up the dead and pickle organs in jars?

Sárkány: Practising as a pathologist has been rather difficult for me lately.

Mengele: Yes, I expect it has. By the way, look at this beauty. I've had it polished by one of the camp jewellers. What do you think?

Sárkány: It's stunning! Is it human?

Mengele: It's Roma.

Sárkány: How did they die?

Mengele: Die? No, we removed it along with the rest of her gall bladder.

Sárkány: You perform cholecystectomies on Gypsy patients?

Mengele: Yes, indeed. It was a fascinating operation.

Sárkány: Do you still stitch up lacerations? Or have you become too distinguished for such trifles?

Mengele:	No, I still suture. Things have changed for me of course. I've had to move with the times.
Sárkány:	Me too, Dr. Mengele, me too.
Mengele:	Well, we're still close in many ways.
Sárkány:	Except I'm a Jew.
Mengele:	You're a Jew of sorts, yes. But you're really more German. You studied medicine in Frankfurt for Christ's sake! And you speak our language beautifully, with such panache.
Sárkány:	Thank you, *Herr Doktor*.
Mengele:	József... it's difficult... you must understand. You must relinquish your racial heritage. Jewry is not a friend of the *Führer*. Is it not time to put your marriage behind you? Leave your Jewess wife and daughters. Return to the fold. I can help you to become Aryan again, and a distinguished doctor that holds the utmost respect of his peers.
Sárkány:	You want me to abandon my family? Have you already killed them?
Mengele:	No, of course not. I'm just asking you to be realistic. This is an Aryan world. If you want to live in it, you must become part of it. And what better way to begin this transformation than becoming my personal assistant and helping me with my work.
Sárkány:	Your work?
Mengele:	Yes, you can assist me with my experiments. It is incredibly important work.
Sárkány:	What sort of experiments?
Mengele:	Well, I will need to conduct certain tests on specific groups of people.
Sárkány:	You mean Jews.
Mengele:	Well, yes, but not just Jews. There are others – Gypsies, dwarfs, giants, twins...
Sárkány:	You know I have twin daughters.
Mengele:	Do you? No, I didn't know. Are they identical?

Sárkány:	Yes, they're monozygotic.
Mengele:	Splendid! Well, yes – twins hold a particular fascination for me.
Sárkány:	So, what would you like me to do?
Mengele:	I'd like you to come and work for me here, in Birkenau's first and greatest crematorium.
Sárkány:	Do you have patients here?
Mengele:	Yes, lots. All dead of course – but you're a pathologist, and one of Europe's finest.
Sárkány:	Thank you, *Herr Doktor*. And if I do this for you, will you help me to find my wife and children?
Mengele:	Of course! Do we have a deal, Dr. Sárkány?
Sárkány:	We have a deal, Dr. Mengele. Is that all?
Mengele:	Just one more thing. I'm hearing all kinds of rumours about planned escapes and revolts amongst the *Sonderkommando* who work in the crematoria. We suspect the Jewish prisoners are planning some sort of uprising. Persuade your people that any form resistance will only result in death. And if you happen to hear anything – rumours, gossip – well, I would very much like to know.
Sárkány:	So you want me to be your pathologist and your spy? You'd like me to be an informer?
Mengele:	Telling me the names of dangerous criminals is not informing! And besides, you were more than happy to collaborate with the Jewish Council and Gestapo in the ghetto.
Sárkány:	But are the *Sonderkommando* really dangerous criminals or just desperate victims?
Mengele:	As if you really care! No József – they are the *Untermenschen*. These inferior races will be conquered and enslaved. Others will become extinct. It is a matter of racial hygiene, of natural selection… of eugenics.
Sárkány:	You're different. The years of National

	Socialism have changed you.
Mengele:	I've grown up, for sure. I was young and naïve back then. Now I am a man, much wiser – and with great responsibilities. I've seen far more of the *Führer's* Brave New World since those cloistered and halcyon days in Frankfurt.
Sárkány:	All roads now lead to Auschwitz.
Mengele:	For Jews, yes. But for us Germans, all roads lead to Berlin. Yes – German law, medicine, science, engineering, architecture, art, music, literature – the list is endless! Germany is the glorious future of the human race.
Sárkány:	I still don't know if I can become an informer.
Mengele:	Look, let me spell it out to you. The *Führer* is watching us, judging us constantly. At this very moment, he scrutinises every move we make. This is my great opportunity, and yours too if you're shrewd and ambitious enough. You can rise with me, I promise. And just think where it might end? Berlin! Yes, perhaps at the side the *Führer* himself.
Sárkány:	But neither Hitler nor Berlin believes in the future of the Jewish people.
Mengele:	What future do you speak of? You're a conquered race! There's no Noah's Ark to save you from the deluge of Nazism. The tablets of Moses are nothing but dust. King David's glory is gone. Solomon is just vanity. Don't fool yourself any longer. Turn your back on the *Talmud.* Turn your back on Éva! Look to Berlin and to the glory of National Socialism!
Sárkány:	And you promise that I will rise with you?
Mengele:	You have my word.
Sárkány:	You're a liar!
Mengele:	I warn you, A-7938.
Sárkány:	Or what? I'm already a dead man.

Mengele: But there are other facets to the life of Dr. József Sárkány.

Sárkány: Meaning?

Mengele: It's a small world, József: and the medical fraternity is far more insular than even you realise. People talk, I listen. And I too have enjoyed the forbidden fruits of Hannah Fischer. She is a remarkable woman in more ways than one. Whilst your wife must surely know of your sordid little affair, I'm certain that the lethal extent of this adulterous relationship is at present unknown to her.

Sárkány: What are you talking about – *lethal?*

Mengele: Come, come Dr. Sárkány, you're being obtuse. The word is plain enough; adequately describing the conspiracy of assassins who took the life of your handicapped son.

Sárkány: András died of wholly natural causes: 'bronchopneumonia' to quote the official death certificate.

Mengele: You forget who you're talking to. I was intimately associated with the Mercy Killers of *4 Tiergartenstrasse.* Death certificates were falsified, children were killed. I even have the Bernburg dossier on your son after the Euthanasia Centre was mothballed last July. He was suffocated by Dr. Hannah Fischer, under the supervision of Dr. Irmfried Eberl. But you know this; you were part of this plot. You betrayed your son to curry favour with Eberl and Brandt, in a vain attempt to further your own career. Dr. József Sárkány is the greatest oath breaker of them all!

Sárkány: I thought... I thought that his death would liberate Éva from a lifetime of servitude and fear... But I was so wrong! András meant everything to her. His death only created

	another kind of bondage: a cage of inconsolable grief.
Mengele:	And yet this distressing revelation of her husband's filicide would undoubtedly light the touchpaper of her own death instinct; dramatically decreasing her will to survive, especially in a place like this.
Sárkány:	She wouldn't believe you. She trusts me. She loves me too much!
Mengele:	I see. Then I'll put another question to you. How old are your daughters, József? They must be, what – sixteen years old? I'm sure they're lovely young ladies; both beautiful and intelligent, like your dear Éva. It would be a tragedy indeed for such a triumvirate of Sárkány Jewesses to perish in the gas chamber of this very building. And who knows? I may be inclined to have them dissected and dismembered; even immortalised in my museum of pathological curiosities.
Sárkány:	Very well, Dr. Mengele. I will do as you wish. Now, may I go?
Mengele:	Yes, of course. I'm glad that we now have a complete understanding. But first a little toast. It's dreadful Hungarian wine, but there's a war on. To the loyalty of old friends: will you drink to that?
Sárkány:	I will drink to that, *Herr Doktor Mengele*.

MENGELE'S PATHOLOGIST

Diary of Dr. József Sárkány, Auschwitz, Poland, 1944

<u>Tuesday 30th May</u>

I bade farewell to the hospital block this evening. It had only been a short stay, but I'd learnt enough about camp life to know that my wife and daughters must be suffering terribly. I ached to find out where they were, and how they were faring under these impossible living conditions.

Krömer was attending to a dying patient when my escort arrived. I approached the kind doctor and thanked him.

"What for?" he asked.

"For caring," I replied.

We shook hands. He wished me luck. His yellow eyes began to moisten, and I knew why. This poor shadow of a man hadn't got long to live, perhaps three months at most.

"I've put a few little extras in your bag," he said. "You know how it is, nothing fancy – some medicines, dressings, ointment… even a couple of small turnips."

I thanked him again and we embraced. If more doctors were like him, then the world would certainly be a better place. I departed with my Gladstone bag and guard escort.

We walked at a brisk pace through the cosmopolitan city of the Birkenau men's camp, illuminated by a dazzling blaze of *klieg* lights. His Majesty Mengele came to collect me in person from the administration office.

"It's no luxury hotel where I'm taking you!" he jovially remarked. "However, it is quite a tolerable position compared to the rest of the main camp."

We proceeded to walk in silence towards Crematorium I, my new home. As we travelled up the central main street of the camp, I saw the vast unloading ramp. It sent a cold shudder through me. A few weary inmates were stirring here and there, loading the last suitcases onto trucks. Next to them, forty cattle-cars stood ominously still and silent, like a colossal black basilisk disgorged of its prey. These pathetic wagons were once the temporary abode of entire communities, families, friends… lovers. These cursed chariots of our ultimate destruction now melted away into the gloom of another balmy night in Birkenau.

The main road passed through various sub-sections. First was the men's quarantine zone, followed by the Czech camp, and then the Hungarian women's transit site. There followed the men's sector, then the Gypsy camp, and finally the men's hospital barracks where I had been staying since my arrival. The Gypsy precinct housed a medical experimentation block. Like the Czech enclosure, prisoners were allowed to keep their hair and clothes, and were also permitted to live together as family units.

At the southerly end of the hospital barracks was a football pitch where the SS and special camp prisoners played a weekly game of soccer on a Sunday afternoon. To our right was the new camp extension, only partly constructed. This was nicknamed 'Mexico' and it functioned mainly as a transit zone and quarantine. In other words, it was holding area before the gas.

We finally arrived outside Birkenau's Crematorium I. A guard hurried over and presented himself to Mengele with a click of the heels and a Nazi salute. Crossing the courtyard, we passed through a large door into the bowels of this enormous red brick building.

We were greeted by the SS head of Crematorium I. His name was *Oberscharführer* Muhsfeldt. He was an ugly man, with a weasel-like face and bulbous blue eyes.

"Is the doctor's apartment ready?" asked Mengele. Muhsfeldt answered in the affirmative, and we made our way there directly.

We entered into a spacious and freshly whitewashed room on the ground floor. Overlooking the front courtyard was a large window with heavy iron bars. The furniture made a peculiar impression after the squalor of my previous dwelling. A pinewood bed, a white wardrobe, a long table and some chairs made up the room's furnishings. On the table was a red velvet tablecloth, and underfoot, on the concrete floor, were splendid thick-pile rugs.

Mengele left us. Muhsfeldt looked visibly relieved, and continued with a tour of the facility.

Passing through a long corridor, we arrived at a bright, double-windowed dissecting room. The floor was of reddish concrete, and in the middle of the room, on a grey concrete base, stood a marble-slab dissecting table with several drainage channels cut into its surface. Installed near the edge of the table was a tub with nickel-plated taps. Three porcelain sinks were mounted along the wall. The walls were painted light green. In the glass windows, behind the iron bars, green-meshed screens kept the flies, mosquitos and prying eyes out.

Next door was the laboratory. This was an elegant room fitted with comfortable armchairs and a long work desk covered by a shiny grey cloth. On the table I counted three microscopes and a microtome for cutting sections. A tall bookcase stood in one corner, filled with medical and technical volumes in the latest editions. An elegant glass cabinet also stood in the room. This contained various bottles of chemicals and tinctorial dyes for preparing histological sections. The room was also equipped with a large medicine cabinet and a spacious linen closet containing surgical gowns, aprons, gloves, towels and face masks.

In fact, the laboratory before me was a perfect replica of any modern anatomical institute in Europe.

After handing me the medicines key, Muhsfeldt bade me a good night and left. I eagerly unlocked the cabinet and found it fully stocked with injectable vials of morphine. A box of ampoules labelled 'Compound P' was also stored on the bottom shelf.

It was getting late. I was famished and thirsty. I headed up to the first floor of the building, to the living quarters of the *Sonderkommando*. It was an enormous well-lit annex under the eaves of the roof, directly above the oven room, and lined on either side by rows of comfortable-looking triple bunkbeds. The bunks were made of unpainted pinewood, but each was richly covered with cushions and silk coverlets in different styles and patterns. This brilliantly colourful bedding stood in sharp, even jarring, contrast with the surroundings. It was obviously pillaged from the belongings left by the daily Jewish transports.

Only half of the men were currently in the annex; I estimated around a hundred or so. Most were in bed, either asleep or chatting quietly. The remaining members of *Sonderkommando* were covering the night shift and were no doubt busy in the underground gas chamber and ground-floor furnace room.

A long dining table with around fifty chairs ran down the centre of room, spread with a silk brocade cloth. Fine china plates, porcelain jugs, glasses, and all manner of cutlery covered the table. These too had been salvaged from the transports. A large sink with running tap water was situated in one corner. Next to this was a gas stove.

The dining area was currently occupied by three inmates who were eating and drinking. There was an abundance of food strewn across the tabletop which made my mouth water. There were preserves, smoke-cured bacon, salami, marmalades, pastries – even chocolate. From the labels, I saw that these were provisions left behind by recent Hungarian deportees.

I tentatively sat down at the table. Two men introduced themselves as Levi and Shlomo. Both spoke good German. Levi poured me a glass of dark liquor. He was a senior stoker and one of the Old Guard. Arriving in a transport from Poland two years ago, he'd been in the *Sonderkommando* for nearly one and a half years. Sitting directly opposite me was another old timer called Shlomo. He was also a senior stoker in the furnace room below us.

At the far end of the table sat a young man – dark, rugged-looking and moody. He didn't speak, but stared at me with an air of suspicion.

"The talkative fellow over there is Malkin," whispered Levi. "He's been here the longest and tends to keep himself to himself."

I helped myself to some bread and cheese, and emptied my glass in one gulp. The fiery fluid caused me to cough and splutter. It burned all the way down to my stomach.

"Good man!" said Levi, topping up my glass. "That's my own secret blend. Have some salami and olives: they're fresh in today."

I ravenously tore at the bread with my teeth and crammed a huge piece of smoked sausage into my mouth.

"Slow down, Doc!" laughed Shlomo. "You eat faster than a Jew at a buffet!"

Both Levi and Shlomo were accomplished raconteurs, and were eager to tell me their life stories. They'd been drinking heavily and broke the momentary silences with bursts of song.

"Anyone for a cup of tea?" asked Levi. "Don't worry; I'll add some of my special rum to spice it up a bit."

"I'd prefer a cup of coffee," Shlomo replied. "What I wouldn't give for a cup of freshly ground coffee – sweet, no cream."

"Sorry Shlom, but we're right out of cream: how about with no milk?"

"I really must have a drink of water," I said apologetically, explaining my thirst and fatigue.

"I'm also tired and thirsty," said Levi. "But's that's probably my diabetes."

We got onto the subject of family. I told them that I was hopeful about seeing my wife and twin daughters again.

"Twins, you say?" interrupted Malkin. He grimaced and said no more. I knew exactly what he was thinking.

"Ignore misery guts over there," said Levi. "His wife divorced him for religious reasons. She worshipped money and he didn't have any!"

"Daughters, eh?" said Shlomo. "Well at least they were

spared the cut."

"Circumcision is an essential part of our religious culture," said Malkin in earnest.

"*Ach!*" replied Shlomo. "Our Jewish women won't touch anything unless it's got twenty percent off!"

He laughed to himself. Malkin growled and relit a cigarette that was sitting behind his ear.

"That's it, Malkin," said Levi. "Waft that fag over here. The Doc likes his sausage smoked! Anyway, talking of daughters; I remember a rumour that was circulating in my town before we got deported. A Christian girl had been murdered just outside our ghetto. Naturally, we all feared reprisals, so several important council members met up to discuss a plan of action. Just as the meeting was being called to order, an old Rabbi hurried into the room, very out of breath. 'My good brothers,' he cried. 'I have wonderful news! The murdered girl was a Jew!'"

Suddenly the lights went out and a deafening siren filled the room. Everybody jumped up. Two men had electric torches and there followed a stampede towards the exit.

"It's another air raid," said Shlomo. "Come on! Let's head on downstairs."

"No, wait!" said Levi, frantically searching his pockets. "I can't leave without my dentures."

"Get a grip!" yelled Shlomo. "What do you think they'll be dropping – *matzos* and *knishes?*"

"May your teeth fall out!" replied Levi. "Except for one, so you can get a toothache!"

We headed down into the recently emptied underground gas chamber. The sense of unease was palpable.

"One day the archaeologists will be digging all this up," muttered Malkin. "But when they expose all the rubble and concrete and rusted iron, they'll have no idea about the genocide that went on here in this small bit of God's earth."

Shlomo and Levi looked at him in the torchlight and nodded solemnly. Then a twinkle returned to Shlomo's eyes.

"Talking of archaeology…" he began. "I read in the

paper that the British have uncovered an ancient mummy in Palestine that they believe died from heart failure. When questioned about how they could be so certain, a scientist explained that they'd found a piece of papyrus clutched in his hand. Written in Aramaic, it read: 10,000 shekels on Goliath!"

"Was that one of your feeble jokes?" asked Malkin.

"What do you think?" replied Shlomo.

"Why do Jews answer every question with a question?" said Malkin.

"Why shouldn't they?" said Levi.

I caught Malkin's eye as we eventually left the chamber and I invited him back to my new private quarters for a nightcap. He accepted. He told me that Levi and Shlomo were both alcoholics, and that they would vacillate between days of light banter and silent melancholia. They both took to drink after discovering their dead wives and children lying under a pile of gassed bodies.

Malkin went on to say how the crematoria were factories of genocide, and that *Krema* I specialised in women and children. He looked down and began to mumble, as if talking to himself:

"I have an intimate relationship with these forsaken people. I observe their final moments of life – directly, closely, day in day out. It is a foul, dirty death. I wash the body and purify it… watch it burn… feel the heat, smell the flesh and hair and bones. But with time, little by little, I get used to it. It becomes routine, a daily chore that I don't even think about. Only in the quiet moments, in the dark and the shadows, does the quiescent human conscience bite back."

Transcript of secret recording (unknown source) in Crematorium I, Auschwitz, Poland, dated Wednesday 31st May 1944

Shlomo:	*Ach*, no! Get away from me! I don't need no medic! Please leave me alone!
Levi:	Let him be, Doc: he's ready to go. The poor sod has had enough.
Sárkány:	How many did he take?
Levi:	The whole frigging packet… about thirty pills.
Sárkány:	He's becoming drowsy. He'll soon lose consciousness. Then his breathing will cease and his heart will stop.
Levi:	Yes, that's right. But it's what he wants, Doc. We're all dead anyhow. It's just a matter of how and when.
Sárkány:	What will Muhsfeldt think? Mengele will want an autopsy for sure.
Levi:	And you can tell Mengele that he died of a heart attack. I doubt he'll be watching while you spill open his guts.
Sárkány:	But he's fit and healthy; and if Muhsfeldt gets wind of what he's taken, then questions will start being asked.
Levi:	Am I my brother's keeper? Shlomo was the best stoker we've ever had. He's been here longer than most, even the SS. He was here on the first day when he had to burn his own convoy… his own family. He first carried his wife off the freight elevator, then his son, then his daughter, then his mother, and then his father. And in just two hours, his entire family – his heritage, his identity – had disappeared into smoke and ashes. But you can still kill yourself. That's the only choice we've got left!
Sárkány:	As new Doctor-in-Chief of this crematorium, I'm personally responsible for the welfare of

the *Sonderkommando*.

Levi: Look, he's going! Farewell, dearest friend. Wait for me on the other side.

Sárkány: He's Cheyne Stoking. Alright, he's not going to make it. But don't ever call me again. I'm a doctor, not a murderer!

Levi: Really? Is that so?

Sárkány: What's that supposed to mean?

Levi: Forget it! None of us have got long anyway.

Sárkány: The SS won't kill this *Kommando*. You're the best group of men they've ever had.

Levi: Says who? We all count for shit at the end of the day. We're all dispensable, even you, Doc. The chain breaks, you repair it. You'll always find another link.

Part III

A Tale of Two Doctors

UNTO DUST SHALT THOUGH RETURN

Diary of Dr. József Sárkány, Auschwitz, Poland, 1944

<u>**Wednesday 31st May**</u>

A train of dishevelled pilgrims trudged sleepily over stone and clay towards the crematory gates, groaning under heavy bags. They were dejected, exhausted, apathetic and broken. The great brick chimney loomed incongruously over them, but they were all too shattered to care. They'd hardly eaten a morsel for days. Just a few sips of water had moistened but not quenched. This was a pilgrimage of the damned: the final road to oblivion.

An SS escort hovered around them like blow-flies over tainted meat. The Jewish carrion was ripe and ready.

The travellers descended the twelve stone steps, swallowed one by one into the subterranean belly of the concrete Leviathan: an oubliette of naked deceit. The throng began to fill the changing room, oblivious to the false reassurances and disinfection signs. It was all a blur for them – bustling, bumping crowds of women and children, voices, signposts, gazing around, disorientated, disbelieving. They huddled next to clothes pegs, gazing up at tall pillars and blinding artificial lights in that vast underground cavern.

The voices of a dozen translators echoed around the chamber, goading and guiding with blasphemous lies, all vile and obscene. But the passive pilgrims didn't listen. They were too tired to care. They just wanted it all to end. Some ruminated upon half-remembered *Bar Mitzvahs*, of Passovers in spring, of *Hanukkah* candles and *Kaddishim*. But these were distant memories now, more akin to echoes from another time, another world.

Shouts from guards harried and rebuked, compelling them to undress. They began to strike out, barge and push.

But who cared? It was all going to end very soon. Their threats were just vacuous words in a world of futility and nothingness. Lie after lie rained down, spewing revolting falsehoods about cleanliness. As if they cared anymore. These Jews had been suckled on pretense and weaned on betrayal. Who cared about nudity, about hygiene? Who cared about life?

Mengele entered and looked impatiently down at his immaculate new watch: a *Bethge & Söhne*. He murmured in the ear of an SS guard who nodded. The doctor donned a fresh white coat and made his way to the centre of the room before stepping upon a kind of dais. Like a seasoned preacher, he began his sermon. A Sonder-man stood next to him and translated:

"*Shalom* to you, my splendid Jewesses and children: *ma nishma*? There's absolutely nothing to fear. We just want you to be fresh and clean. I hear that the water's lovely and warm today.

"You will notice that individual clothes hooks are numbered. Please make a careful note of your peg number in order to facilitate a speedy return. Kindly ensure that all footwear is placed neatly underneath the wooden benches. You may wish to tie shoelaces to prevent any mix ups later on. Spectacles, walking sticks, umbrellas, prosthetic limbs and the like can be safely left on the benchtops. For security reasons, we advise that all jewellery stay on your person. Wrist watches can be securely placed in any available pocket – but be sure to remember which!

"What is your occupation my dear *Fräulein*? A dressmaker! Wonderful – we have an urgent need for all such skilled workers. Which reminds me: could all seamstresses please report to *Obersturmführer* Hössler after you've had your fill of bread and hot soup. And would any diabetics with special dietary requirements please come and find me after your shower. Excellent! Thank you so very much for your kind cooperation."

The speech had an invigorating effect on the women

who began to mumble excitedly amongst themselves. Others became suddenly aware of their nakedness and covered themselves to preserve their modesty. Like a revitalising placebo, Dr. Mengele's address had me momentarily lured into his mesmerising web of deceit and misinformation.

Doctors are surely the greatest liars of them all. I imagine the honeyed tongue of Mengele coaxing the crowds forward and saying, 'This way to the gas, my sweet Jewish ladies.' They'd still go, like enchanted lemmings, I'm sure.

It took over an hour for everyone to fully disrobe. At the opposite end of the steps, the chamber narrowed into a short corridor, which led through double doors into an underground foyer. This gave access to the gas chamber through a set of heavy airtight doors.

As soon as the last of the loiterers had left the changing room, dozens of *Sonderkommando* wasted no time in rummaging through the piles of clothes and shoes. Boxes were brought in and started to quickly fill with all sorts of paraphernalia – spectacles, hairbrushes, combs, mirrors, toothbrushes, perfume bottles, scissors, spoons, forks, hat brushes, shoehorns, spice jars, ornaments and watches.

In the adjacent part of the building, the brightly illuminated gas chamber began to fill. It was arranged perpendicular to the undressing room. Several SS men had entered and surreptitiously kept their eyes on the door.

The crowd was expertly crammed together in neat, tightly packed rows. The Germans couldn't resist a little last-minute sport by flicking the lights on and off, sending ripples of panic and fear through the room. The enormous underground bunker was now approaching capacity. The SS and *Sonderkommando* began to slowly make their way to the exit. Still the women and children piled in, pushed together ever tighter and tighter.

"Please be careful, I'm eight months pregnant!" exclaimed one expectant mother, holding desperately onto two little ones.

Many now stared up at the dummy shower heads above them, praying for a refreshing stream of water to quench their raging thirsts. Finally, the frail and disabled stragglers were herded in. The guards now had to push and shove to get out. Once safely outside, a rapid headcount was performed.

I had never seen a thousand humans sandwiched together in such an inhumane manner. Many had to lift their arms above their heads. Children tried to climb onto mother's shoulders. But still no water came. The bitter realisation that this was no shower room must have surely now taken hold. Whatever glimmer of hope they might have had after Mengele's speech had now evaporated.

At the very last minute, the gargantuan deceit was shatteringly exposed as seven babies were lobbed into the chamber over the packed peoples' heads. They had been hidden amongst the bundles of clothes in the changing room. A great yell now erupted as the solid double doors were slammed shut behind them. The sound of heavy metal bolts was quickly followed by frantic screws being tightened to make the rubber seals airtight. Muffled wails and cries of despair could now be heard, mixed with begging, pleading... imploring.

Finally, the lights went out – and stayed out.

Piercing screams erupted as the four trapdoors in the ceiling were opened. Once the concrete slabs had been removed, the Red Cross disinfectors donned gasmasks and then punched open each cannister of *Zyklon B*.

Mengele paced outside like an excited schoolboy. I overheard him mutter: "Give the Jewesses their fodder!"

The message was quickly relayed to the two medical service corporals on the roof. Upon receiving this go-ahead signal, they proceeded to empty a cannister of the poisonous granules into each of the four wire-mesh columns. They were overseen by Theuer and Koch, who assisted in immediately closing up these holes of death.

An enormous panic now ensued within the gas chamber

as frantic hordes made for the exit, beating and hammering upon the impenetrable doors. Derisive laughter was the only reply. One of the guards shouted: "Is the water too hot?"

The nightmare lasted for twenty minutes and was timed with a stopwatch. Finally, the lights were switched back on and the gas pellets extracted through mesh baskets in the roof. Wearing a gasmask, Mengele peered in through each of the roof apertures to check for any signs of life. He then signalled for the extractor fan to be switched on, and the chamber was ventilated for another twenty minutes. A dull throbbing noise became audible as the foul air was mechanically cleansed.

At last, the great doors were swung open and a potent stench filled the outside vestibule as a heaving mass of befouled bodies spilt and splashed out of the chamber. Now another kind of hell commenced as the *Sonderkommando* began to unpick the twisted and tangled morass of clawed flesh. Armed with gasmasks, nooses and hooks, they worked with frenzied activity in emptying the chamber. The first to enter formed a vanguard quartet equipped with rubber gloves, aprons and tall rubber boots. They also carried rubber-bulb syringes that dislodged pockets of trapped contaminated air from between the corpses.

Once the mountain of corpses had been cleared from the doorway, ferocious jets of water now flooded the room, hosing down the walls and washing the bodies of blood, urine and excrement. Others now entered, frantically looping belt straps around wrists and ankles before dragging the bodies, still slippery with water, towards a small lift in the foyer. Here, they were laid out in rows before being loaded onto a mechanical hoist and conveyed up to the ground floor ovens.

Mengele was loitering by the lift shaft, smoking a cigarette. He smirked at the body of a young woman who was laid out before his feet:

"Sarah, Sarah, come on, get up!" he merrily remarked. "Don't you realise that your soup is getting cold?"

The elevator stopped at the cremation hall where the wet corpses were dragged towards the ovens using the hooks of walking canes lodged in gaping mouths or under jaws. A specially constructed slipway with an irrigated gulley facilitated the transport of bodies.

And now began the final phase of looting and pillaging. Eight men of the tooth-pulling *Kommando* stood before the furnaces, with crowbar in one hand and monstrous pliers in the other. They turned the bodies face upward, wrenched open the mouths, and with gruesome alacrity, proceeded to not so much pull out as smash out, any gold teeth and bridges they could find. And yet these brutish men with their brutal instruments were all qualified dentists and oral surgeons.

Any gold teeth wound up in a zinc bucket, where they sat in a corrosive solution of hydrochloric acid in order to dissolve any residual fragments of jawbone and soft tissue. The other items found on the dead – gold, silver and platinum trinkets, pearls, necklaces and rings – all went into a closed strongbox set aside for this purpose. Malkin estimated that about two kilograms was collected daily from this crematorium alone.

Before being handed over to the Cremation Squad, the barbers first got to work on shearing the dead flock. Women's hair was coveted for its length and tensile strength. The vast jumbled quantities of hair – strands, braids, curls, ponytails – were carefully laid out to 'cure' on the warm loft-space flooring above the ovens. It was then cleaned and spun into fibre before being shipped off in twenty kilogram bales that fetched forty pfennigs per kilo.

I shuddered to think of this versatile human fibre – this highly personal human fabric – being used to manufacture such impersonal objects as textiles, ropes, carpets, mattress stuffing, felt insulators and detonator fuses. For hair is not only part of the human body; it is an integral component of human personality, culture and identity. Hair is so simple and yet infinitely complex to the intricate human psyche.

In front of every muffle, three stokers were busy burning bodies, day and night, in a kind of conveyor belt of annihilation. I stood next to Malkin and watched over his grisly work. When he opened a muffle door, I beheld the inferno within and the glowing mass of flesh, sinew and bone. The body hissed and boiled. The flesh cracked and the fat spat and popped. Then, as if possessed by some final remnants of life, the cadaver appeared to move and sway. I perceived the occasional quiver, a sudden twitch. It was almost as if the corpse was in the process of a resurrection, like an incubated phoenix gestating in the flames.

Was there to be no rest for these wretched people, even in death? If you bury a corpse in a cemetery, the body is ritually laid to rest, with dignity and ceremony. He or she no longer feels a thing. They are at peace in their grave, asleep for eternity. But in the oven, it is wholly different. It seems to me that the body becomes agitated and animated once more, reinvigorated by the thermal energy of the flames. How ghastly it appears, as if writhing and thrashing in a new igneous agony; a new torture devised by the enemy. And so, the form changes – again and again – in a fiery flux of incineration and metamorphosis. It is nothing like watching a glowing coal fire or an inanimate log of wood: the human body fights disintegration to the very last, with a medley of sounds and movements in an orchestra of fire.

A middle-aged Rabbi stood nearby reciting the *Kaddish*. A respectable and religious Jew, he was the former *Dayan* of Maków. Malkin asked him why God had abandoned his Chosen People:

"Do not worry, my son. This is the Lord's will and we cannot change His will. The Jews have sinned, and this is our divine punishment."

"What about the thousands of infants, the innocent babies? What is their great sin?" he asked.

"They have surely imbibed their mother's sins," he replied.

"You bloody fool!" Malkin cried, in utter disbelief at

these words. "You call yourself wise and learned! How can you, a man of God, stand here before me and spout such a blasphemy of lies? Really, Rabbi! No such justification, whether it is scriptural or philosophical, can be made in the presence of so many dead children! Judaism is nothing but ashes!"

"Yes, that is true," he calmly replied. "And hear my prophecy when I tell you that a new Israel will be built out of the ashes of Auschwitz-Birkenau."

CHARITY & MALICE

Diary of Dr. József Sárkány, Auschwitz, Poland, 1944

<u>**Thursday 1ˢᵗ June**</u>

This afternoon I noticed a workforce of women labouring on a new pathway just outside the crematorium precincts. They numbered around a hundred, and were guarded by five female guards with dogs. Haggard and emaciated, they toiled in the afternoon heat, lugging buckets of gravel and rocks by hand. I anxiously checked to see if my wife and daughters were with them, and felt both relieved and disappointed to see that they were not.

I now witnessed something quite extraordinary. Five senior members of the *Sonderkommando* approached two SS sentry guards at the gate. The Sonder-men were each holding partially filled potato sacks. A concealed exchange then took place and the crematory gates were opened. An SS man approached one of the female guards and there was another rapid exchange. She half-nodded before approaching the chief *Kapo*, who gave a signal to the working prisoners.

Everything appeared to be carefully arranged as five women, each holding a bucket, approached the gate. Without stopping, each container received a pre-prepared parcel from one of the Sonder-men. After accepting the consignment, the women walked casually back to the working party as if nothing had happened. This well-rehearsed routine continued as another five received their packages and concealed them under their dresses. Within twenty minutes, all of the women had been furnished with a parcel. The *Kapo* gave a final signal to the SS guards who proceeded to close the crematorium gates.

I later discovered that this relief aid was going on outside all four crematoria and *Kanada*. It was a small piece of charity and human kindness that almost touched me, although no doubt dependent on a network of bribes and a certain understanding between the guards and *Sonderkommando*. I also learned that the contents of these parcels varied according to availability, but generally comprised bread, margarine, beetroot jam and cheese.

I asked – more out of obligation than anything else – if I might be able to add some medicines to the next batch of parcels. However, my empty gesture was taken seriously by the *Sonderkommando* seniors, who unfortunately agreed.

I reluctantly began to make my own little bundles wrapped in muslin gauze. These precious little packages purported to contain a precious assortment of vitamin pills, sulphonamide powder, iodine ointment, dressings and small pieces of soap. Most of the contents were in fact no more than placebos.

Friday 2nd June

From two large windows in the dissection room, I noticed a tipper truck pull up outside the gates just after seven. On board were some eighty or so women. The courtyard was filled with dreadful cries as the emaciated truckload glared up at the soaring brick chimney. All looked gravely ill, some stuporous and moribund. None of them moved, no doubt paralysed by a mixture of exhaustion and terror. The SS guards barked orders to descend from the truck's high platform. The vexed driver – an alcoholic NCO called Glutz – got out of the front and hurled abuse at them. His face was bright pink and I noticed a glistening film of sweat over his corrugated brow. His impatience was evidently turning to rage. Do these uncooperative Jewesses not realise that his shift is over and that his dinner's getting cold?

Cursing and swearing, Glutz dashed back into his cab and restarted the engine. He chuckled to himself. He'll show them!

The back of the truck began to pivot as the front was raised upward on hydraulic pistons. As the gradient grew ever steeper, the helpless women spilled out of the back and crashed onto the concrete in jumbled heaps. These miserable, half-dead human beings were unceremoniously dumped outside the crematorium gates, devoid of all dignity and compassion. Some tumbled backwards, smashing their heads. Others flipped horribly forwards, face first. Many now slithered and slid haphazardly, elbows clashing with knees, and feet with heads and hands.

An inhumane cry erupted. The *Sonderkommando* began to scoop up the skeletons and accompanied them inside. Those unable to walk were mercilessly dragged. A few of the lesser soiled were tossed over shoulders and carried.

I stood motionless by the window until the last of the women were taken into the building. The sound of muffled gunfire shortly followed. The shots appeared to be coming from the large washroom at the back of the building. I was filled with fear as I counted shot after sordid shot – twenty, forty… sixty – and still it went on.

Silence fell. I then heard footsteps pass my door on the corridor. It was Muhsfeldt; I recognised the limp.

My morbid curiosity once again got the better of me. I plucked up the courage to leave the dissecting room and quietly made my way through the foyer to the washroom. It was a bare and gloomy chamber with concrete flooring. A small, barred window looked out onto the back courtyard. I occasionally used it as a temporary morgue, storing bodies until they were autopsied.

Heaped outside the entrance was a pile of tattered and dirty women's clothes; battered wooden clogs caked in filth, headscarfs, spectacles, and stale pieces of bread. I braced myself and entered the room.

A horrifying picture unfolded as I looked upon the dim chamber. The bloodied remains of eighty naked women were sprawled out before me. The bodies lay every which way, slumped over one another. I moved closer and realised that many were still alive. They made slow movements with their arms and legs, some trying to lift their heads.

I examined one of the women close up. My God! No, it couldn't be? I recognised that face! It was that of my former au pair, Lena Herschell. She glared at me through bloodshot eyes and gurgled as if trying to speak. But instead of words, blood dribbled from the sides of her mouth and ran in two crimson rivulets down her chin. Her teeth were pink and bloodstained. She began to cough and splutter before making one desperate effort to say something thar was clearly important to her. I held her hand as words formed in her bubbling throat:

"Tell Éva, I'm sorry."

She attempted to squeeze my fingers as her eyes began to bulge and her lips darkened to a dusky lilac. Finally, she stopped breathing. It had taken almost an hour for her agonal suffering to end.

Turning her head to one side and wiping away the congealed blood, I was fascinated to learn that Lena had been shot in the back of the neck; just like my father-in-law and the other unfortunate folk of Munkács. There was a 6mm entrance wound fired from a small calibre pistol, commonly used in slaughterhouses. The blackened powder-burns indicated a shot fired at point-blank range, perhaps up to four centimetres away but no more. No exit wound was apparent, suggesting a soft lead bullet that flattened out inside the skull base. Such a wound did not always cause instantaneous death if the trajectory of the slug was off by one or two millimetres, narrowly missing the brainstem.

This was all the work of *Oberscharführer* Muhsfeldt. He was repellent in both appearance and smell. An unwholesome blend of sociopath and psychopath, this barbarous baker from Brandenburg was the antithesis of human enlightenment. He had a conceited disregard for others, be they Gentile or Jew. Wholly devoid of a moral backbone, Muhsfeldt was as manipulative and deceitful as he was sadistic.

~

At nine o'clock, the Ober visited me in my room. He looked flushed and clammy. His eyes were watery and bloodshot; his breath reeked of strong liquor and cigarettes. Taking off his jacket, he complained of a headache and ordered me to examine him. His pulse was rapid and irregular: I suspected auricular fibrillation. I measured his blood pressure at 180/105 mm Hg, consistent with essential hypertension. His heart sounds were normal and his chest was clear.

I began to examine his cranial nerves, but he lost patience and demanded a diagnosis. I suggested that his headache may be due to high blood pressure, which was no doubt related to the 'little job' he had performed only two hours earlier.

Muhsfeldt sprang up from the chair and stared at me indignantly:

"Your diagnosis is *Scheisse*! *Juden* quacks – you're all the bloody same! Let me tell you something, Doctor Sárkány: killing your people is a pleasure, not a chore. It certainly doesn't make me stressed! On the contrary, it's actually quite relaxing, even therapeutic. I'm equally calm whether I shoot eighty or a thousand of you bastards! Anyway, today's little killing spree was nothing compared to Majdanek's Harvest Festival last November. You know why my blood pressure's up? Well, I'll tell you! It's because I drink too much! Jesus Christ! I'd have thought it was fucking obvious!"

Muhsfeldt stormed out of my room. Shortly after, I went up to the attic and drowned my sorrows in a tumbler of Polish vodka. I asked one of the *Sonderkommando* escorts where the ill-fated women had come from:

"They are medically selected from the women's hospital barracks. Every evening at seven a truck brings eighty over. A queue of naked women lines up outside the washroom; some propped up by one or two Sonder-men. The Ober stands inside the chamber to receive his guests one at a time with a small-bore *Kleinkaliber* he stole from a Gleiwitz abattoir. He always wears the same green rubber gloves.

And one by one, like sacrificial lambs, the women receive a single bullet to the back of the neck. Once she's been 'knocked down' – as Muhsfeldt calls it – the Sonder chaperone brings in the next in line. In a matter of twenty minutes, all eighty women have been shot. Some occasionally go on suffering throughout the evening, but volunteers from the nightshift usually go in around midnight to finish them off."

I retired to my room on the verge of nervous collapse. I took a hit of morphine and guzzled back two Luminal pills. Drug-induced sleep is the only antidote to yet another harrowing day.

Sabbath 3rd June

Muhsfeldt was in a perversely talkative mood this afternoon. He plonked himself down by one of the microscopes and ferreted around in his jacket pockets. I was quite a distance away but I immediately detected the pungent smell of body odour and alcohol. His eyes were glassy and red. His voice was somewhat slurred and punctuated by hiccups.

"Look what I've got for my dinner tonight," he said, showing me a handful of potatoes. "Fresh out the earth! They'll be lovely with that bit of fish I caught this morning."

"Where do you fish?" I asked.

"Wouldn't you like to know, Jew? Well, it's no secret really. There's a small river just north of *Krema* IV. It's not ideal though: too near to Moll's cremation pits and all that fucking smoke!"

I hesitated for a moment. I wanted to know more about these pits. I'd already heard ridiculous tales about rivers of boiling fat:

"Are the rumours true about Moll throwing live babies into the flames?"

The Ober scoffed and laughed, knocking over a jar of formaldehyde. I quickly attended to the spill. As I bent down, I could sense his psychotic eyes burrowing into the back of my neck:

"What Otto gets up to is his business. Anyway, he gets the job done and that's that! You should keep your big Jew's nose out of it!"

Muhsfeldt belched and stashed his prized potatoes back in his pockets:

"I'm just waiting for a ration of butter and then it's bye-bye to these beauties – straight into my gut! Ha! Moll likes my potatoes too. He once asked me the difference between a newborn baby and a new potato. I made up some crap about them both having smooth skins. Do you know what he said? Ha! He said potatoes don't scream when you cook 'em!"

INFERNO

Diary of Dr. József Sárkány, Auschwitz, Poland, 1944

<u>Wednesday 7th June</u>

Muhsfeldt entered the laboratory in a good mood this morning. He seemed to delight in informing me that some 130,000 Hungarian Jews were gassed and cremated last month alone. With an average of 9000 people arriving every day, the vast majority were cremated in the outside incineration trenches. To every train were attached four open freight cars, two containing timber and two with coke. One car usually carried a load of around twenty-five tons of fuel. Transportation of materials and machinery around the camp was the remit of the Central Construction Office, which had eighteen trucks and eight tractors at its disposal.

A telephone call mid-morning ordered me to pick up first aid and medical supplies from Station V. This was formerly called Bunker II, which had now been reactivated due to the sheer volume of Hungarian transports. Postcards were written by the few that made it into quarantine. They were sent back to relatives in Hungary with the generic sentence: 'Arrived safely, all is well'. The sender's address was given as 'Waldsee'. The objective was to lull the Jewish families still awaiting deportation into a false sense of security. It was just another deception.

A single path led out of the camp to the west. This was an extension of the main camp road, which ran alongside the new railway ramp, passing between Crematoria I and II. About eighty metres past the two entrance gates, this road exited the camp and merged with another road running along the outside of Crematorium III. It then ran west for about half a kilometre before arriving at a crossroads that led to the area of Station V. This was surrounded by trees in a pentagonal area located some two hundred metres west of the Central Sauna. A large chain of watchtowers ran along

178

the western boundary fence.

Outside the complex, situated in a vegetated area near the north-west corner of the perimeter fence, were four bulldozed linear excavations, precisely orientated and running north-south. These mass incineration trenches were perhaps two hundred metres north of *Krema* IV and were connected to the camp complex by a bulldozed trail leading to, and through, the perimeter fence to another area of smaller hand-dug trenches. The larger trenches were at least a hundred metres long, ten metres wide and perhaps three metres in depth.

Two of the larger pits were currently being filled with corpses from Station V. At the bottom of the pit, thick wooden logs were piled up, followed by increasingly small branches and twigs. Corpses were thrown on top of this base. After petrol was poured into all four corners of the trench, the SS lit rubber combs and threw them onto the spots moistened by petrol. 1200 corpses were placed into the trenches in three layers of 400 each. The cremation of the bodies took between five to six hours, depending on the weather.

From the bunker to the trenches, a narrow-gauge track was laid, by which the gassed corpses were transported on flat cars. On separate carts arrived large amounts of wood in small chunks which were laid out in the trenches. From the nearby forest, the workers also brought fir branches.

The other two trenches were in full blaze and kicked out an incredible heat and smoky stench. Along the edge of these ditches facing the wooded path from the undressing barracks stood rows of SS guards, about two metres apart.

I reported to *Oberscharführer* Moll, who was busy shouting orders, and explained that I was here to collect medical supplies from the undressing barracks. He nodded slightly, eye twitching, face bright red and drenched in sweat. He pointed towards a *Kapo* standing nearby and told me to go with him.

"And don't fuck about!" he shouted, as I turned away.

Moll appeared to be everywhere at once, moving tirelessly around the trenches and along the path to the undressing room. It was then that I realised to my horror that this morning's victims were not going to the gas chambers of Station V. I'd heard rumours about the dwindling supplies of *Zyklon B*, but dismissed them as idle gossip. But now I saw it for myself: long columns of naked women, children and men moving ever onward towards the inferno.

Then I saw Moll grab four screaming babies by their legs, dangling them upside down, two in each arm, like a brace of pheasants. He walked over to one of the swimming pools of fire and proceeded to toss the infants high into the flames. I stood still, paralysed to the spot; my numbed brain in knots, desperately trying to make sense of what I'd just witnessed.

Escorted by *Kapo* Krupp, I staggered in a daze towards the barracks area. I asked him what happened to his bandaged arm. He told me that Moll had shot him from a distance of twenty metres for smoking on duty.

We passed a group of forty or so Sonder-men pulverising bones with wooden pounders. Others were sieving the ashen grey powder for any gold, and to identify residual bone fragments that required further crushing with mortar and pestle. Moll had fashioned an enormous concrete platform, some thirty metres long and ten metres wide, for this bone-grinding *Kommando* to work upon. The tons of ash were finally loaded onto trucks and dumped into the confluence of the Sola River and the Vistula.

Krupp took me to a separate block next door to the undressing barracks. Inside was a vast array of valuables and jumbled clothes. He showed me the collection of medicines, no doubt dispensed from hundreds of apothecaries across Hungary. He went on to tell me that a record number of bodies were cremated yesterday across the four crematoria and incineration ditches around Station V and *Krema* IV. The total amounted to 24,000 Hungarian Jews!

I asked him about the high groundwater in this area and how the cremation trenches were kept dry. He said that Moll had worked closely with the Central Construction Office in designing a grid work of drainage canals and the mother of all ditches called the *Königsgraben*. The groundwater, he went on to explain, was now three metres deep around Station V and a good two metres beneath the surface in the vicinity of *Krema* IV. Furthermore, the warm summer weather and relative sparsity of rainfall would further reduce the water table and buffer any periods of summer rain. On the subject of fuel, he said that the corpses essentially fuelled these fires themselves due to the enormous latent heat of the charcoal embers and ashes.

My God! What am I writing? I'm sounding like a Nazi – a machine, a perpetrator. Am I a man or robot? Today I feel more binary than biped: an automaton and lifeless shell that obeys orders and keeps silent. I am a faceless android; a mechanical functionary, an instrument, an ineffectual blob of humanoid nothingness in this factory of futility. There is no happy ending, no *deus ex machina* to make everything right. I am an engine of the underworld.

Arriving back home, I dumped the wheelbarrow of drugs in the morgue. I will sort them out in the morning. I then headed straight for my room and vomited. I took some Luminal and a generous shot of morphine before finally going to bed.

BUSINESS AS USUAL

Diary of Dr. József Sárkány, Auschwitz, Poland, 1944

<u>Thursday 8th June</u>

My new assistant, Michał Kowalsky, is an odd chap – and certainly well-nourished compared to most. He is short and has a kyphosis which gives him a slight hunchback. He has a remarkable intellect and extensive knowledge of morbid anatomy. He tells me that he studied philosophy before entering medical school at the University of Warsaw, which he had to leave after contracting tuberculosis. After almost two years of therapy and convalescence, he decided against completing his medical studies and eventually found work as an anatomy demonstrator and pathological technician. I must say that his evisceration technique is second to none, and he is fully adept at special procedures that include removing the brain and spinal cord.

I have not been given a prisoner's uniform but rather an excellent civilian suit. It follows that the important position reserved for me is one that requires a neat and tidy appearance. I carry with me on my rounds my new elegant doctor's bag. A Sonder-man recently brought it to me from the undressing room, where it was discovered amongst a pile of clothing belonging to some unfortunate Hungarian doctor, now gone to the gas. Inside are a blood pressure gauge, a stethoscope, fine quality syringes, instruments and injections necessary for first aid.

There is a separate *Kommando* whose task it is to open the hand luggage of the transports and to collect any medicines found therein. I note that a large majority of the drugs are various forms of sedative, especially a barbiturate called Luminal. This must surely typify the nervous condition of Hungary's persecuted Jewry.

A meadow path and the dead-end tracks of the new unloading ramp separate Crematoria I and II. The two buildings are essentially mirror images of each other. However, the room corresponding to the laboratory is a pathological museum and there is no dissection hall in *Krema* II. Instead, three goldsmiths work there in what can only be described as an Aladdin's Cave. For this is where all of the gold teeth, coins, jewellery, precious stones, wristwatches and cigarette cases are cleaned and classified. The gold is then smelted in graphite crucibles and converted into one kilogram bars.

The dentists who remove the gold teeth are supposed to put them into a sealed container of acid. However, it's not uncommon for the odd item of precious metal or jewellery to find its way into the pockets of the SS guards. By this route all sorts of fresh products flow into the crematoria, such as butter, cheese, eggs and milk.

Gold procurement occurs on a collective basis, so distribution of the smuggled goods happens collectively as well. By the same route, the *Völkischer Beobachter* arrives at the gate. The price of subscription to this official newspaper of the Third Reich is one piece of gold. I quietly read the paper in my room at the end of the day, and relate the news to Malkin the following morning. He passes it on to his comrades so that everyone is fully aware of recent events.

Friday 9th June

Whilst my own morphine habit continues to grow, I've come to realise that *Oberscharführer* Muhsfeldt is addicted to both alcohol and violence. My relationship with this former pastry chef from Brandenburg is complex and capricious, and largely borne out of trial and error. He is extremely vicious when drunk, which is practically all the time.

In a recent exchange, I dared to ask him by what right he exterminated my fellow Jews. He glared at me, clearly irritated, but fully aware of Mengele's invisible protection:

"I'll give you my answer, Jew! The *Führer* orders me to do it – it's as simple as that! And in a National Socialist sense, killing you lot isn't even murder: it is sacred extermination!"

Another time, he unloaded on me the circumstances of his abusive marriage to a poor woman called Herta Grunow. He went on to tell me about his handicapped son who he beat on a regular basis. There was no remorse in those intoxicated Aryan-blue eyes of his, but why should there have been?

Sabbath 10th June

A *Dayan* of Maków tends to the bonfires outside Crematoria I and II. These are where the hundreds of thousands of photographs are burned in the company of prayer books, Torah scrolls, diaries, diplomas, passports, marriage certificates – and all other combustible paraphernalia from the endless Jewish transports. These great mounds burn continuously.

In almost every single prayer book, the *Dayan* has found handwritten entries containing birthdays, holidays and anniversary dates. Pressed flowers plucked from all the Jewish cemeteries of Europe are devoutly preserved. Prayer shawls, kippahs and phylacteries also lay here in a sprawling heap awaiting incineration.

The *Dayan* is the aesthete of the *Sonderkommando*, eating nothing but bread, margarine and onions. His assignment was to have been an oven stoker, but with a lot of persuasion and bribes, Muhsfeldt eventually granted him exemption from this soul-shattering work.

Sunday 11th June

Two trucks pulled up in front of the crematorium this morning. They carried a group of weary and dejected male prisoners with yellow-tinged faces, all wasted away to skin and bones. They numbered around two hundred. Amongst them were victims of vitriolage, with hideous facial burns and disfiguring scars. Others had black streaks around their mouths, blackened tongues, red eyes and crumbling teeth. The Ober saw me looking and informed me that they were factory workers that made sulphuric acid. They were evidently suffering from severe sulphur poisoning and had been selected for Muhsfeldt's Special Treatment.

Shortly after noon, a black lacquer hearse arrived. The deceased was an SS officer from Gleiwitz. A gleaming silver Mercedes appeared shortly after, containing a commission of four men in splendid uniforms. The group included an SS doctor, two Gestapo officers, and a military court clerk. Mengele appeared a few minutes later.

I offered seats to my distinguished guests before they engaged in a brief discussion. The inspectors presented the circumstances of the body's discovery. The cadaver was laid out on my dissecting table where a bloodstained gunshot wound testified to suspected assassination. The dead officer's loaded pistol was still hanging in its holster.

That it might be acceptable for me to defile the body of an Aryan officer seemed incredible. I was therefore astonished when Mengele turned to me and ordered an immediate postmortem.

I carefully undressed the body with Kowalsky and began my analysis of the external findings. Most ballistic injuries involving a high-velocity projectile caused a small entrance wound and a larger exit wound due to the increased kinetic energy of the departing bullet. In the case at hand, I noted two lesions of equal size; one below the left nipple and the other at the upper edge of the left shoulder blade. So why was there uniformity of the entrance and exit wounds?

Mengele was enjoying the attention and lively debate, handing out his finest cigarettes. He suggested that the wound patterns could be due to two separate gunshots; one fired from in front and the other from behind.

I began to explore and probe the wound canal. The bullet's trajectory, having penetrated the left ventricle and vertebral column, proceeded at a 40 degree angle towards the left scapula where, breaking off a bone shard, finally exited the body at the back. This suggested a single gunshot fired from in front since the channel proceeded upwards and from front to back. The wounds were the same size because in its trajectory the bullet had lost kinetic energy as it abraded the spinal column and fractured the scapula. Thus spent, it did not tear a larger wound when exiting the body.

It was therefore apparent that the shot had been fired from a high-velocity 8mm pistol pointing upward at close range, but far enough away not to leave any powder burns.

The delegation was satisfied with this conclusion and departed just after four. Mengele didn't thank me, but looked at me with an air of approval, even pride perhaps, in his excellent choice of pathologist.

Upon leaving, he said: "*hic locus est ubi mors gaudet succurrere vitae.*" The Latin translation reads: "This is the place where death rejoices to teach those that live."

Monday 12th June

This afternoon I performed comparative autopsies on a pair of 13-year-old twins, Jenö and Zoltán Kovács. I incised the pericardial sac of the first twin and noticed a blood-tinged effusion. I transected the great vessels and lifted out the heart. It weighed 205 grams unopened. A curious lesion was present over the left ventricle, situated midway between the left anterior descending and left marginal coronary arteries. A tiny round spot, caused by a pinprick, was discernible. The lesion was slightly oozing blood and appeared fresh. Yes, there could be no doubt: a needle had punctured the heart. But who administered an intracardiac injection? There was no reference to the procedure in the notes.

I exposed the left ventricular chamber. I was able to follow the penetrating needle tract as it spanned the entire thickness of the wall. The ventricle was in a contracted state, indicative of systolic cardiac arrest. A coagulated bolus of blood and fibrin filled the cavity and was impacted in the aortic vestibule, thus occluding exit through the aortic valve. This would have caused massive instantaneous left ventricular failure and death from cardiac arrest.

With a long pair of tweezers, I teased the blood clot apart and sniffed. A curious and pungent odour of phenol filled my nostrils and I almost passed out. So, the child had received a lethal and undoubtedly painful phenol injection directly into the heart.

Kowalsky helped me to complete the evisceration. There was a mild ascites and generalised abdominal distension. The gall bladder was mildly inflamed. There were no stones, and the bile drained freely into the duodenum. The distal ileum displayed punctate mucosal ulcerations over the Peyer's patches. There was sloughing and surrounding inflammation, but no fibrotic stricturing. The spleen was mildly enlarged, with congestive softening of the pulp. The colon contained offensive stools, reminiscent of pea soup.

My findings were pathognomonic of abdominal typhoid in its third to fourth week. This correlated with the documented fever chart, dicrotic pulse and abdominal pains. Similar clinical and postmortem findings were noted in the second twin, who had also died directly from an intracardiac injection of carbolic acid.

At the usual hour, Mengele arrived. Both cadavers were lying on the marble dissection table, with body cavities opened, eviscerated and swabbed out. The organs had been weighed, dissected and cleaned, and were neatly presented on two separate chrome trays. I concluded that the findings were consistent with enteric fever.

My diagnosis alarmed Mengele:

"Are you certain?"

I replied that I was confident both twins were suffering from typhoid fever.

"This is grave news indeed!" he said, and left shortly afterward.

I later heard from Muhsfeldt that Mengele had put this particular children's barracks under strict quarantine.

"They'll all be coming here tomorrow," he said, grinning to himself. "The quickest cure for typhoid is a lead tablet injected straight into the back of the neck!"

Tuesday 13th June

This morning I dissected the corpse of a Jewish woman who died of obstructive jaundice. Mengele was worried about malaria and ordered me to perform an autopsy. There was no splenomegaly, and the blood film was normal.

What I did find was a large gallstone impacted in the cystic duct, so-called Mirizzi's Syndrome. I knew that Mengele was a passionate collector of such objects. I washed and dried the calculus, and lovingly placed it in a glass-stoppered vial. I also attached a label containing a succinct description of this pathological curiosity.

During his visit this afternoon, I proudly presented the gallstone to Mengele. This pleased him immensely and he even gave me a small bar of Swiss chocolate.

"Do you know the ballad of Albrecht von Wallenstein?" he asked. His question appeared entirely random. I said that I'd heard of General Wallenstein but not the ballad.

He smiled to himself and said: "In the possession of the Wallenstein family, you'll find more gallstones than gemstones!"

Wednesday 14th June

This morning I examined a pair of 12-year-old Gypsy twins. One of the girls had been hideously disfigured by *cancrum oris*, which undoubtedly took her life. Intricate coloured illustrations had been added to the clinical notes by the Czech painter, Dina Gottliebová. These vividly captured the rapid and inevitable progression of the disease over several days. The mouth was gnawed by rodent-like *noma* abscesses, which had ulcerated and fissured into the cheeks and jawbone.

Mengele had ordered me to decapitate the child and send her head to the Bacteriology Section of the Institute of Hygiene in Rajsko. He wanted the head to be preserved and put on display at the SS Academy of Medicine in Graz.

The other twin appeared externally healthy, but I noted the tell-tale sign of intracardiac needle trauma. She had been killed solely in order to perform comparative autopsies.

Mengele arrived at noon to review my findings. He had difficulty reading my handwriting and I told him that I had always formerly used an Olympia Elite typewriter.

"Very well!" he said. "I sow to all winds, and Dr. Sárkány shall have his Olympia Elite typewriter by tomorrow."

Thursday 15th June

Mengele pulled up outside the crematorium just after 2 o'clock this afternoon. He was on his motorbike and had come directly from the ramp. His normally pristine dark green tunic was crumpled and his boots covered in sandy dust. He looked tired and grimy from his work.

"It's fucking hot outside!" he muttered. "Four hours on the ramp and I'm stinking like a Yid!"

He removed his cap, which was tilted rakishly to one side. His face was flushed and his fringe damp and sticky with perspiration. Walking over to the sink, he removed a bar of soap from his attaché briefcase and proceeded to wash his hands and face. The water invigorated him and he began to whistle a few bars from Wagner's *Rheingold*.

"This is bloody good soap!" he said. "None of that Polish shit! This is proper *Sonnenlicht Seife* from Germany. You wouldn't think I have degrees in philosophy and medicine. All I seem to do these days is flick my hands left or right, left or right. It's so incredibly dull when there are no twins or defectives to get my hands on!"

Unlike his personality, Mengele's dry sense of humour was as constant as Eichmann's train timetables. I attempted a little banter to get us through the long afternoon:

"I thought you liked playing God and having the power of life and death over us Jews."

"My doctor's oath instructs me to remove a gangrenous appendix. The Jews are the gangrenous appendix of mankind. That's why I cut them out. And especially if they're from Hungary!"

"Is it death to the left and life to the right? I can never remember."

"It depends on my mood, even the weather. I would hate to become predictable. Dr. Hermann Voss is currently collecting guillotined heads from the Stapo in Posen. He has wagers with his medical students as to which direction the heads will roll. He invariably gets it right. He tells me that his winning form is an algorithm of probabilities based on anthropometric and morphological cranial data, coupled with atmospheric pressure and what his wife ate for breakfast. Again, it's just a bit of fun. Variety is the spice of life, is it not?"

I nodded and laughed submissively.

I now wonder if Mengele is more unhinged than not. He's certainly egocentric, neurotic, obsessive compulsive – probably manic depressive. But his behaviour, even for a Nazi doctor, is bizarre and unpredictable. Rumour has it that he suffered a prolonged concussion when he fell off his motorbike and fractured his hip. Some of the Sonder-men swear blind that he changed after contracting spotted fever. This, so camp legend tells, was brought on by a laundry worker sprinkling typhus-infected scabs into his uniform.

Friday 16th June

In the countless infirmary blocks throughout Birkenau, grisly experiments are performed by a malevolent group of SS doctors. Dr. Thilo is Mengele's deputy, and can usually be found in the operating theatre of Camp F where he performs surgical procedures without anaesthetic. He observes all the rigours of aseptic technique and the patient subsequently receives meticulous postoperative monitoring. But sooner or later, perhaps a week, a day, sometimes as little as a few hours, Thilo makes special arrangements for the patient's discharge. This release invariably emanates from a syringe full of poison or from the muzzle of Muhsfeldt's abattoir gun.

I dissected a young woman this morning marked up with the usual ZS on her chest. She'd come from Block 30 of the women's camp and had severe burns around her perineum. Infected horizontal incisions were also present over the lower abdomen, either side of the pubic symphysis.

The clinical notes indicated that she'd been under the joint care of Dr. Schumann, Dr. Dering and Dr. Wirths. The woman had been subjected to a battery of experimental procedures, including enormous doses of X-rays over both ovaries. These had then been surgically removed, and the specimens sent to Breslau for histological examination in order to assess how effective the ionising radiation had been. A subsequent gynaecological examination discovered a cancerous growth on the cervix which was vivisected – without anaesthetic.

A second female patient arrived this afternoon from Clauberg's Block. She was still alive! I accommodated her in the laboratory. She was in terrible agony and begged me in Hungarian to end her suffering. I gave her a good shot of hexobarbitone and she gradually settled.

Whilst I waited for further instruction from Mengele, I perused the clinical dossier and read that the woman had been subjected to a catalogue of tortuous procedures under Dr. Carl Clauberg. Her 21-week pregnancy was first aborted by Dr. Porkorny upon arrival. This didn't surprise me. Indeed, both abortion and infanticide were the norm here.

What did astonish me however was what happened after the termination. The eminent Dr. Clauberg followed this up with an intrauterine injection of formaldehyde '… in order to sterilise and fix the reproductive apparatus *in vivo*'.

Has the world gone mad? What has happened to human

ethics? Can German medicine, once unrivalled in the civilised world, steep any lower into the mire?

Mengele arrived and peered through the laboratory door. He looked flustered and gestured me over:

"What the hell's going on? You should have dissected that piece by now!"

I explained that the 'piece' arrived at the crematorium in terrible pain and that I'd given her some Evipan. He shook his head and ran a gloved hand through his untidy hair:

"Find Muhsfeldt! As soon as he's done, get to work! I'll be back around six. There's a transport arriving at two, so I'll be busy on the ramp until then."

"What questions do you need me to answer with the postmortem examination?" I inquired.

"Fuck knows! She's Carl's case. He should have finished her off before she arrived here. Find out if he wants to join you in the dissection room, and make sure you don't damage the pelvic structures when you eviscerate!"

Muhsfeldt did his duty shortly after Mengele's departure. I performed the autopsy without Dr. Clauberg's presence as he was giving a lecture at a medical conference in Posen. He had left instructions for me to perform an *en-bloc* pelvic exenteration and to preserve the organs in a bucket of formaldehyde for his inspection tomorrow. To what ends I really wasn't sure, but I obeyed the order without question.

Kowalsky soon got to work and did an exceptionally neat job. The remainder of the autopsy was unremarkable. I had to fabricate a natural cause of death. I decided upon 'sepsis' secondary to 'pyometra'.

Sabbath 17th June

What has become of the medical profession? We are doctors, not destroyers. Dr. Herta Oberhauser kills children with benzene, petroleum and Evipan injections. Dr. Helmuth Vetter conducts sponsored trials in which he studies the effects of Ruthenol and Substance 3582.

This evening I received a message to join Mengele in his office. The SS guard recorded my tattoo number and I eventually left the complex through a heavy iron gate in the direction of Sector B-IIf. I passed along the barbwire fence of the women's camp and beheld a handful of skeletal figures aimlessly coming and going. They were all alike and repulsive with their shaved heads, skin sores and tattered clothing. I thought despairingly of my wife and daughters…

I arrived before the gate of Camp F. A sentry guard with a large port-wine stain on his face sat by an open window in the guardroom. I ambled up to the little window, rolled up my left sleeve and announced the number on my tattoo. The guard immediately saw that I was wearing a wristwatch. I had permission from Mengele to wear it for my work. He sprang angrily out of the guardroom:

"You piece of shit! How did you get that wristwatch?"

I stood undaunted and looked him right in the eye:

"I'm here on the orders of Dr. Mengele. He wants to speak to me, but if it's not possible then I'll return to the crematorium and telephone him. What is your name?"

The mention of Mengele caused the guard to flush and he became instantly pacified. He politely asked how long I wished to stay. I looked at my watch and savoured the moment's silence:

"I'll stay until seven, or until I'm finished."

I entered the barracks and waited in the anteroom. I was soon escorted into a large and ornately furnished study. A desk sat in the centre, covered in charts, tables, graphs and maps. Above a bookcase teeming with medical records and journals hung a photographic portrait of Heinrich Himmler. This mugshot of the bespectacled *Reichsführer* was captured on a large rotogravure print, set in an ornately decorated frame. Was this a gift to Mengele from the SS Chief himself?

Three men were sitting around the desk: Dr. Mengele, Dr. Thilo and Dr. Wolff. The latter had a specialist interest in everything gastrointestinal, with a particular penchant for dysentery. But rather than preventing the disease with basic hygiene and sanitation, he exacerbated the condition by omitting vital salts and minerals from the diet. The most basic intervention of adding sodium chloride – common table salt – to the daily food rations would save countless lives. Even a 2% solution of hydrochloric acid added to the drinking water would undoubtedly improve gastric digestion and help to prevent chronic diarrhoea.

Dr. Wolff was quick to inform me that he had a special interest in anatomical pathology. He went on to explain how chronic diarrhoea was endemic in Birkenau and that the affliction had a ninety percent fatality rate. He boasted how he was thoroughly versed in the pathogenesis and course of the disease, and how he had performed thousands of clinical examinations and investigations. He claimed to have made meticulous clinical notes that included blood tests, stool analyses and X-ray imaging. He also had a comprehensive set of medical illustrations specially drawn up by the artist, David Olère of Drancy.

"This ground-breaking research is not yet perfected," he said, pausing for effect. "For it lacks the scientific gravitas of postmortem analysis in a large cohort of patients."

So, this was the cause of my summons. Amid this toxic atmosphere of gas, gore and genocide, the infamous Dr. Wolff also wanted to profit from the disease and death. He too wanted his slice of Birkenau *Blutwurst*, requiring me to open up dozens of desiccated corpses in the hope that I could shed some scientific light on the cause of their intractable dysentery.

And yet these causes were well known.

The formula for producing chronic diarrhoea is as follows: take a group of normal persons; evict them from their home; plunder all their possessions; starve them down in an overcrowded ghetto; pack a hundred of them into a cattle-car for a two-day journey with a single latrine bucket and some stagnant water; cram them with thousands of others into unheated horse barracks, and feed them starvation rations devoid of milk, fat, flour, salt and sugar.

And as if by magic, the flux is flowing freely after four-to-five days. Very soon, the victims lose fluid and vital salts as their flesh and spirit melt away. Finally, Dr. Wolff's patients are cured of all maladies. The dripping bowels dry up as the withered carcasses shrivel and contort before an agonising death.

My heart sank when Wolff expressed the view that, for the pathological aspect of his groundbreaking scientific work, autopsy material from at least 150 cadavers would be required. An enthusiastic Mengele joined in at this point, reckoning that I could get through seven autopsies per day, and therefore complete the task in just three weeks.

I didn't share his view on this, and aired my concerns that if Dr. Wolff required accurate work, which I did not doubt, then under no circumstances would I undertake the dissection of more than three corpses per day. On this we eventually all agreed. I was then dismissed.

Monday 26th June

One after another, Dr. Wolff's diarrhoea patients have gone under my scalpel. Sarcopaenia and cachexia are profound. Some of these *Muselmänner* weigh as little as 30 kilos. They lack iron, vitamins, sugars, fats and proteins. The skin is thin, dry and withered; almost translucent in areas, like parchment. Their gaunt faces look vacant and simian.

They are all products of Birkenau's 'Hypo-Syndrome' – hypokinesia, hypotonia, hypovolaemia, hyponatraemia, hypokalaemia, hypoglycaemia, hypolipidaemia, and hypoalbuminaemia.

Clinically the victim is devoid of all vivacity and personality. They exhibit inertia, amnesia and somnolence. There is total passivity and apathetic obedience, accompanied by mute indifference to food, water, personal hygiene and pain. They are the useless mouths, the ballast, the rotten and the living dead.

I have reached the twenty-fourth autopsy already. In

every case, the mucous membrane of the stomach displays an inflammatory process; the consequence of which is complete atrophy of the glands which secrete digestive enzymes and hydrochloric acid. I also note the inflamed condition of the mucous membranes of the small bowel, with villous atrophy and thinning of the intestinal wall. The pancreas exhibits variable degrees of inflammation, atrophy and decreased secretions. The liver appears contracted and pale. The gall bladder is devoid of green bile and is instead filled with colourless mucus that scarcely tints the stools. Finally, the large intestine is papery thin, with inflammation and atrophy of the mucosa.

My Polish assistant seems most put out by what he calls this 'Dysentery Brigade'. I'm clearly not in his good books, and I regularly hear him moaning to himself during these difficult daily eviscerations. He tells me that a rate of three bodies per day will take him seven continuous weeks.

Kowalsky often tears the bowels when eviscerating. This is not a product of poor autopsy technique, but simply because they are so fragile and friable; often no thicker than cigarette paper. Such inevitable rips and faecal soiling are always accompanied by a cascade of Polish expletives that echo throughout my ground floor rooms.

And so, the alimentary canal in these cases is no longer a healthy gastrointestinal system with adequate digestive juices and muscular tone. Instead, the atrophic guts are no more than flaccid sewer pipes, connecting mouth to anus and discharging their liquid contents indiscriminately, day and night. These observations constitute, in broad terms, my pathological findings: a very monotonous, unpleasant and uninteresting job.

THE FAMILY CAMPS

Diary of Dr. József Sárkány, Auschwitz, Poland, 1944

<u>**Sabbath 29th July**</u>

The façade of Birkenau's Czech family camp was liquidated today on the Jewish Sabbath. Many of the starving inmates had already been decimated by dysentery and petechial typhus. The barracks lockdown was declared this morning and several SS detachments surrounded the perimeter fence. The prisoners were subsequently ordered outside before being loaded onto Red Cross trucks. The howling of those awaiting transport to the crematoria was dreadful to hear.

The victims had all originated from the Theresienstadt model ghetto in Terezín, and were the second generation of Jewish families to be sent to Birkenau. I had read in the newspaper how Dr. Maurice Rossel of the International Red Cross visited the ghetto only last month. He appeared to have been completely taken in by the orchestrated propaganda machine; no doubt following an intricately choreographed and beautified inspection path through the complex. The IRC had subsequently cancelled its scheduled visit to Birkenau, and was even looking to endorse some kind of Nazi propaganda film about the ghetto.

The first generation of camp inmates went to the gas last March. They were initially housed in relatively good conditions, and families were not separated. A man called Freddy Hirsch was appointed the first Camp Elder, but was soon replaced by the German arch-criminal Arno Böhm. Hirsch was later suspected of planning an uprising just before liquidation. Malkin thinks that this caused unrest in the Camp Resistance, who quickly had him poisoned.

Sunday 30th July

This morning I performed parallel comparative autopsies on two fifteen-year-old twin girls from the Gypsy camp. They were not much younger than my own daughters.

Today's cases had been killed with the usual intracardiac injection of phenol. An early curious observation was that the eyes were of different colours; a condition referred to as ocular heterochromia. Both left eyes were blue and the right eyes were a distinct chestnut brown.

When Kowalsky rolled the bodies over, I also noticed thick tufts of dark hair protruding from dimples in both lower backs.

I proceeded to examine the anterior mediastina. Both twins had a condition called *thymus persistens*. The thymus gland is normally identified in much younger children and babies, and sits under the sternum over the heart. There is a gradual atrophy of the tissue with increasing age until only a small amount of epicardial fat remains.

Deeper dissection revealed discrete, rounded swellings about the size of a walnut. Each was smooth, soft and fluctuant. I delicately compressed one such lesion with my forceps and a thick pustular secretion oozed out. This confirmed my diagnosis of a Dubois abscess, itself a morbid manifestation of congenital syphilis. The entity was first described by Dubois in 1850. Tuve later developed the concept that the abscess was a result of ischaemic necrosis secondary to a syphilitic vascular infiltrate.

More important were my lung findings. Both twins had pathological hallmarks of pulmonary tuberculosis. This was more advanced in twin 2, with fibrocaseous disease and a chylous pleural effusion. This girl also showed left sided rheumatic heart disease, with a scarred mitral valve.

Returning to the hairs on the lower backs, I asked Kowalsky to dissect the lumbosacral regions of both spinal columns. The fourth and fifth lumbar vertebrae, as well as the sacral portions, displayed a condition known as *spina bifida occulta*, or closed spina bifida.

Another curious finding in both girls was the presence of a floating tenth rib, so-called *costa decima fluctuans*. In normal cases this rib is fixed. Its fluctuation was therefore another developmental anomaly in the caudal direction of the spinal column.

I spent the afternoon with Mengele debating the morning's findings. This turned out to be a lively discussion, with careful analysis and clarification of the morbid anatomy. The phenomena of heterochromia and closed spina bifida interested him greatly; the Dubois abscesses intrigued him still more. I referred to the bench-books provided, and generally got my way in matters of clinicopathological correlation.

"This is excellent work," he said. "Your findings unequivocally support the concept of neurological degeneracy in Gypsies, made manifest in hereditary syphilis, spina bifida and heterochromia. The cause of death is your own business, but pulmonary tuberculosis would seem like the obvious candidate."

I am delighted with my work today, and fully agree with Mengele's conclusions on the degenerate nature of the Gypsy. In the dissection room and in the laboratory, I elaborate and defend my own point of view in fluent German. For a brief moment, I am no longer an inferior Jewish prisoner, but rather, a highly qualified and experienced doctor who is able to argue and refute the opinions of my SS interlocutor.

Dr. Mengele even offered me one of his cigarettes this afternoon, and for the first time, saluted as he left the laboratory.

I was instructed to preserve the lungs, thymus, eyes, brains and spinal cords. The organs were to be packaged and shipped to Berlin-Dahlem. The Kaiser Wilhelm Institute of Anthropology, Human Heredity and Eugenics houses many experts in their respective medical fields, including Julius Hallervorden, head of neuropathology.

I later observed Kowalsky removing the eyes. For each, he made an incision in the sclera and used this flap to grip the eye with toothed forceps and pull it forwards. Then with curved blunt-ended scissors, he skillfully cut through the optic nerve and divided the ocular muscles, thus enabling the eyeball to be lifted out of its bony socket.

Mengele had ordered me to send the eyes directly to Dr. Karin Magnussen in the Department of Experimental Pathology of Heritage at the KWI-A. With funding from The German Research Foundation, she is currently working under Professors Nachtsheim and von Verschuer, and is focusing her research on the inheritance of eye colour in rabbits and humans.

The boxed parcel was finally stamped with the words, 'Urgent, important war material.' I have sent many such packages during the course of my activity in the crematorium, and I receive replies about them with exhaustive scientific commentaries. Kowalsky has helped me set up a separate dossier to file all such correspondence.

~

This evening I received an odd telephone call from Mengele. He informed me that today marked the Jewish holy day of *Tisha B'Av*. I'd completely forgotten. It was supposed to be a day of solemnity, mourning and fasting. Being evidently familiar with the Jewish religious calendar, Mengele ordered Sonia Vinogradova, the leader of the women's orchestra, to prepare a special concert for tonight.

I was perversely invited to join Mengele's party, which included Kramer, Moll, Mandl and Grese. With such illustrious company, how could I possibly refuse? In this cynical mockery of Jewish custom, Mengele made sure that I personally violated the main prohibitions commonly observed on this day. He therefore delighted in making me shower and shave before the evening performance, and personally brought food and wine into my room. He also lent me a pair of leather boots, and talked lecherously over dinner about his sordid affair with Irma Grese.

Monday 31ˢᵗ July

This morning I accompanied Mengele to the God-forsaken Gypsy camp. The SS have rightly tossed into this sector everything that is dirty, dishevelled and strange. It is a bubbling cultural hotbed of multilingual exotica and raw diversity, now concentrated and caged. These nomadic Romani tribes are called the *Cigány* in my tongue; to the Germans called *Zigeuner*, but to the Nazis they are the *Untermenschen*. In their doctrine of social Darwinism, the racial hygienists cry pariah – and for once I agree with them.

Whether rightly or wrongly, the *Cigány* thus await their imminent *Porajmos*: a corporeal violation and a cultural rape. Through the long and miserable months of their own Babylonian captivity, they now rot with the rest of us.

I beheld mothers in brightly coloured clothes and headscarves. Others sat jumbled together and sang snatches of old folk songs in a collective air of fragile nostalgia. The half-naked menfolk stood idly in the shade, whilst dozens of dirty children ran around and played naked in the mud. They rampantly scratched their scalps through matted clumps of lice-infested hair. Others raked scabs on their faces, which oozed and suppurated and putrefied. And before too long they'll be hospitalised as the gangrene takes hold. And there, with half-eaten faces, they'll writhe and wail in a febrile agony before the kind Angel of Death sees fit to release them.

For these will be Mengele's Children. He will adopt them, not out of care or compassion, but as scientific specimens to inject and dissect. These sub-human samples of *noma faciei* will undoubtedly be subject to an array of novel treatments. For within this sector is the experimental block of Birkenau. Here, the medical apostate reigns supreme. With healer's hands, he works with loving and indefatigable passion to advance his theories of racial degeneracy. He conducts his research with the assistance of two inmate physicians, Professor Epstein of Prague and Doctor Bendel from the Faculty of Medicine in Paris. They work in concert with a talented Czech painter named Dina Gottliebová, who prepares detailed and annotated medical illustrations. She enjoys a range of privileges in the camp, and due to her close relationship with Mengele, is one of the camp *Prominentia*.

A prodigy of von Verschuer at the Kaiser Wilhelm Institute, Mengele is indefatigable in the exercise of his medical duties, fully immersed in his pioneering work. He spends endless hours poring over books and writing in his private journal, which must run in to hundreds of pages. His current hypothesis on the cause of *noma* – which he always refers to as *Wasserkrebs* – is the innately corrupt fabric of Gypsy children. This he postulates is due to a mixture of defective hereditary traits coupled with the pathological effects of congenital syphilis, which he claims to be endemic within the population. Whilst this seems entirely plausible, he does somewhat neglect the counterarguments of inadequate sanitation and malnutrition in the pathogenesis of the affliction. Coupled with other childhood diseases like diphtheria, measles, scarlet fever and tetanus, the microbial burden on such immature immune systems – degenerate or otherwise – may well be the root cause.

Gypsy twins are a particular passion for *Onkel Josef*, who even brings them sweets and toys before injecting them with experimental serums, neosalvarsan and other magic bullets. His favourite children's medicine is an intracardiac injection of phenol, now generally administered – and on my own recommendation – after a preliminary dose of barbiturate.

~

Upon entering the Gypsy hospital, Mengele immediately walked over to Dr. Rabinowitz and rapped him over the knuckles with his leather gloves.

"You lazy and second-rate prison doctors are all the same!" he shouted, in full earshot of the other staff. "You're only interested in extra food rations and looking after your mediocre selves. I have here with me this morning, Dr. József Sárkány – a proper doctor."

Mengele threw down the hospital notes of a pair of female twins from the infirmary. I had autopsied them yesterday after they'd both been killed with injections.

"Look at your notes on twin number 2 if you don't believe me!" exclaimed Mengele. "You clearly state that the child is suffering from chronic asthma, complicated by rheumatic heart disease. For your information, she also has fibrocaseous tuberculosis, with a left-sided Ghon complex and pleural effusion! You are correct about the heart: there is mitral valve stenosis due to scarred leaflets and chordae, no doubt secondary to rheumatic fever at the age of three. However, your inability to recognise and diagnose pulmonary tuberculosis is frankly unforgiveable!"

"Please, *Herr Doktor*," said Dr. Rabinowitz. "I can only apologise for my misdiagnosis of this case. May I kindly ask how your diagnosis of tuberculosis has been made?"

Mengele shook his head and produced my autopsy report in an almost matter of fact gesture of reproach.

"You see!" he exclaimed, pointing to my paragraph on the respiratory system. "There it is, plain as day. You can't argue with a pathologist!"

Tuesday 1st August

I returned to the Gypsy Camp with a petulant Dr. Mengele who dismissively mentioned that the entire *Zigeunerlager* will be liquidated tomorrow. Taken aback by his flippancy, I inquired why.

"Why the fuck not?" was his curt reply.

I then asked how many people currently inhabited the sector. He growled and said that it was none of my business. Lighting a cigarette, he complained about the summer heat.

We entered the hospital barracks. The prison doctors stood rigidly to attention whilst Mengele washed his hands and donned a white coat. He approached Dr. Rabinowitz and stared at him.

"Where are they?" he asked.

"In the clinical room, *Herr Doktor.*"

As we walked towards the clinical room at the far end of the building, I could hear Mengele muttering and cursing under his breath. Still agitated by yesterday's misdiagnosis, he asked me rhetorically how any doctor worth their salt could miss such an advanced case of tuberculosis.

We finally entered a small side-room adjoining the operating theatre. Two German Gypsy children were sitting quietly on stools in one corner. They were non-identical twins; a boy and girl of about five years old.

Like some Jekyll and Hyde, Mengele miraculously transformed into a kind and avuncular personality, speaking softly and bending down to address the pensive children:

"Hello Guido. Hello Ina. Look what Uncle Mengele's brought for you on this lovely sunny day. After you've finished these two delicious lollipops, I'd like you to come with me into my special room where only good children can go. Inside this room, you'll have a nice relaxing sleep and dream about gingerbread and candy. I'll give you both a piece of chocolate and then you'll feel a slight scratch and fall fast asleep. After some lovely dreams, you will both wake up and I'll give you some of my own special cake.

"But first, let me tell you a little story about two children called Hansel and Gretel. Now Hansel and Gretel miss their Mummy and Daddy very much. One day, they decide to go looking for them in the woods, near to a big chimney they are always talking about. But when they get there, all they can see is smoke and an old Gypsy woman feeding ashes to the crows. They ask the woman where they can find Mummy and Daddy. She laughs at them and points up to the chimney top.

"'Come with me children, and I'll show you my lovely

house,' she says. 'There you can eat lots of cakes and sweets and gingerbread! For I do a lot of baking in my home and have lots of hot ovens that burn all day and night.'

"But when they get to the house, Hansel and Gretel find out that the old woman is really an evil witch. She has told them a pack of lies! The witch puts Hansel into a horrid metal cage and makes Gretel become her slave. She feeds Hansel lots of cake and chocolate to make him really fat. Why? Because she wants to eat him for her Sunday dinner!

"After a few days, the witch prepares her biggest and best oven for Hansel to roast in. She also decides that she's hungry enough to gobble up Gretel as well! Pretending that she is going to bake some hazelnut streusel cakes, she orders Gretel to check if the oven is nice and hot.

"But Gretel is a clever little Gypsy girl. She tricks the witch in to looking inside the oven. Then, as quick as a flash, she pushes the old hag straight into the fire – and slams the oven door. Bang! The screaming witch is burned to a crisp!

"Inside the house, the children find a box of golden teeth which makes them rich forever more. They finally leave and watch the last few puffs of smoke rise out of the chimney. And that is the end of my story."

Mengele looked at me and grinned. His face was pouring with sweat. He gestured for me to escort the children into the adjoining operating room. After a heavy dose of barbiturate, they both lost consciousness and the SS doctor got down to work.

Not fully comprehending what he was about to do, I asked permission to leave. He nodded but rebuked me for not being up to the challenge. I tentatively departed and returned to the main hospital wing, frantically groping in my pocket for a cigarette to calm my nerves.

After three hours, Mengele arrived back on the ward. He was drenched and thoroughly subdued.

"It didn't go well… you'd better finish it!" he muttered, and then left though the main door.

I quickly went in search of the children, only to find

them lying on the operating table in a terrible state. They had been crudely sewn together, back-to-back, like Siamese twins. There was blood all over the floor and I slipped and nearly fell. The twins were still drowsy, barely breathing, but clearly in agony. I rapidly drew up two syringes of barbiturate. The drug acted quickly – thank God – and soon their suffering was over. Hansel and Gretel were no more.

Wednesday 2nd August

By seven this evening, the hour of annihilation had arrived for the Gypsy families in Sector B-IIe. Over a hundred SS guards surrounded the perimeter fence following lockdown. With the usual lies and false promises, they evacuated the barracks and lined up the prisoners into files of men and women. Children were always assigned to their mothers. To embellish the deceit, bread and sausage rations were distributed. Everyone received three portions, food for a three-day journey.

And so, the once bustling and suppurating family camp of European *Cigány* was soon to become silent and empty.

I ventured outside just before bedtime in an opiate-induced torpor. There was a light east wind blowing in from the Volhynian steppes. Birkenau was quiet and still, except for the ceaseless hum of electrified wire.

SKELETONS

Diary of Dr. József Sárkány, Auschwitz, Poland, 1944

<u>Tuesday 15th August</u>

I spent a quiet morning catching up on some paperwork and filing. It had just turned noon when a middle-aged Jewish man and his teenage son were brought to the crematorium under SS escort. They were from this morning's transport of Jews from the Łódź ghetto. The man, in his fifties, had a pronounced kyphoscoliosis, rendering him a 'hunchback' and 'cripple' in the vernacular of the Swastika. His son was a tall, handsome-faced youth of around fourteen or fifteen. He had a congenital deformity of his right leg, which had been corrected with an externally fixed steel-plated frame and a reinforced orthopaedic boot.

I escorted them both into the laboratory and told them to make themselves comfortable. I had Kowalsky bring them tea and biscuits which they greatly appreciated. Mengele soon entered, carrying a pile of papers for me to fill in. He excitedly informed me that father and son were a textbook example of Jewish degeneracy, and must be treated with utmost care. He told me to examine both of them from head to toe, and to record precise measurements of height, weight and limb parameters.

I returned to the laboratory and began to take a clinical history. The father told me of his background, and I learned that he was a wealthy textile wholesaler from Litzmannstadt. He went on to explain how his son had undergone a difficult birth which left him with a permanent hip deformity. This handicap had been monitored and corrected over many years by a distinguished Viennese Professor of Paediatrics.

My inquiries clearly established that the boy's condition was in no way hereditary, but a consequence of obstetric trauma. Likewise, the man's spinal curvature was not congenital but a product of tuberculous osteomyelitis and childhood rickets. Both patients were otherwise fit and well, with normal hearts, lungs, abdomens and nervous systems. Even upon closest clinical scrutiny, I was unable to detect any evidence of organic disease, and certainly no features to suggest genetic 'degeneracy'.

The only pathology I elucidated was psychological. The man told me about his harrowing experiences in the ghetto and how he'd lost both his eldest son and baby daughter. He asked me where his wife had been taken and I falsely reassured him that she was safely registered in the women's camp.

The teenage son was less forthcoming with his conversation and typified the obstinate adolescent. When I pressed him about any future aspirations, he suddenly broke down and burst into uncontrollable sobs. His father hugged him and told him that it was perfectly normal to cry; especially after all that he'd been through. I should feel pity for him, but all I can think of is my own teenage daughters and how frightened they must feel.

Trembling with anxiety and in a monotone voice, the boy began to tell me about the painful events of his wasted childhood years in the ghetto. I could almost empathise with his isolation and despair. He related to me how he'd lost his older brother last year. He was just eighteen years old, with a potentially bright future ahead of him. But he was unable to endure the hardships and daily ordeals of ghetto life. After months of self-harm, he fell into a deep depression and was found dead one morning having slashed his wrists.

What a dreadful catalogue of misery and depravation. And still, I must listen and record and examine with clinical precision and detachment.

But I began to falter. I could feel myself trembling as a wave of panic and nausea overwhelmed me. I ran next door to the dissecting room and vomited in the sink. Kowalsky was in there and asked me if I was sick.

"Yes, I'm very sick!" I replied. "I am sick with grief, with disgust... with guilt."

I asked Kowalsky if he would deal with the couple next door. I explained my findings and told him to inform Muhsfeldt that they required his immediate attention.

"But first, give them some food – and lots of it," I added. I knew that this would be their final supper together, but I'd like them to experience the joy of a full belly before the end.

I hurried back to my room and collapsed on the bed. I covered my head with a pillow but it was no good. After half an hour, the sound of two gunshots filled my ears and exploded inside my brain.

Journal of Michał Kowalsky, Auschwitz, Poland, 1944

Tuesday 15th August

Sárkány ordered me to remove the thigh and calf muscles of two Gypsies who were autopsied yesterday.

"Why?" I asked.

"Because I told you to!" was his haughty reply.

Once I'd dissected off the thigh muscles, I tackled the gastrocnemius and soleus by incising up the leg surface from medial malleolus to patella. The exposed calf muscles were then cut away from the tibia and fibula.

Muhsfeldt appeared to take an interest in my work. He told me that the flesh was used to culture bacteria at the Rajsko Bacteriological Institute.

"They used to use horsemeat," he remarked. "But this was considered to be a waste of valuable resources."

~

The Doc was in a right state this afternoon. I caught him chucking up his guts in my pristine clean dissecting room. He'd been dealing with a couple of newbies from the morning's convoy. I fetched them some meat stew and macaroni, laced with a couple of crushed sedatives. They polished it off in seconds.

The soused Ober finally appeared after a lunchtime carouse and directed them both into the washroom. They were both already drowsy, and he told me to assist them in undressing. After two shots it was all over. The kid bled like a stuck pig, but death was thankfully instantaneous. The father refused to get up off the floor so our resident chief neck-shooter did him sitting down. As he walked over to the man, he slipped on the concrete floor and nearly put a fucking slug in me! Cursing, he eventually fired his second bullet and the man crumpled forward to join his son in some hideous form of bloody union.

The Doc was nowhere to be found. I knocked on his bedroom door and found him sobbing on the bed with a pillow over his face and a used syringe by his side. I asked if he wanted me to crack on with the prepping. He said yes.

I eviscerated the dad first, adopting the Rokitansky-Letulle method. For the kid, I decided upon Virchow's triple block approach. Both bodies were lean and warm. Long gone were the salad days of the fridge-cold obese brigade.

The Doc eventually came out of hiding and began work on the organs. He found nothing wrong! I asked if he'd like me to strip the dura and remove the pituitary glands.

"Yes, of course," he replied. "And I'll also need the testes."

I'd just finished with the bollocks when Mad Fucking Mengele made his big entrance onto this sickest of pantomime stages. He listened carefully to the postmortem examinations. He was seriously pissed off when the Doc admitted that there was nothing wrong with the organs.

"These degenerates must not be cremated!" he blasted. "They will be defleshed and the skeletons sent to the anthropological museum in Berlin."

As soon as Mengele had fucked off, I asked the Doc about what to do next. I suggested that cooking was the quickest and most reliable method. He reluctantly agreed and told me to deal with it as I saw fit.

"You can use the copper baths that are stored in the

210

small washroom," he said.

Then he too sodded off back to his room and left me to do all the hard graft as usual.

I ran it past the Ober and explained that I needed his permission to boil up a couple of corpses. He sniggered at first and then burst into raucous laughter. The unusual request clearly amused the vicious cunt on so many levels.

"You doctors are all fucking crazy!" he spluttered, taking a long fat swig from his hipflask. "You wait 'til I tell Moll."

Muhsfeldt reflected a little before belching in my face. He recommended that I have brick stoves built in the backyard in which to heat the containers from underneath.

So without much ado, I got to work on constructing the outside ovens with the assistance of four Sonder-men. The two copper tubs were carried outside and placed on each brick stack, under which were piled logs of firewood doused in petrol. The corpses were carried into the courtyard and lowered into the containers which were then filled with water from a hosepipe. The fires were finally lit, and we all waited for the bathwater to boil. My assistants now acted as stokers, helping to carry extra wood and tend to the flames.

It was just after seven and some five hours later when I was satisfied that the cooking was complete. I hate to admit it but the meaty aroma from both tubs was making my mouth water. I prodded a long fork into the simmering thigh of the man and was able to separate muscle from bone. My comrades extinguished the two fires, and we left the tubs to cool off while we got a bite to eat in the annex. The smell of cooked meat had given us all an appetite!

Urgent repairs to the crematory ovens were nearing completion, and we passed a half-dozen stonemason prisoners packing up their tools for the day.

After a delicious meat stew supper, I returned to my cooling cauldrons, this time accompanied by the Doc himself. Sárkány was eager to see how the process had worked, and seemed to have shrugged off his earlier feelings of remorse. My assistants had gone down shortly before us in order to remove the carcasses and pour out the broth.

As we entered the yard, a great commotion confronted us. A panicky Sonder-man ran up:

"Come quickly! The Poles are eating the bodies!"

We all rushed over. The stonemasons were hovering over the tubs. They were all stunned and immobilised with shock and disbelief. Half-starved and ravenous, I learned that they'd been waiting for their SS escort back to camp for over an hour. Thinking that they'd surely missed their evening meal, they began to wander around the courtyard in search of food scraps and edible vegetation. It was then that they stumbled across the simmering aromatic cauldrons, temporarily left unmanned whilst we were all inside.

Thinking they were large vats of bubbling soup for the *Sonderkommando*, these sorry men began to guzzle down the broth. When they came across chunks of pork, they couldn't believe their luck and greedily got to work on devouring the tender flesh and gristle.

The SS escort finally arrived to take the men away. They'd all eaten well this evening.

The stewed remains were hurried back to the dissection room. The Doc assisted me in stripping the bones, and we left them overnight in a strong bleaching solvent.

Wednesday 16th August

I got up early with the Doc to give the bones a final clean and polish. We laid out both skeletons on the floor and waited for Mengele's arrival. The Ober popped his head round the door and congratulated me on a sterling job. He'd already got word of yesterday's incident with the Polish stonemasons, and asked me to give him a blow-by-blow account of the whole affair.

"These Poles are really something else!" he laughed. "I wonder who got the parson's nose?"

Mengele entered late morning and seemed to be very satisfied with my work, although Sárkány took all the credit as usual. The SS doctor was accompanied by three other medical bad boys – Wirths, Clauberg and Thilo.

Mengele eagerly examined the deformed spinal column of the older man, fiddling self-importantly with individual vertebrae and making spurious anatomical statements. The Doc nodded obsequiously and suggested that the skeletons be thoroughly photographed before being sent away. The doctors all agreed, and Wirths also mentioned the possibility of a scientific paper that will no doubt turn into another piece of anti-Semitic propaganda.

Just as I was thinking about a well-deserved cigarette and early lunch, Mengele decided to subject us all to one of his longwinded monologues. Whilst his normal state was that of moody passive aggression, today he was full of beans and even smiling. He told the Doc to record his words for posterity, although the unenviable task was quickly delegated to me. I took it down in shorthand:

"Under the direction of August Hirt, the Jewish skeleton collection will be an anthropological masterclass in racial hygiene, showcasing the sub-human nature of the Hebrew nation. The assemblage is to be proudly housed within the Anatomical Institute at the Reich University of Strasbourg.

"Professor Hirt is a remarkable individual, who has performed some excellent research into mustard gas. His doctoral thesis examined the sympathetic ganglia of dinosaurs, but this professor is no fossil, believe you me! He is working closely with Rudolf Brandt and Wolfram Sievers from the Ahnenerbe division of medical research. They are responsible for procuring and preparing the specimens.

"We currently have around ninety suitable subjects, with the initial selections and preliminary work carried out by Dr. Beger and Dr. Fleischhacker. Furthermore, they have also procured a considerable number of skulls from Bolshevik Commissars who display the prototypical characteristics of the Jew, as specified on the Fischer-Saller scale."

After the tedious bullshit was finally over, I boxed up the two skeletons and included the autopsy protocols, together with the clinical data. The packages were stamped: 'Urgent, important war shipment' – and off they went!

CATHARSIS

Diary of Dr. József Sárkány, Auschwitz, Poland, 1944

Monday 28th August

I heard from Malkin that Chaim Rumkowski arrived at *Krema* II this afternoon. Camp intelligence had long known about his corruption and collusion with the Nazis as head of the *Judenrat* in the Łódź Ghetto. Such compliance resulted in the deportation of 20,000 Polish children to the extermination camp at Chełmno. Rumkowski and his family were on the last transport to Birkenau.

The *Sonderkommando* bludgeoned him to death in the changing room.

Monday 4th September

I've slowly come to realise that Mengele's psychosis is a manifestation of the decay that permeates Nazi Germany. For a civilisation is best judged on how it treats its weakest and most vulnerable members of society – the infirm, the handicapped, the mentally ill, the outcasts and the poor.

This genocide is a product of a sick society. And sickest of all are the nation's bastions of compassion – the doctors. From the early days of carbon monoxide to the lethal application of hydrogen cyanide; from the euthanasia centres to the Reinhard camps: all are fuelled by medical monstrosities and their plethora of lies.

And finally, in hell's lowest ditch that history will forever remember as Auschwitz, there resides the devil incarnate: his name is Doctor Josef Mengele. This former physician who spent years assimilating the healing arts has cast aside his Hippocratic Oath. Once trained to care for the sick, Mengele – this pretender, this diabolical travesty of a doctor – now maims and mutilates and murders.

Mengele is now embroiled in a menacing flux as his Auschwitz-self strives to dominate over his increasingly quiescent doctor-self. Like two diametrically opposing forces, one side wants to kill, the other wants to cure. But instead of healing his patients, his *alter ego* enables him to derail and detach himself from the self-destructive forces of being a mass murderer. He has somehow managed to maintain a pseudo-sense of professional integrity and respectability in the deluded belief that he is still very much a doctor. It is precisely this juxtaposition of doctor and psychopath – this cure-kill paradox – that makes Mengele's dual personality so impenetrable, erratic and utterly lethal.

I hear stories of how he treats patients with the utmost care before sending them off to the gas chambers. A little girl is born in the transit camp. After delivering the baby using strict aseptic techniques, Mengele asks the mother for the child's name. When she replies 'Mia', he shakes his head and says that a German name just won't do. He personally swaddles the infant and gently suggests the name 'Kezia'. The woman agrees. Two days later, he sends mother and daughter to the gas. Such is the disordered nature of this Angel of Death who can readily transform from kindly carer into kindly murderer.

~

Mengele was in an unusually cheerful and talkative mood this morning. Whilst I caught up with some paperwork in the laboratory, he told me about his delightful dinner with Dr. Aribert Heim yesterday evening.

Seizing upon his good mood, I decided to broach the delicate subject of my wife, and asked for permission to finally locate her. Even as I made my request, I noticed a change in Mengele's temperament. His jovial expression became suddenly serious and his black eyes drilled into mine. Had I gone too far? I knew it was a dangerous request, but now was as good a time as any. He continued to glare at me in silence. Then he grinned, sat down at the table and lit a cigarette. He cupped his head in one hand and appeared to deliberate. After several long draws of tobacco smoke, he finally broke the silence:

"I will give you a universal camp pass. You may search for her, but…"

He put a finger to his lips and looked at me ominously.

"Understood," I murmured.

Mengele eventually departed. With the camp pass in my hands, I went happily to my room and read:

'Prisoner A-7938 is authorised to circulate within the grounds of *Birkenau KZ* without an SS escort. This authorisation is valid until revoked. Signed: *SS-Hauptsturmführer* Dr. J. Mengele'.

I was beside myself with excitement. Such a thing had surely never happened in the history of the camp; a prisoner receiving authorisation to seek out his spouse and go without escort into the women's camp.

I didn't even know where to begin. The women were in Sectors B-IIc, B-III and the *FKL*. The majority of the Hungarians, so I'd heard, were in Camp B-IIc however.

Tuesday 5th September

Today is the day that I hope to find Éva. It has been four months since we last saw each other, and I miss her dearly.

I first went to the SS office and announced my departure to Muhsfeldt. It was a warm September morning as I set off. Leaving the crematorium, I passed a pair of broken eyeglasses and crutches by the side path. C-Camp was much closer as the crow flies, but I had to negotiate my movements within the extensive guard chain, and bypass other precincts of the camp to arrive there.

With an uncomfortable sense of nervous anticipation and fear, I ventured out onto the path leading between two rows of electrified wire. Camp Police on noisy motorcycles patrolled the area. Turning right on to the main street, I continued for a short while before turning right again to enter Sector B-IIc – the Women's Camp. It was ten o'clock in the morning when I arrived at the north gate.

Two SS soldiers were sitting on a bench basking in the autumn sunshine. They looked me over. I was an unusual guest, but they did not speak. They didn't meddle in the duties of their senior colleague who sat in the window of the sentry hut. I approached him and announced my number. He looked me up and down disdainfully. I took Mengele's chit from my pocket and handed it to him. He read it carefully before ordering his companions to open the gate. He asked me how long I intended to remain in the camp. I replied that it may be a while, and we agreed that I return to the gate by 4pm. That was six whole hours, but a ten-pack of *Spezial Mischung Josma* was a good *Passierschein* in any part of the Birkenau complex. I handed them over to him and headed down the sector in a southerly direction.

The central thoroughfare continued lengthwise through the camp, cutting it into two all the way down to the latrine blocks at the south end. There were thirty-four shabby barracks, seventeen on each side of the road. Groups of women were carrying the empty breakfast cauldrons back to the kitchens. On both sides of the street, many were basking in the morning sunshine. Their emaciated bodies wrapped in dirty rags presented a pitiable sight as they sprawled out on the ground, picking lice from themselves or from their companions.

I tentatively made my way to the first hut. The prisoners were in a shocking state of neglect. They were stripped of all femininity, all dignity. A naked woman with wild eyes and black teeth approached me and began to dribble. She was covered in sores. Her back and legs were caked in faeces.

I was quickly rescued by Zofia, the Polish Block Elder, who swept me into her side room and pulled across the curtained partition. She told me that the creature outside was an 'Hourglass', destined shortly for the gas.

This charming Pole was talkative, and excited to receive

her unusual guest. She was pretty certain that my wife did not dwell in her barracks, but suggested that I double check with a quick search myself. First, however, she insisted upon telling me all about her life in the women's camp.

Zofia explained that most of the inmates were starving to death. The watery swill the Germans called soup merely enabled them to survive a little longer, but certainly not to thrive. Their bodies bloated up with dropsy and their swollen ankles became as heavy as lead. Malnourishment made them constantly drowsy, lethargic and forgetful. Their menstruation stopped and caused anxiety and irritability. Many of them fainted during roll call and always had the latrine buckets poured over them. Others suffered from terrible migraines and frequent nosebleeds.

I learned that the women's long day began at four o'clock in the morning. After roll call, those barracks selected for work formed various labour squads. Whilst they marched out of the camp, the orchestra played in a parting mockery. The working day was eleven hours, from six in the morning until five in the evening, with half an hour break for lunch. Many prisoners perished at work; their comrades having to carry their bodies back to camp at the end of the gruelling day. The sound of gunshots often broke the night silence, signifying that the spiritually broken had gone to the wire in despair.

Maria Mandl was in charge of the entire women's camp and all female guards. Zofia told me how she supervised daily roll calls and corporal punishments. The women's orchestra was Mandl's creation, and was used to accompany musters, selections and executions.

Mengele sometimes even appeared at roll calls. He was irritated when he found siblings or mothers and daughters standing next to each other. He always separated them. An attractive woman similarly vexed him, as such a thing ran contrary to his contrived notions of Jewish degeneracy. These women were invariably selected for the gas chambers.

Zofia told me how Mengele was pathologically obsessed

with skin lesions. He was particularly averse to scabies and the women tried desperately not to scratch, lest they abrade the skin and create an infected sore. Just before an inspection, they pinched their faces to bring back colour to their cheeks. Others tinted their faces with beetroot juice or blood from a pricked finger. Healthier inmates who were still menstruating often shared their blood with the weak and emaciated. Seasoned prisoners puffed themselves up with a feigned exuberance and cheerful volition.

Zofia went on to inform me about another infamous guard called Irma Grese. She was a vicious sadist and nymphomaniac, sleeping with SS and inmates alike, both male and female. She bribed prisoners to keep watch as she raped other inmates, and relished flaying the nipples off young women with her bespoke plaited whip. I learned that Grese was sexually aroused just watching the women suffering. She arbitrarily beat prisoners until their faces were raw, and kicked them with her hobnailed jackboots until they were swamped in blood and bruises. Her meticulous grooming, tailored uniforms and excessive use of designer perfumes were all part of a deliberate act of sadism directed toward the ragged and neglected women prisoners.

After a mentally exhausting half-hour, I was finally able to take my leave of Zofia and continued with my search. As I walked down the centre of the barracks, wild shouts and cries greeted me from the women who were too sick to work today. The clumps of rags lying in the bunks suddenly sprang to life and, leaping up, ran toward me. There might have been thirty who recognised me, urgently inquiring about their husbands and sons.

Many identified me because I had a normal, human appearance, but they themselves were very difficult to recognise. My situation in the crowd started to become uncomfortable. They kept coming, more and more of them clamouring around me, desperate for any news.

These poor wretched creatures had endured the most squalid conditions for the past few months. Many asked if the gas chambers were real and if the crematoria were really burning thousands of murdered Jews. I denied everything. Doctors are good liars – and I am no exception:

"Besides, the war will soon be at an end and we'll all be going home to our families once more."

I didn't believe a word of it of course: how could I? But it was somehow comforting to pretend that everything was going to be fine. The visible relief and calm on many faces filled me with content, but it was only a momentary happiness that was tainted by guilt.

My first visit to C-Camp ended at the tenth hut. It had taken me six hours of searching and I'd nothing to show for it. I left the sector just after four. I planned to return again tomorrow if I was able to. I had to find Éva at all costs.

Wednesday 6ᵗʰ September

I arrived once again in the women's camp this morning and recommenced my search for Éva. It was 5.30am. I'd decided to come much earlier from now on, before most had to leave for work. I entered the next hut and approached the Block Elder, a Slovak woman with a harelip and stubble.

Block 11 was a particularly overcrowded barracks, with at least a thousand inmates squeezed together in stacked bunk boxes arranged on either side. It was difficult to call out names here. The din of a thousand women overwhelmed the searchers' voices. They returned after a few minutes and reported on the fruitlessness of their efforts. I thanked them for their kindness and entered the next hut, number 12. Here it was the same situation; the previous scene repeated itself: no success in here either.

And so I arrived at Barracks 13. It was beginning to empty as the women joined their various work parties for the day. The Block Elder put a call out, sending two young women on their way along both sides of the hut. One of them quickly returned and told me that she'd found Éva Sárkány, prison number B-6789. I almost fainted.

After what seemed like an eternity of waiting, I glimpsed the frail form of a woman walking slowly towards me. As she drew closer, the face of my wife gradually materialised out of the gloom. I barely recognised the skeletal visage that presented itself before me, with hair shaved and eyes wide open with fear. She suddenly recognised me and stopped as if frozen with shock and disbelief. I rushed toward her and embraced and kissed her all at once. She couldn't find her voice, but instead burst into tears.

I gradually calmed her, whispering words of comfort and reassurance. Already a crowd of the curious was gathering around us. I couldn't speak with her like this. I asked the Block Elder to allow us into her little side room. She agreed. At last we were alone.

Éva began to sob hysterically. I again tried to placate her fear and sat her down. She began to speak, at first in a kind of mumbled gibberish, but lucidity gradually came back to her. She desperately wanted to unload her past few months upon my shoulders. I must patiently listen and be a passive instrument of this catharsis, this purification. For without it, my wife may never regain her sanity.

I broached the subject of our daughters. It was as if she'd forgotten them:

"Éva, my love – I can't locate the girls. Dr. Mengele has them, I'm sure. But he's keeping their whereabouts from me. He enjoys that sort of thing."

"No, you're wrong József," she replied. "The girls are here, in the hospital barracks."

"Dear God! You're sure? I must find them!"

"They're both here, I can assure you. Lily contracted dysentery a fortnight ago and Emilia shortly after her. I managed to hide them during selection and a kindly doctor called Ella Böhm has them in Infirmary Block 17. I'm able to visit them occasionally. They're sharing a bunk with two sisters. I don't think you should see them, József. They're both proud and deeply private girls. They wouldn't want their father to see them in such a state. Please promise me

222

that you won't try to seek them out."

"If you're sure, then I promise. You have my word. Are they very bad?"

"Well, they're not good. They are very frightened and withdrawn, often tearful. They're malnourished of course, and badly infected with scabies."

"Will they make it through another selection?"

"That's my worry… I'm really not sure. They're both young, but…"

"I shall see what I can do for them. Do you have their prisoner numbers?"

"Yes, they're directly after mine. Olivia is B-6790 and Emilia is B-6791."

"That's good. I shall speak with my contacts. I'm pretty sure I can get you all out of here, hopefully to another camp altogether."

"Thank you my darling… but what about you?"

"That's complicated. I'm one of the *Sonderkommando* in *Krema* I. I'm a secret bearer and therefore unable to leave the camp, lest I tell the world all that I've seen."

"Are they killing innocent Jews over there?"

"I'm sworn to secrecy, but let's just say that the fires are burning day and night."

Éva glazed over and became silent. She looked famished. She was also damp and caked in filth. Here, even my wife – so gentle, decent and kindhearted – had been stripped of her humanity.

An hour passed by, mostly in silent embrace. At last, it was time to part. She panicked and clung on tightly, imploring me to stay a little longer. I reassured her and promised to return again tomorrow. As I stood up to take my leave, she began to weep again and regress into her stupefied state, mumbling incoherent words and staring wildly, like some poor hunted animal.

Thursday 7th September

I arranged with Muhsfeldt to spend the next few mornings out of the crematorium. Any autopsy work for that day was to be fully prepped by Kowalsky in order for me to perform the organ dissections at noon before Mengele's arrival shortly after lunch.

"Very well, Dr. Sárkány – you shall have your little sabbatical," said Muhsfeldt. "Just be sure not to lose that precious pass of yours."

Kowalsky looked vexed by this arrangement, knowing full well that the real hard graft would have to be performed by him alone. He was still moaning about all those dysentery patients he'd had to eviscerate in the summer, and constantly reminded me how I'd got the much easier job.

I'm never quite sure how much of his petulance towards me is genuine or just banter, as he certainly has a dry and highly unusual sense of humour.

~

Again, it took me a while to recognise the wretched creature that was my wife. The past four months in Birkenau had changed her. Apart from her bestial physical appearance, she showed a hitherto unknown brutishness and crudity. Of course, there were tantalising moments of her former eloquence and sophistication, but those sparkles of light were always punctuated by outbursts of dark despair.

Who was this person, this thing that sat hunched over before me? I must bring her back from the abyss. I want Éva the loving wife and mother: not some concentration camp aberration; some mockery of womankind.

Before I left the women's camp, I made a brief visit to Block 17 where my daughters were being accommodated. I was greeted by a French nurse called Geneviève de Gaulle. She introduced me to the *Blockärztin*, Dr. Ella Böhm, who had just performed a late termination of pregnancy. Covert abortions, she explained, were generally carried out at night, and the products of conception thrown out with the surgical waste on the following morning. This was an urgent case however as the fetus had died *in utero* and was causing painful contractions with fever.

Dr. Böhm took me into a side room and we chatted over a cup of ersatz coffee. She told me how pregnant women were asked to report to Dr. Mengele on the ramp in order to procure extra rations of milk and eggs. Her voice fell into a subdued, chant-like cadence: "They're never seen again".

I informed her of my two children and inquired after their health. She reassured me that both were doing well and were over the worst of it. She went on to explain how Mengele ordered routine blood tests if he suspected any form of infectious disease that might lead to an epidemic. It was therefore common practice for the inmate doctors and nurses to bleed themselves in order to save the lives of their patients, and possibly the entire barracks.

Dr. Böhm was naturally aware that my daughters were twins. She had wanted to separate them, but they insisted on staying together.

"Fortunately, Mengele hasn't paid much attention to the girls," she said. "For when it comes to his prized twins, he insists on drawing the blood himself, often fanatically, several times a day."

I thanked Dr. Böhm for her time and the coffee. I explained that I didn't wish to see my daughters, but asked her to give them a parcel of provisions I had with me. She promised to hand them over once I'd left. I believed her.

Friday 8th September

Day 3 with Éva began with her usual sobbing. I held onto her hand as she laid her stubbly bald head on my shoulder.

"The toilets are awful!" she murmured, in between hiccups. "We use a bucket at night and latrines by day. Some shit in their food bowls. I piss in mine. But it's impossible to wash them out. Heh, but who cares? Kitty and Zena drink their own piss. Many do. Some even share it. Disgusting! Is it wrong?

I've not showered since the sauna. All my lovely hair… shaved off… everywhere! Then we're marched off to quarantine. It starts to rain. I feel drops bouncing off my bald head. I begin to feel frightened. I share a top bunk with eight others. The damp boards are our only mattress. We share one filthy blanket. We look and smell like rotten sardines in a tin. When someone wants to roll over, everyone else has to turn. It's torture! I just want to die…"

Sabbath 9th September

Éva seemed forlorn and withdrawn today. Her rambling eventually continued:

"We all live in shit! The whole place is crawling with filth. The windows are black with fleas and the blankets alive with bedbugs and lice. We're all awake by four. Some go to the wire at night. We see them lying by the electric fence at roll call. We are starving. The soup is rancid – weeds, mud and gravel. I once had a piece of turnip but some bitch filched it! Fuck her, she's dead now! The kitchen girls wash their foot sores in the soup cauldrons. Who cares?

"We don't work here, in this Block. We all just sit around and rot. Supper follows another fucking muster – stale black bread and margarine that smells like petrol. I bolt down my bread ration straight away. A lady once saved up a whole week's worth. Then some bitch stole it in the night. Poor cow lost all hope after that; she soon withered away. But her bread was delicious!

"When a group is selected for the gas, they might leave us their extra bit of bread. I actually look forward to this. Yes! Is this wrong? No, it's not right – is it? Can you imagine waiting for someone to die, just so you can stuff your face? Ha! I used to feel ashamed, but not anymore. I've changed from a butterfly into a vicious caterpillar – bald and bristly and brutal! But I am what I am – alive and speaking to my husband!"

Sunday 10th September

I got an opportunity to visit the *Kanada* this morning. Éva was in desperate need of my help and I was determined to make her well again. From the clothing department I packed together some warm clothes, underwear and stockings in a knapsack. From the toiletries department I took a toothbrush, toothpaste, soap, nail clippers and small mirror. I packed medicines, vitamins, ointments and bandages; in fact, anything that might be useful. I also pilfered sugar cubes, butter, apricot jam, salami and white bread. Thus equipped, I headed out again for the women's camp.

Éva seemed a little brighter today and was overwhelmed by my parcel of goods. She immediately attacked the food and tore into a piece of sausage like a rabid dog. After draining a flask of coffee, she soon got to work on the bread and jam. Gradually, a light came back into her eyes. The calories and fluid gave her a new vigour and lease of life.

I gently washed her face and cut her nails. I cleaned her sores and applied various salves and ointments. I helped her into some new clothes. Her face lit up when she saw a pair of clean underwear, woollen stockings and a pretty blouse. I put socks over her stockings and then produced a pair of soft leather shoes. They fitted perfectly. I covered her excoriated scalp with a soft blue headscarf, pristine clean. Finally, I foraged in my pocket and produced a miniature bottle of *Emeraude Coty* perfume. I left shortly afterwards as Éva was anxious to share her gifts with others, despite my objections. I was slowly getting my wife back.

Monday 11th September

Éva's catharsis continues. She told me how she's part of a group that goes foraging for kitchen scraps after roll call.

Anything goes, apparently, and they often resort to eating grass and weeds to appease the gnawing hunger pangs.

"Beetroot is the most prized treasure of all," she remarked. "Not to eat, you understand, but to smear on our lips and cheeks in order to look rosy for inspections."

I tentatively asked about Mengele and these inspections. "Maybe tomorrow," she said.

Tuesday 12th September

The extra rations and medicines have done wonders for my wife. She is composed and has a newfound eloquence.

Today I heard about Mengele. In what must be terrifying weekly selections, these poor women see an immaculately groomed doctor who is the antithesis of themselves:

"We look and smell like zoo animals in a cage, with our shaved heads and grimy rags. Mengele glides in, all dashing and handsome, like some German Prince Charming or Hollywood film star; impeccably dressed in his kid gloves and long leather boots. His charisma and good looks sometimes create disturbing psychological paradoxes. A girl once remarked that she wanted to kill him and fuck him at the same time. She didn't last long.

"The doctor greets us in his usual cordial manner: 'Good afternoon, ladies. How are you? Are you comfortable?' No one dares say a word. There's an uncomfortable silence. Mengele senses our fear and enjoys every second. Then a naïve bottom bunker plucks up the courage to ask when she'll get to see her children. 'In a few weeks, please don't worry my dear.' I almost believe him. I want to believe him. He looks so elegant, so benign, so civilised. Compared to us lepers, he feels more like God – ethereal and untouchable. He always talks to the new arrivals with such kindness and affection. The women are all touched by his courtesy and manners, for nobody has talked to them as civilised human beings for months, even years. He tells them not to be afraid and from now on things will be much better for everyone.

Lowering their guard, many now lose their inhibitions and unload their multiple ailments. He leads them away for private consultations. None return.

"The weekly selections require us to run naked with raised arms in front of Mengele, who is usually accompanied by Grese and another woman called Drechslerka. He often hums or whistles to himself. He once told me to dance naked before him while he hummed the Blue Danube Waltz! There are no golden rules to follow. Mengele has a double personality that's impossible to understand or predict. Thin or plump, both can spell selection and death."

Wednesday 13th September

Today was my final morning visiting Éva. Knowing that our meetings were about to come to an end, she was eager to tell me one more story. It involved a second selection that occurred outside the Central Sauna on her very first day in Auschwitz-Birkenau:

"Like some kind of demigod, Mengele stares at me. Eichmann is standing next to him, flaunting a horsewhip from under a black leather coat. Can you imagine how I feel as a woman, a respectable Jewish woman, standing naked, exposed, humiliated? Irma Grese just hovers there. I can still smell her perfume. She has a stick in one hand and a ferocious dog on the other. With the thin end of her cane, she flicks my hand away from my groin. I feel the implement caress my pubic area. It glides upwards inside me. I wince with pain. Grese looks excited, even sexually aroused. Her eyes are wide open and transfixed on the point of the cane.

"Eichmann feigns a cough and she finally snaps out of her twisted trance. Mengele snatches the cane and waves the offending end over his nostrils. *Juden fotze!*' he mutters. Grese laughs. 'Please, kind *Herr Doktor!*' I beg. 'I am young and healthy.' Grese strikes me on the face. She catches me over the left eye which instantly begins to water and swell. 'What do you think, *Herr Eichmann?*' Mengele asks. 'Shall we let the puffy-eyed Jewess live?' 'You'll be going up the chimney, my dear,' says Eichmann, shaking his head. Mengele looks irritated by this remark. Only he wields the power of selection, of life or death. 'Mm, maybe,' he says. Eichmann thrusts his whip handle under my swollen eyelid and barks in German: 'Keep those fucking pig eyes open!'"

"I am bewildered and confused. Nothing seems to make sense. There are no rules, no codes of conduct to guarantee survival. Without warning, Mengele thrusts his pistol into my mouth. He cracks my front teeth and rams the barrel to the back of my throat. I gag and choke. Blood fills my mouth. I begin to suffocate. He pulls the trigger. I wince and shudder as a loud click resounds in my ears. Everybody laughs as the empty barrel is retracted from my mouth. The fun and games are finally over. I'm still alive."

~

I bade my farewell to Éva just before noon. My daily visits had undoubtedly been expedient in bringing her back from the void of despair and suicide.

However, her flattering descriptions of Dr. Mengele bother me greatly, and fill me with a growing sense of jealousy and betrayal. Does she forget who she is? She is my wife, and that must command loyalty and fidelity at all times.

Whether Mengele is dashing and handsome is really beside the point: she is plainly viewing him through the lecherous eyes of an adulterous. I begin to wonder whether she actually enjoyed parading naked in front of him during those weekly camp selections. Was she flirting with him as she danced like Salome before her King? Did her gyrating breasts and buttocks tease and titillate?

And then there is today's final revelation outside the sauna. She saved this story for our last meeting. But why tell me at all? Is she toying with me? Is this some kind of emotional payback for my own infidelities?

I ruminate over the simulated intercourse with Grese's

cane and that final violent act of fellatio with his gun barrel. She must have seduced them with her lewd Jewess eyes... No, don't be ridiculous! Éva is the victim. Yes... she has always been the victim.

Transcript of secret recording (unknown source) in Crematorium I, Auschwitz, Poland, dated Saturday 16th September 1944

Grese:	Do you want me, Prisoner A-7938?
Sárkány:	Want you?
Grese:	For sex.
Sárkány:	I'm a Jew, a prisoner.
Grese:	I know you are. It's forbidden, taboo and deliciously dangerous. That's what makes it so fucking exciting, no?
Sárkány:	I don't know what to say.
Grese:	Don't you find me attractive? Am I too Aryan for you? Don't you like golden blondes with blue eyes? They say I'm beautiful. Am I beautiful?
Sárkány:	You are, *Oberaufseherin*.
Grese:	Do you like women in uniform? This dress has been custom made for me by Madame Grete. It accentuates my hips and breasts, don't you think? And if I just lift this up, you can see my gorgeous black stockings. Yes, you like my legs. Or is it my tall leather boots that turn you on? I can see you're enjoying the show. Yes, indeed. Smell my neck. Yes, that's it. Do you like the perfume? It's *Vol de Nuit* by *Guerlain*.
Sárkány:	It's exquisite, *Fräulein*.
Grese:	Would you like to touch me?
Sárkány:	I would, *Oberaufseherin*.
Grese:	Yes, I bet you fucking would. I'm ravishing. I'm going to be a film star after the war. I'd

	change my name of course. Irma Grese isn't sensual enough. I like the sound of Katherine von Drexel or Madam Kitty for short.
Sárkány:	I'm sure you will be fabulous, *Oberaufseherin*.
Grese:	You have nice manners for a Jew. But I've not come here to be flattered and charmed. I require your services as a doctor.
Sárkány:	How can I be of assistance?
Grese:	There's something I need you to get rid of.
Sárkány:	I see. How far gone are you?
Grese:	I'm not sure. I'm two months overdue.
Sárkány:	That's fine. You're still first trimester.
Grese:	Whatever. I'll need you to do it here. Is there anywhere more private?
Sárkány:	Well, there's my sleeping quarters. I don't have a lock on the door…
Grese:	That's fine. I'll have one of my girls guard the door. I trust you'll tell no one.
Sárkány:	No, of course not, *Oberaufseherin*.
Grese:	That's good. I can be quite cruel if I want to. By the way, will it hurt?
Sárkány:	A little. I can inject some local anaesthetic and give an injection to dull the pain.
Grese:	I'll think about it. There's nothing wrong with a little pain, especially when experiencing pleasure at the same time. There is something wholly erotic about inflicting pain. I feel my pulse racing. My hips begin to move, rhythmically back and forth. It makes me wet.
Sárkány:	Sorry, *Frau Oberaufseherin*. What does?
Grese:	Torture. Ah, the ecstasy of pain; the cries, the intoxicating blood! The panting, pulsating pleasures of ripe raw flesh being spanked and flayed! Man or woman: it makes no difference. Are you a sadist, A-7938? I suppose you must be, being a doctor. What's your dark fetish? What arouses you above everything else?

Sárkány:	You do, *Frau Oberaufseherin.*
Grese:	Yes, that's right. I am truly delectable… yet so out of reach. Anyway, Jew, I shall return at nine tomorrow evening. I'll bring my own instruments. I just need your hands on the end of them.
Sárkány:	Are you sure? I'm not a gynaecologist. There must be other…
Grese:	I want you. I shall bring along Dr. Perl to assist you, but I want *you* to do it.
Sárkány:	May I ask why?
Grese:	Because I say so, it's as simple as that. Besides, Dr. Mengele speaks quite well of you. And if you do a good job, you might get to fuck me when the bleeding stops.

Part IV

Disintegration

REVOLT

Diary of Dr. József Sárkány, Auschwitz, Poland, 1944

Erev Yom Kippur, Tuesday 26th September

Just before sunset, our resident *Dayan* put on a shawl and recited the evening prayers. We organised everything that was needed and then chanted the *Kol Nidre* as follows:

"Regarding our promise and holy vows, we utterly repudiate them. All of them are undone, abandoned, cancelled, null and void, not in force, and not in effect. Our vows are no longer vows, and our prohibitions are no longer prohibitions, and our oaths are no longer oaths."

Yom Kippur, Wednesday 27th September

The *Dayan* meditated in silence throughout the morning, completely and absolutely focused on the quest for atonement with his God. I was personally not fasting for *Yom Kippur*. It was a private protest against Him, against the Lord and Father and His silent quiescence.

I overheard two Sonder-men talking in the attic. They were brothers, Gideon and Seth. Seth was black with soot, having just finished his nightshift. He was eating a hearty breakfast. The conversation went something like this:

Gideon:	Don't you know what day it is?
Seth:	*Feh!* I know what day it is. He thinks I don't know what day it is.
Gideon:	What day is it, then?
Seth:	You tell me, brother!
Gideon:	It's *Yom Kippur*, you *schmuck!* You know? Today is the Sabbath of Sabbaths!
Seth:	I knew that. He doesn't believe me. Just look at him shaking his big bald *boychick* head! But what does it matter? We're in Birkenau if you

	haven't noticed. Anyway, it's the Germans that should be doing all the atoning.
Gideon:	You should be fasting!
Seth:	Don't be such a *kvetch*. Anyway, I'm *chalisching* from hunger. How would you feel if you'd had to *schlep* corpses all night? You've got a busy day ahead of you. Get some of this *nosh* down your neck.
Gideon:	Do me a favour and shut up! There's bound to be some sport today. And camp selections too. I expect Mengele and his posse can't wait!

Gideon was right. It was common practice for guards to come up with special forms of torture on Jewish holidays. Mengele and Eichmann thoroughly enjoyed the custom which they cynically referred to as Goebbels's Calendar. Mengele was especially fond of selections on Jewish high days and holidays.

True to form, at three o'clock, all the Jewish boys in the camp were called to muster on the football field, some five hundred in all. Mengele proceeded to inspect the ranks. He stood one boy against a goalpost and gave orders to knock a plank of wood just above his head. He then made each boy walk under the plank in single file. About half failed to reach the required height. These unfortunates were later incarcerated in Block 25, a halfway house to the gas.

And so, Mengele's demonstration made a mockery of Holy Scripture as it is written in the prayer of Ezekiel:

'I will lead you out into a desert world, and there plead my cause against you, as I did with your fathers long ago, in the desert confines of Egypt. I will force you under my sceptre, chain you to my covenant.'

In Birkenau, Mengele was God.

Transcript of secret recording (unknown source) in Crematorium I, Auschwitz, Poland, dated Friday 29ᵗʰ September 1944

Malkin:	Camp Intelligence has informed me of another cull – the Hungarian women.
Kowalsky:	It's good for them really. They're all starving.
Malkin:	I'd rather starve than drown in cyanide and shit! Give me some of that vodka will you.
Kowalsky:	The Resistance dropped off more firearms by the fence last night. That makes eight in total, together with the twenty pineapples. What about the powder?
Malkin:	The factory girls are on it. The payload is coming with the next corpse cart.
Kowalsky:	The powder's essential. We must take out these death factories!
Malkin:	And then what?
Kowalsky:	We get out. But we take the machinery first.
Malkin:	You want to escape?
Kowalsky:	If I get the opportunity, fuck yes – you bet.
Malkin:	Come on Kowalsky, let's keep this real. You're not gonna live through this. You won't even make it to the Vistula.
Kowalsky:	Others have. What about Vrba and Wetzler?
Malkin:	Yeah, but we don't know if they made it. Anyhow, they weren't Sonder-men. We're different. We're the untouchables. No, they'll hunt us down! They won't stop until every last one of us is silenced forever.
Kowalsky:	Muhsfeldt is snooping around more than usual. Do you think he knows something?
Malkin:	I doubt it. What about the Doc? You work with him every day.
Kowalsky:	Sárkány knows shit. He can't be trusted though. Muhsfeldt calls him Mengele's Bitch.
Malkin:	Muhsfeldt is bloody dangerous. He's sharp as

	a knife, even when he's pissed. Be careful! We must be vigilant... Are you scared of death?
Kowalsky:	Fuck yeah! But I'd rather die a free man than be slaughtered like some circus animal. But we MUST do the buildings first! Anyway, I'm not gonna croak, not now.
Malkin:	Let's suppose, just for a moment, that you do manage to get out alive. What's the point?
Kowalsky:	What do you mean – the point?
Malkin:	Isn't it bloody obvious? It's the end of the world for us Jews. There's nothing left to escape to. We've lost our families, our homes, our possessions, our jobs. And worst of all, we've lost our dignity. Even if you do find pockets of your family amongst the rubble, can you honestly look them in the face after what you've seen? Can you carry on as normal knowing what you've been a part of? And for what? For a bit more time, a bit more living.
Kowalsky:	I want revenge above everything else. I don't care how many Nazis I take out, but Mengele will be top of my hit list!

Transcript of secret recording (unknown source) in Crematorium I, Auschwitz, Poland, dated Saturday 30th September 1944

Muhsfeldt:	I'm hearing rumours of a possible uprising. Have you heard anything?
Sárkány:	An uprising? Are you certain?
Muhsfeldt:	Don't take me for a fool, doctor. They think we're going to kill them.
Sárkány:	Are you? I've heard about culls every four months or so.
Muhsfeldt:	This is a complete myth. It's true that we like to inject new blood into each crematorium every so often, but the men who are replaced

aren't killed. They are simply relocated somewhere else in the camp. And you must know by now that there are many experienced stokers who've been working here since the building first opened. We'd be stupid to cull so much knowledge and experience. No, you must reassure the men.

Sárkány: Why don't you tell them yourself?

Muhsfeldt: Its better coming from you. You're the doctor. They trust you.

Sárkány: The men tell me nothing. They think I'm in Mengele's pocket and do his spying.

Muhsfeldt: See! They're clever, these Jews – are they not? Why would we want to liquidate such fine minds? Yes, I suppose you're right. You may be their doctor, but they know exactly what you do; who you are.

Sárkány: And what exactly am I?

Muhsfeldt: You're a piece of Jewish shit, just like the rest! But Mengele seems to like you, for the time being at least. Don't think I haven't noticed how he talks to you. And all this preferential treatment you get: your own room, your own laboratory – Christ! You eat, sleep and shit better than me – and I'm the fucking Aryan! Anyway, if you do happen to hear anything…

Sárkány: As I say, I'm not in their inner circle.

Muhsfeldt: The cargo keeps coming, and Mengele's Bitch keeps cutting. He splices and dices, whilst his fellow Jews all go up in smoke. Have you mentioned my drinking to him?

Sárkány: No, *Herr Oberscharführer*, I would never...

Muhsfeldt: That's right; you would never – because you really don't want to upset me. Who knows? Working in this place is full of dangers, and no one would be blamed if you were to have a tragic accident one day. There are always other

doctors, other pathologists. Yes, you're just as
disposable as I am. The only difference is that
I have the gun and you the scalpel blade. How
is your neck these days? Not too stiff, I hope.

Sárkány: I understand, *Herr Oberscharführer*.

Muhsfeldt: I know you do, Jew. And just remember where
you are. You're in a place that pillages, gasses,
mutilates and burns hundreds of thousands of
your kind. Mengele knows this. I know this.
Your men upstairs know this.

***Transcript of secret recording (unknown source) in
Crematorium I, Auschwitz, Poland, dated Thursday 5th
October 1944***

Muhsfeldt: What did my blood tests show? Is my liver
holding up?

Sárkány: Your liver function is mildly deranged, but no
permanent damage.

Muhsfeldt: That's good to hear. Anything else?

Sárkány: Your Wassermann reaction is positive.

Muhsfeldt: Wazza? What the fuck is that?

Sárkány: Nothing of concern. I was thinking out loud.

Muhsfeldt: I don't like the way you think to me.

Sárkány: Is my German hard for you to understand?

Muhsfeldt: Don't patronise me, Jew! You may spout
haughty German, but you're still a subhuman!

Sárkány: I understand, *Herr Oberscharführer*.

Muhsfeldt: What's this specimen? It's very pretty.

Sárkány: It's called a strawberry gall bladder, filled with
cholesterol stones.

Muhsfeldt: What are you keeping it for? Are you going to
eat it?

Sárkány: He takes an interest in such things. He likes
human stones – be they biliary, renal or even
alimentary.

Muhsfeldt: What? We have stones in our gut?

Sárkány:	They're called faecoliths, and you can find them in the appendix and colon.
Muhsfeldt:	Only Jews could make stones out of shit! Anyway, what does Dr. Mengele want with a Jew's gall bladder?
Sárkány:	He collects them for his anatomical museum.
Muhsfeldt:	Sounds fucking weird to me. Keeping bits of body in jars reminds me of Frankenstein.
Sárkány:	Have you read it?
Muhsfeldt:	Read what?
Sárkány:	Frankenstein is a book by Mary Shelley.
Muhsfeldt:	Thank you, doctor, for enlightening me once again. I'm only a simple butcher after all.
Sárkány:	I thought you were a baker.
Muhsfeldt:	You're a patronising cunt and I'm tired of your insolent manner.
Sárkány:	I understand, *Herr Oberscharführer*. I apologise.
Muhsfeldt:	Your apology is accepted, but don't overstep the mark. Anyway, I'm sure Dr. Mengele will be delighted with your pickled strawberry. Now what about the other matter?
Sárkány:	I told you, the men don't speak to me.
Muhsfeldt:	I'm glad to hear that you've found your wife. That pass he gave you works like magic. What do you think of it over there in C-Camp?
Sárkány:	It's horrible. They're starving.
Muhsfeldt:	But your wife isn't, surely? Not with all the parcels you've been taking to her. Did you tell her what goes on here?
Sárkány:	Of course not.
Muhsfeldt:	Does she have any ideas about the cargos?
Sárkány:	Everybody talks. There are rumours. But they know nothing of the transports.
Muhsfeldt:	You're sure?
Sárkány:	Yes. They only suspect those women selected in the barracks are sent here.
Muhsfeldt:	And what do they think happens once they're

	here? Do they know about the gas chambers?
Sárkány:	As I said, there's a lot of talk. They're women after all. Well… just.
Muhsfeldt:	But you denied everything?
Sárkány:	Yes, categorically. Doctor Mengele has put his trust in me. I don't intend to break that trust.
Muhsfeldt:	That's very good, Doctor Sárkány. Trust and loyalty are everything. So, what about your daughters? Do you know where they are?
Sárkány:	Do you?
Muhsfeldt:	Ah, that would be telling! If he hasn't said anything, then it's not my place to divulge any information. Of course, if you were to help me, with information, I mean…
Sárkány:	You want me to spy, is that it?
Muhsfeldt:	Any intelligence regarding a potential mutiny would be helpful for us both. And any information that I may or may not know about your daughters, well, I'd consider that a fair exchange. You scratch my back; you know how it is. There's a war on.
Sárkány:	Not for long.
Muhsfeldt:	What was that?
Sárkány:	Nothing, I was thinking out loud again.
Muhsfeldt:	Look, I'm feeling generous. I'll give you a free piece of information to whet your appetite.
Sárkány:	Please go on, *Herr Oberscharführer*.
Muhsfeldt:	They're going to be liquidating C-camp.
Sárkány:	No! That's impossible. Who said?
Muhsfeldt:	It's all down to the Russian advance. There have been cuts in our supply chains in the east. There's not enough food. So, the Hungarian women will be first to snuff it. In the next fortnight, might even be sooner.
Sárkány:	The entire sector! In two weeks?
Muhsfeldt:	That's what he told me.
Sárkány:	Mengele? Mengele told you this?

Muhsfeldt:	Yes, it was his decision. He had a meeting with the bigwigs. As for your wife and daughters, you need to act quickly.
Sárkány:	Mengele knew this? Why didn't he tell me?
Muhsfeldt:	Doctor Mengele is a complex individual. But you must know this by now.
Sárkány:	What can I do? I thought Mengele was my…
Muhsfeldt:	What? You thought Mengele was your friend? Ha! And I thought you were the clever one.
Sárkány:	I'm a naïve fool.
Muhsfeldt:	No, it's not that. You're a Jew. And that is all. However, I'm prepared to help you get your family to safety. I'll need to pull some strings, but there's time to arrange for a transfer.
Sárkány:	How?
Muhsfeldt:	They'll soon be moving healthier prisoners west, back into Germany, away from the Russian offensive. I need to clarify which are the safe convoys out of here. Then all they need to do is volunteer.
Sárkány:	You'll do this for me? You're sure it's safe?
Muhsfeldt:	Yes, and yes again. I will make it safe. That's what I'll do for you.
Sárkány:	Thank you. I'm in your debt.
Muhsfeldt:	Precisely doctor. You get me the information I require and I might even throw your good self into the bargain. You must of course keep it a secret: if everybody starts volunteering…
Sárkány:	I understand, *Herr Oberscharführer.*
Muhsfeldt:	*Ausgezeichnet!* Well, I must be off. It's almost time for the next truckload. I hope he likes your Jew's gall bladder.

Boger:	Welcome to the Gestapo kitchens, *Fräulein*. As you can see, we have a whole gamut of knives, tenderisers and other utensils. And kindly note the clean tables, meat hooks, chopping boards, wall plugs, sinks and stove. We butcher our own *kosher* meat here, and keep the room tidy and spotless. Please also notice the floor drains for washing away blood or stray bits of offal. We also have an eclectic range of condiments at our disposal – including paprika, pepper, mustard seed and horseradish.
Mengele:	Hello, my dear.
Boger:	If you haven't already met, this is Dr. Mengele. He will be your personal physician during your visit here. He will ensure that you're in the best possible care. He will administer any injections required and revive you if you should faint.
Gärtner:	What are you going to do to me?
Boger:	That depends on you, *Fräulein*. I am reluctant to cause you any pain. I appreciate that human memory is fragile and fallible. But I truly want to listen. Tell me what you know and I'll have you out of here in no time.
Hoffmann:	We're gonna beat you up then split you open!
Gärtner:	Fuck you!
Boger:	Now, now. Let's not get off to a bad start. Hoffmann here is not a very nice person, if I'm perfectly honest. He would appear to have a penchant for violence, so try not to provoke him. He likes to hang women upside side.
Hoffmann:	I learnt it from Eichmann. He calls it the *Judenstrafe*.
Boger:	Anyway, let's get down to business. Sharpened interrogation is a dark art known only to a

244

select few. Men like me are born, not made. So what do we have here in our box of delights? Goodness, there's quite a selection of toys in order to facilitate any questions that might happen to materialise during our little chat.

Mengele: She's fine. You can proceed.

Boger: Now, are you hanging comfortably? Splendid! Then we'll begin. So, Prisoner 62913, you've been here for some time, a little shy of two years. I think it would be perfectly acceptable to comb the camp for any of your family members: your husband, Jacob, for instance. Ah yes! And your children, Rachael and Beth: I'm sure they'd all like to share in the fun.

Gärtner: They're already dead! I'm not fucking stupid!

Hoffmann: Who wants the powder? Who is your contact?

Gärtner: Fuck you! You're going to kill me anyway.

Hoffmann: Ha! We'll liquidate your stinking barracks first! That's a thousand women. Can you die with so many innocent people on your conscience?

Gärtner: I... I can't...

Boger: Revive her. Yes, that's better. Welcome back *Fräulein*. Now, where were we? Ah, yes – the powder. Who?

Gärtner: I... I don't know who. Nobody knows who these people are.

Boger: They're Polish Resistance, suicidal partisans. But you do know this, of course. They've infiltrated the camp somehow. I need names! No, nothing? Silence doesn't solve anything, really. It just hurts you even more. Mengele! She's fainted again.

Hoffmann: The bitch isn't going to talk.

Mengele: That's because half her tongue is now missing.

Boger: Very well, liquidate her. I don't want to smell her anymore.

Transcript of secret recording (unknown source) in Crematorium I, Auschwitz, Poland, dated Saturday 7th October 1944

Tauber: Doc, come quick! There's a girl, a young girl downstairs. She... she's alive! I mean to say... well... she survived the gas! She's still breathing. I can feel a pulse.

Sárkány: Don't be ridiculous man! This is hydrogen cyanide we're talking about.

Tauber: Honest to God, Doc. This one's living all right. I think the gas men only poured in two tins. They must be low on supplies. I don't know. Just come!

Sárkány: Very well, I'll come.

Tauber: Thank you, Doc. She'll be burned alive otherwise. The cargo's been half cleared. The barbers and dentists are already busy.

Transcript of secret recording (unknown source) in Crematorium I, Auschwitz, Poland, dated Saturday 7th October 1944

Darius: Just let me get at the hair.

Tauber: Leave her be! The Doc is here.

Darius: She's a twin. I've already got the sister's locks.

Sárkány: Twins go straight to Mengele – alive! He must have missed these two at the ramp. Anyway, let me see her.

Tauber: Right you are, Doc. You'll need to put a mask on. You can borrow my gloves.

Sárkány: My God! She's still alive!

Tauber: Didn't I tell you. I'm no medic, but even I can see if someone's still breathing.

Darius: What about the hair?

Tauber: Fuck off scissor-man! We're taking her, with hair. Go shear someone else!

246

Sárkány: Let's get her out of here. We'll take her somewhere private. My room is best.

Tauber: And what do we do with her after that?

Sárkány: We'll worry about that later. Could we just wash her down first? That's it. Hey! Go easy with that hose! We don't want to drown her!

Transcript of secret recording (unknown source) in Crematorium I, Auschwitz, Poland, dated Saturday 7th October 1944

Sárkány: Right, that's it. Careful! You can lay her on my bed. That's it, good. Let's cover her up.

Malkin: Can somebody tell me what's going on?

Tauber: We've got a live one! Poor kid survived. She's had twenty minutes of gas.

Malkin: Have you all lost your minds? Really! What were you thinking? We do not have time for this. Look at her! She's not even conscious, barely breathing. She'll never make it. Let's finish her off right now. Use the pillow.

Sárkány: We're not killing her! We're not murderers.

Malkin: Ha! Look at Doctor Death there, standing all high and mighty!

Sárkány: She's fitting! Hold her down. Good, that's it. Fetch some sweet tea. And a spoon, I'll need a spoon. I'm going to give her a shot of adrenaline. What she really needs is oxygen.

Malkin: What's the cargo?

Tauber: They're Hungarians, from Monor.

Malkin: Who found her?

Tauber: I did. She was at the bottom of a pile by the door. I found her on her belly. I don't know how the gas didn't get to her. It's a mystery.

Sárkány: It's a bloody miracle. Hello there! Can you hear me? What's your name?

Malkin: Let me do the kindly thing…

Sárkány:	I said NO! You summoned me and I came. This wasn't my idea. But I've revived her. I shall give her some dextrose and yes, here it is – some vitamin B12.
Malkin:	So now what?
Sárkány:	I'll have to tell Muhsfeldt. He'll understand.
Malkin:	Like fuck will you! No, not on my watch. He'll flay the lot of us. No, we must kill her – now!
Sárkány:	The Ober needs to know. With a bit of careful bribery, she can be absorbed into C-Camp. Once she's been shaved and tattooed, no one will know. Nobody needs know, especially him. We'll need cigarettes and gold of course.
Tauber:	Gold isn't a problem. We're shitting gold! But fags are in short supply.
Malkin:	My answer's still no. I want her out! Out! She's a fucking distraction, especially when things are so critical with the planned Action.
Sárkány:	What are you talking about? What Action?
Malkin:	Shit! Okay, but you breathe a word of this and I'll personally cremate you alive! There's going to be… an uprising.
Sárkány:	You're joking! When? Who?
Malkin:	We're gonna blow the *Kremas* and take out as many as we can.
Sárkány:	Then what?
Malkin:	Well, some of us are planning to escape. Once we're across to the river, the Polish Resistance will help us to disappear.
Sárkány:	When?
Malkin:	Tomorrow afternoon.
Sárkány:	You're all going to die.
Malkin:	We're all to be killed by the week's end anyway.
Sárkány:	What? How do you know?
Malkin:	I make it my business to know. Anyway, the transports are drying up. Once they've finished off the Hungarians, then we'll all be

out of a job. So, we're practically dead already. Our time's up!

Sárkány: And when were you planning to tell me about this little enterprise?

Malkin: To be honest, we didn't trust you. We thought you'd blab to Mengele as soon as you got wind of it. I mean, you practically live up his arse.

Sárkány: I never asked to be doing what I do.

Malkin: You volunteered, didn't you?

Sárkány: He wanted a pathologist. I'm a pathologist.

Malkin: You knew exactly what you'd signed up for. Mengele wanted you to work for him in the main crematorium of Birkenau. Birkenau! The biggest death factory the world's ever known.

Sárkány: That's as maybe, but I do not kill!

Malkin: What? And I suppose we do?

Sárkány: You're putting words in my mouth.

Malkin: I'll put more than words in your mouth if you don't shut the fuck up and get rid of this girl!

Kowalsky: Hey, I've got news... What's going on in here? Who's she?

Malkin: Never mind who she is. What news?

Kowalsky: They've got two of the powder girls.

Sárkány: Michał, what are you talking about?

Malkin: This day's going from bad to worse. Where?

Kowalsky: They're in the cells of Block 11. It's horrific, believe you me. I've been there! The wet detention cell is tiny. The women will be naked and cold. The floor is kept perpetually damp. You can't lie down. I remember coming face to face with Boger. He was fucking brutal. He broke my teeth.

Malkin: Will you shut up! Have they said anything? Hello, is anybody there?

Kowalsky: Sorry Boss... No, they've kept *schtum*. But they're threatening to liquidate the barracks.

Malkin: Right, this changes things. We're gonna have

to act right away. Put out word to the other *Kremas*. It's now or never. Shit! We're running out of time. We need to rally the men. Come on! Let's go. Leave the Doc with his patient. We must get moving!

Transcript of secret recording (unknown source) in Crematorium I, Auschwitz, Poland, dated Saturday 7th October 1944

Muhsfeldt: It's cold outside. Poland is miserable this time of year. I wouldn't be surprised if it starts snowing. I need something to warm me up. Do you want to join me for a drink? I've got a new bottle of Cognac in my room.

Sárkány: Thank you, *Herr Oberscharführer*, but I've been asked to help downstairs. They're struggling with the high volume of bodies today.

Muhsfeldt: No, it's filthy work down there. The whole place stinks of shit! I'll get some of the nightshift to... heh? What's that?

Sárkány: She... survived the gas.

Muhsfeldt: *Verpiss dich!* Our gas kills everyone, with no exception. Ah, that's it. You were fucking her!

Sárkány: No, *Herr Oberscharführer!* She's barely fifteen. She survived the gas chamber. She's been fitting on and off. I've given her some drugs, but she's yet to regain consciousness.

Muhsfeldt: Who is responsible for this? I want names!

Sárkány: I have some more pressing news. The *Sonderkommando* are going to revolt. They've got explosives, guns... it's all happening this afternoon.

Muhsfeldt   *Mein Gott!* Then it's true!

Sárkány: You knew already?

Muhsfeldt: About the revolt? No, indeed – that is news, although I've had my suspicions for a while now. No, I was referring to you, Dr. Sárkány. I had a wager with Mengele that you'd never betray your companions. Mengele thought you would, I said not. I now owe the doctor that bottle of Cognac. How disappointing. But, then again, I should have known better. You doctors are all the same. You're full of deceit and treachery. And a Jewish doctor is the worst of all. I was never an anti-Semite you know. In fact, I used to like Jews before the war. But now I see you for what you really are! You steal, you lie, and you betray each other. And how easy it is to make you do what you do in this place: to your own people. And to do it so well, so efficiently – it's incredible.

Sárkány: I told you because you promised to help save my family.

Muhsfeldt: Very true, yes that's right. But what if I were like you? What if I told lies and broke all my promises? Anyway, I must thank you for this information. I will of course make sure you are unharmed in the skirmish. It shouldn't last long. And then we can all get back to business as usual. Thank you.

Journal of Michał Kowalsky, Auschwitz, Poland 1944 (Encrypted Final Entry)

Saturday 7th October

We meet with Stakło. He thinks the women are going to crack. David has the camera. He's going to attempt to get some shots of the outside cremation pits. Alter and the Dragons are going to help.

This will be my last entry. Today is *the* day. We have a box of explosives, five machine guns and twenty grenades in the weapons cache.

I want to live. I want to escape from here, but I know my chances are slim. I shall pass this journal onto the Doc for safekeeping. He isn't going to run, but he's got a much better chance of getting out of here alive than me. I just hope that these memoirs will one day come to light. People need to know what went on here. We owe it to the dead.

THE UPRISING

Diary of Dr. József Sárkány, Auschwitz, Poland, 1944

<u>Sabbath 7th October</u>

A teenage girl was discovered in the gas chamber – alive! Although battered and bruised, I observed the shallow rise and fall of the thorax in synchrony with expanding and contracting bubbles of frothy blood in her nostrils. She was horribly scratched about the face, and one eye was swollen and closed. I felt for a carotid pulse. It was weak and thready, but just palpable. After rinsing off the excrement and blood, the Sonder-men transported the unconscious girl to my bedchamber. We dried her off and covered her naked body with a blanket. She had a *grand mal* seizure and almost bit off her own tongue. I gave her morphine, adrenaline, dextrose and cobalamin. After several minutes, the girl showed signs of revival. Her breathing became stronger and more regular, and her pulse fuller. I recorded a blood pressure of 90/55 mm Hg. As she regained the first signs of consciousness, I spooned a few drops of sweet tea into her mouth. She swallowed. There followed a protracted paroxysm of coughing as her airways began to open.

Muhsfeldt entered and saw the girl. I quickly managed to divert his attention and disclosed the intelligence I'd only just heard. He thanked me for this information, but appeared to be almost expecting it. He left me alone with the girl, who was still drowsy and fell in and out of consciousness. I continued to attend to her and managed to turn her onto her side when she vomited.

My concerns about her aspirating proved futile however when a knock on my door this afternoon announced the arrival of *Rottenführer* Baretzki. He picked up the semi-conscious girl and threw her naked body effortlessly over one shoulder. After just five minutes, I heard the echo of gunfire. Baretzki was generous today and mercifully fired off two bullets. I paced the room with feelings of guilt mixed with fear and hopelessness. Then I burst into tears.

I was incapable of working for the rest of the afternoon. I took a large hit of morphine and smoked one cigarette after another. I later visited the furnace room. The men of the day shift performed their work sluggishly, even though several hundred corpses were laid before the furnaces. Small groups stood around and whispered to each other.

I went upstairs to the annex. It was approaching 3pm and everyone was on their feet. I noticed that the men were wearing warm clothes and boots. They bustled about this way and that; they packed and repacked their suitcases, talking quietly. I sensed the enormous tension.

I entered the head *Kapo*'s side room. Around him sat Malkin, Levi and Kowalsky. They invited me to join them round the table. I sat down. Kowalsky poured me a drink. The amber-coloured spirit was strong to the taste and infused with fennel and cumin. I drank it down in one shot.

I eventually headed back to my quarters. I quietly smoked a cigarette. I looked at my watch; its hands showed half past three. I was drowsy with drugs and alcohol.

Suddenly it began. I heard the rattle of heavy machine guns break amidst several explosions. The SS already surrounded the building and attacked from several sides. My information had warned them to be prepared. German guards poured into every room. A group of four barged into my bedchamber. Under a hail of blows they led me, hands held high, into the courtyard, where they ordered me to lie face down. Several other prisoners were already there.

A few minutes later, I heard from the sound of crunching boots that a large group of Sonder-men were brought over and made to lie down beside me. How many could there be? I really didn't know, for I lay motionless, face pressed against the cold gravel. Three or four minutes later they brought in another group. As we lay there stock-still, we received intermittent blows and kicks amid a thick torrent of abuse. I sensed warm blood on my face; the taste of salt, and of metallic iron which trickled onto my tongue.

I only felt the first few blows. My head buzzed and span. I was unable to think, even to fear as my senses fogged over. I was dissolving into the indifference of disintegration.

For at least thirty minutes I lay there – paralysed, numb – waiting for my shot. I could almost anticipate the intense hydraulic pressure of the bullet as my skull shattered into a thousand shards and my milky brains spilt out and steamed.

Time passed. I heard the engine of a car pull up. It must surely be Mengele. The guards had been waiting for him. I couldn't look up to see. Then I heard a loud shout:

"Prisoner A-7938 – stand up!"

I immediately obeyed the order. Standing to attention, I felt dizzy and almost fainted. I waited. It *was* Mengele! His blurred outline beckoned me over to him. My face and shirt were bloody, my trousers torn and muddy. I hovered and swayed before him. Muhsfeldt was standing to his left, whispering in his ear. Mengele listened. Finally, he spoke:

"Go clean yourself up and then get back to work."

Feeling nothing – no relief, no joy – I proceeded to make for the crematorium door. I heard Kowalsky's number called out. I hesitated as his number and surname were called out a second time, then a third. I momentarily turned round. Nobody arose off the ground.

I staggered to my living quarters. The room was spinning and there was a high-pitched whistle in my ears. I attempted to roll a cigarette but my hands were trembling too much. After tearing five papers, I eventually fashioned a smoke. I lit it with a match and took a deep, deep draw. I felt a rush of euphoria flood my brain. It was a comforting numbness that dulled my senses even more. I felt increasingly dizzy but kept inhaling long draws of tobacco smoke. I stubbed out the butt and tottered over to the bed, collapsing down on the mattress.

I felt dirty. I must shower, but first a lie down. Only then did I begin to perceive the throbbing aches and pains caused by the endless blows and kicks. It was time for morphine.

Kowalsky must be dead. He handed me his journal just hours before. My own salvation gave me no comfort for I had merely gained a short reprieve. As my nerves began to calm, my thoughts inexorably turned to the afternoon's events and a pang of guilt thumped into my chest.

I was a traitor to my people!

I had put myself and my family before all other things. I was an informer and a betrayer of men. The information I had given to Muhsfeldt must have surely compromised the operation and prevented the destruction of all four crematoria. Hundreds had died in the insurrection, and many more will no doubt follow.

It surely won't be long before the Resistance get wind of a traitor in their midst. 'Was anyone pardoned?' they'll ask. 'Yes, one man: the pathologist of *Krema* I'.

I dozed until past eight in the evening. In the furnace room, amidst the naked bodies of my dead comrades, I found the corpse of Malkin. He'd been shot in the back. The *Dayan* of Maków was one of the survivors. He stood over the long lines and recited the Mourner's *Kaddish*.

An SS NCO recorded tattoo numbers from the arms of the dead. He was keen to talk about the events and informed me that the revolt began in *Krema* III.

The *Sonderkommando* were ordered to the oven room, and the building was put on lockdown as the SS prepared to liquidate them. A roll call was taken and numbers read out from a register. Sensing a ruse, the prisoners grew uneasy and impetuous. The guards continued with the register, but nobody answered. A handmade incendiary device erupted from nowhere, blowing the legs clean off one German. After a moment's hesitation, the SS opened fire.

The prisoners made for the exit. It was locked. They began to panic and throw more *Ecrasite* bombs. Sirens went off as armoured vehicles pulled up outside. The door was forced open and dozens of prisoners spilled out. Many were instantly cut to pieces by machine-gun fire whilst a handful of men made a last-ditch attempt at escape.

The SS advanced towards the entrance. It was a difficult task as the prisoners still inside put up stiff resistance. Dozens of glass bottles exploded in the courtyard. There suddenly came a deafening explosion as the crematorium's roof blew open and collapsed in. Four steel barrels full of petroleum had just been ignited in the attic space. Many men – SS guards and prisoners alike – were caught in the blast as the final dregs of resistance crumbled. No quarter was given.

In the other crematoria there were lesser pockets of resistance. Levi, the chief stoker in *Krema* I, ordered his men to muster by the first oven after bludgeoning *Kapo* Töpfer to death. Three more *Kapos* burst in and began to hit out with batons. Levi was dealt a skull-crushing blow. He staggered for a moment as blood poured down his face. From the leg of a boot, he suddenly drew a knife and thrust it into his assailant. But before the *Kapo* could even collapse, two other stokers grabbed hold of him and threw him headfirst into the furnace. Another was quickly stabbed and jostled into the second flaming muffle next to his comrade. The third fled for his life amid cries of liberation. After a few minutes, he returned with SS reinforcements and a fierce gunfight broke out. Many of the SS were wounded and all decided to retreat. Great cheers erupted from the prisoners who now began to run out of the building.

But the guards had time to regroup and set up automatic rifles. The *Sonderkommando* made a final bid for freedom before being mown down in a massacring spray of bullets.

~

I returned to my room and reflected heavily upon the day's catastrophic events. At the cost of so many hundreds of lives, it seemed that not one man had managed to escape. That said, Crematorium III was now just rubble and ashes, whilst Crematorium IV had been rendered non-operational due to the destruction of its machinery.

Muhsfeldt paid me a visit around 10 o'clock. He was drunk as usual and asked me for sleeping pills. I obliged. He went on to thank me for my treachery and told me that my information had prevented many more SS casualties. This made me feel sick with guilt. He swallowed the pills and made for the door. His departing words cheered me a little when he said that two men from this crematorium were still unaccounted for: 88687, Meier Pliszko and 89297, Moszek Soboiko. I knew them both quite well and was unable to suppress a smile. The Ober picked up on this and smirked:

"But don't worry. They'll be soon be apprehended and begging me for the bullet!"

ON & ON, ALWAYS ON

Diary of Dr. József Sárkány, Auschwitz, Poland, 1944

Sunday 8th October

I woke up weary after a restless night. I was in a state of nervous collapse and seriously considered taking a bottle of barbiturates to end all the suffering once and for all.

I reluctantly made my way up to the attic for some breakfast. The airy room was quiet and still. About thirty men sat around the table in a frozen silence. They all knew their time was up. I made my way to the stove. No one spoke. Nobody wished me a good morning. Did they know that I'd betrayed them? Had Muhsfeldt said something? I felt deeply ashamed of my actions, but there was nothing more I could do. I was still alive, and God willing, so were my wife and children.

I returned to the laboratory. The rain hammered on the windows. I kept myself occupied with paperwork. There were no autopsies today, but I was determined to look busy and carry on as usual.

Mengele turned up just after 3pm. He was soaked. His gaze glided over me and hovered on my bruised face.

"What happened to you?" he asked.

From this rhetorical question, I gathered that he'd put the events of yesterday out of his mind. He didn't expect an answer and I happily obliged. We talked about his continued research and got onto the subject of laboratory repairs. Several deep cracks had appeared on the walls and ceiling, and one of the windows was boarded up. I let down my guard and found myself speaking my mind:

"The environment here is far from ideal for the continuation of your important scientific research. I wonder whether you might consider relocating?"

Mengele glared at me. His face hardened:

"You have some sentiments to share?"

I reproached myself for abandoning my hitherto prudent and guarded manner. What I'd liked to have said was that the screams of gassed victims and the shots from Muhsfeldt's pistol disturbed my concentration, not to mention the pervasive stench of burning corpses and singed hair. But then I remembered that Mengele was in his element here. He actually enjoyed it. He spent all of his free time here; he had a passion for what he did, and seemed completely indifferent to the horrors that surrounded him. And with an ice-cold resilience, he ordered me to remove the brains and open the bellies of countless corpses. And then I recalled how billions of bacteria were incubated and cultured on the hunks of human flesh that were hewn off the leg bones. He sat patiently at his microscopes for hours at a time. He spent long days in the experimental blocks, cultivating and expanding his human research material.

Today, however, Mengele appeared tired and forlorn. He had come directly from the ramp where he must have stood for hours in the pouring October rain. He sat at the laboratory bench in his wet coat, bent over with fatigue. He didn't even remove his hat, though drops of rainwater still dripped from its shiny black visor.

"Please, *Herr Doktor*. Allow me to take your damp coat and hat to the furnace room. They'll be dry in no time."

"Leave it!" he snapped. "The water is only skin-deep, and I have very thick skin."

He asked for the most recent autopsy reports. He took the files from me. His right hand was visibly shaking. He tried to read a few lines and then gave them back, remarking:

"I'm tired. You read them to me."

I took the protocols and began to read them out loud. I got to the end of the first paragraph when he interrupted:

"That's enough, József. It's not necessary."

He turned towards the window and stared vacantly at the rain dripping down the misted glass.

What could have happened? Had he received some bad news? Or had he experienced some kind of epiphany; a realisation that the game would soon be up?

"For how long will the killing continue?" I asked

He looked at me and smiled:

"My friend… it goes on and on, always on."

I sensed a quiet resignation in his words. He got up from his seat and left the laboratory.

Monday 9th October

Muhsfeldt informed me that Saturday's insurrection cost the lives of 452 Sonder-men and just 3 SS guards. He named the latter as Josef Purke, Rudolf Erler and Willi Freese. The last handful of escapees had recently been apprehended in the regions of Żywiec and Bielsko. He went on to say that 252 were killed in the skirmish and 200 men later shot. He seemed keen to inform me that he didn't carry out the executions, and that the neck-shooter was Baretzki.

None of the explosives smuggled into *Krema* I were used during the uprising. These were apparently supplied by women prisoners working in the Union munitions factory. Only the inmates of Crematorium II, whose participation in the revolt had been immediately blocked by *Kapo* Lemke, were still alive. There were 212 of us left, but for how long?

THE END IS NIGH

Diary of Dr. József Sárkány, Auschwitz, Poland, 1944

<u>**Monday 16th October**</u>

With the liquidation of the family camps now completed, I was painfully aware that the women's sector would be next. Muhsfeldt's previous comments still haunted me, and I feared for the lives of my family.

This afternoon I was sitting in the laboratory at my microscope when Dr. Mengele walked in. He looked tired and dishevelled. Removing his hat and coat, he hovered by the window. I feigned indifference and continued to look down the microscope. Finally, he broke the silence:

"Kramer informs me that we are no longer in a position to feed the women of C-Camp. We have therefore decided to close the entire sector, and to send the healthier contingent to several work camps in Germany. Muhsfeldt has spoken highly of your actions during the recent mutiny, and I entirely concur with his assessment. I have therefore arranged for your wife to be given safe passage out of here on the first transport to Bergen-Belsen. It leaves tomorrow morning."

"And my daughters?"

"Ah, yes. Your twin daughters that eluded me on the ramp! Of course, they too will join their mother. They are currently in one of the hospital barracks marked up for liquidation, but I'm prepared to allow them to leave with a handful of others. You see József, I'm really a kind man at heart. But I am also a soldier, and appreciate any man that shows loyalty and obedience. You are one such man."

"Thank you, *Herr Doktor*. I am forever in your debt."

"Nonsense, man! You'd have done the same for me, I'm certain of that. After all, we're professional colleagues in the very noblest of professions."

"May I visit my wife before she goes?"

"Of course, that's only to be expected. And please tell her that Dr. Mengele sends his best regards."

I hurried excitedly to C-Camp using Mengele's pass. Éva still looked terribly emaciated, but there was a definite vivacity in those eyes that were once as dead as stone. She told me that the rations had been drastically reduced and asked if I'd brought her anything. I smiled and produced a small bundle out of my pocket. She smelled it and giggled.

"Open it," I said. She carefully unwrapped the parcel. Inside the cloth was a fresh white roll, together with real butter and marmalade.

"Compliments of Dr. Mengele," I told her.

Her face instantly soured and she covered the food.

"Now listen," I said. "I've managed to pull all sorts of strings, and Dr. Mengele has agreed for you and the girls to leave the camp on the next transport west."

"Do you trust him?" she asked. "You know all about his lies and cruelty."

"He's changed, Éva. He seems, well... more human. He's had enough of this place, I'm sure. I genuinely believe that the good side of his personality, buried deep for so long, is finally winning over. He even asked me to pass on his best regards to you."

"O József! He's playing you like a puppet, just as he's always done. And what about the hundreds of other poor women in here? Is the good Doctor Mengele going to save them as well? Of course not. He's prepared to use me and the girls as pawns on his chess board. He's reached the endgame and is wondering how best to achieve a stalemate."

I looked at her perplexed. Had I really been so naïve?

"What do you mean?" I asked.

"The war is nearly over: even I know that. Germany is being attacked from all sides. They're going to lose; it's as plain as the nose on my face. Mengele, like so many other Nazis, is now thinking about damage limitation. He knows he can't possibly win, but with a glowing testimony from you, a respectable prison doctor, he may at least escape the hangman's noose."

Tuesday 17th October

Today I visited C-Camp for one last time. I wanted to confirm my wife and daughters' departure first-hand. Everything had gone off smoothly as I'd hoped. My family was heading west, to a camp called Bergen-Belsen. It sounded like they'd be much safer there as it was not an extermination centre. I really didn't know what the future had in store for them, yet I felt a great sense of relief. Here, certain death awaited them; in this new location, with a little luck, liberation. I prayed that I would see them all again.

I left the women's camp for the final time; my weary eyes running over the sombre barracks in parting. With aching sympathy, my gaze took its leave of the misshapen figures that had once been so vibrant, well-groomed and beautiful.

An icy chill ran through me as I stepped through the gate. Only now as I pulled my jacket together more closely did I feel that winter was on its way. The north wind blew from the already snow-covered peaks of the Beskids. It rattled the miles of barbed wire. Here and there, crows hovered and cawed in the grey skies; the only bird that lived in this infernal place. The cold wind temporarily invigorated me, but I sensed the coming of snow.

Wednesday 18th October

The liquidation of the women's camp began this evening. Fifty trucks requisitioned for this purpose will bring the victims to the gas every evening in groups of a thousand. The long line of floodlit vehicles made for a terrible spectacle as they turned in to the crematorium courtyard with their cargo. One after another, before the entranceway leading below ground, they unloaded the already naked victims. Every one of them was aware that they were going to their deaths, but the rigours of their incarceration and the

264

inexorable collapse of their nervous systems had deadened in them all sensation and capacity to resist.

They let themselves be driven into the subterranean bunker where, weary of their worn-out lives, they inertly awaited the emancipation of death.

Thursday 19ᵗʰ October

I took a turn in the crematory courtyard this morning. The rain was pouring down. Wherever I went, wherever I looked, everywhere there was only electrified wire, concrete and mud. As I walked around the backyard, I sensed a slight movement from amongst an enormous pile of rubbish. I tentatively approached. Crouched amongst the sodden prayer books and photographs, a young woman, soaked to her skin, was shivering. She was cradling something in her shawl. It was the tiny body of her dead infant. A long stump of umbilical cord still hung from the abdomen. The end of the cord was ragged and looked as if it had been bitten off. The placenta was nowhere to be seen.

I spoke to her in Hungarian, for she must have come from the women's camp on yesterday's transport. She looked at me; bone-thin, dripping wet, eyes reddened with tears. But no words came. There was really nothing I could do for her but expedite her death. For die she must. She had crossed the threshold into the inner circle of hell from which there was no return. Although she had been spared the cyanide, she had to watch her newborn infant die in her arms. And now she must go before the *Oberscharführer* and gratefully receive her 6mm ration of lead.

I took her to Muhsfeldt. He was rifling through his office, looking desperately for something to drink. But we were out of alcohol in *Krema* I. He looked up impatiently at me as I entered his office with the woman. His jaundiced eyes were wild looking and twitchy. His pale complexion was ghost-like, his oily dark hair swept back. I perceived a distinct tremor in his hands. I enjoyed his suffering, even rejoiced in it. Yes! Let this man, this alcoholic, this murderer – let him suffer with the *delirium tremens*.

Upon entering the room, the woman ran towards the Ober and fell to her knees. She let go of her dead infant and grasped one of his tall leather boots with both hands. A heart-rending plea for mercy then followed. To my surprise, she addressed Muhsfeldt in German. She told him that she was only half-Jewish, that she had worked in Munich as a doctor for three years, and that her father had fought for Germany in the Great War.

But Muhsfeldt was unmoved. He had his mind on more pressing matters: the acquisition of booze.

"Take your filthy hands off my boot!" he yelled, striking her across the face. "Look at the fucking mess you've made on the floor!"

He grabbed her by the hair and dragged her out of the door. She screamed with pain, still begging for mercy. I heard the crack of his pistol, then another – but only after he'd raped her. This respectable doctor and mother was no more. Fire and chimney now awaited her and her baby.

Friday 20th October

The forgetful hours of morphine and barbiturates ease the pain, for without them I would surely despair. I lay on my pillow in a soporific haze. The overcast sky is bruised by rainclouds, coupled with a benevolent veil of opiate mist. I gaze out of the window in a hypnotic daze on yet another rainy afternoon in Birkenau.

Sabbath 28th October

A large brown van was parked up round the back of the courtyard this morning, partly camouflaged in a carpet of autumnal leaves. Muhsfeldt appeared from nowhere and slapped me hard on the back. I took it as a form of jovial greeting, but it ached for hours after and left me with a bruise. The Ober was drunk. He had evidently managed to find some more liquor, or may well be resorting to methylated spirits knowing him.

"Do you like my new toy?" he asked. "He's called Brown Tony. As we're pretty much out of *Zyklon*, the SS doctors have decided to use another type of gas. Monoxide is a particular favourite of theirs, apparently. They used it in the Euthanasia Centres and Reinhard camps. Anyway, here he is – Brown Tony! Klein wants to use him first on a dozen female patients. I offered to shoot them, but he insists on smoking his birds. Looks like I'm going to be out of a job!"

Tuesday 31st October

The late October sunshine gave way to cold autumn rain. Fog and gloom covered the countless barracks of Birkenau. Only the crows, gaunt from hunger, took to their wings when the north wind howled and shook the barbwire fence.

I decided to take a short stroll in the evening twilight. I wandered around the courtyard several times; my path took me past the gloomy entrance down into the undressing room and gas chamber. I stopped there for a few moments. It then occurred to me that today was All Hallows' Eve, the Night of the Dead. The damp grey stones of the concrete steps disappeared down into the darkness. Thousands upon thousands of people had bid their farewells to the sunlight here. From this point onward, they had all descended into the catacombs and taken their final breaths of fresh air before the suffocating onslaught of hydrogen cyanide.

WITHDRAWAL

Diary of Dr. József Sárkány, Auschwitz, Poland, 1944

<u>Sabbath 4th November</u>

The attic is like a morgue. The remaining few Sonder-men are all mute and sunk into themselves. *Oberscharführer* Muhsfeldt has taken to his room and locked the door.

This afternoon, quite unexpectedly, Dr. Mengele arrived. He told me that Auschwitz was to be liquidated. Not the prisoners, he was careful to stress, but the entire complex itself.

<u>Sunday 5th November</u>

Today was my final injection of morphine. I took it before bedtime, shooting up for one last time. I reclined on the bed, fully narcotised, in the euphoria of Elysium.

There will be no coming down gently: this is going to be acute and exquisitely painful.

<u>Monday 6th November</u>

I awoke this morning with the usual opiate cravings. Just two hours after my scheduled dose, the withdrawal symptoms began. By evening, I was sweating like a pig. My heart began to race and my anxiety spiralled to a full-blown panic attack just before bedtime.

<u>Tuesday 7th November</u>

The first night of withdrawal was totally devoid of sleep. I remained anxious and sweaty into the early hours, with restless legs and horrible muscular spasms. I took several sleeping pills but could not avoid vomiting them back up.

Wednesday 8th November

Diarrhoea blighted me in the early hours. It was explosive and accompanied by dreadful intestinal cramping.

My second sleepless night left me weak and dizzy this morning. My anxiety levels were through the roof. My head was thumping, whilst my racing heart seemed to flutter and surge in my chest. I felt as if I was constantly on the verge of a heart attack or stroke – or both.

Thursday 9th November

I had to endure another sleepless night. My body continued to be drenched and I felt chills right down to the bone.

I went into some sort of convulsion after an episode of projectile vomiting this afternoon. I don't think I lost consciousness, but it certainly left me feeling drowsy.

Just before bedtime, I remembered Éva's birthday. Happy birthday, dearest wife! Then I realised that our son would have been six years old tomorrow.

Friday 10th November

I awoke just after nine to find my pillow covered in blood. I'd almost bitten off the end of my tongue, presumably due to some kind of epileptic seizure. My eyes were blurred and it ached to focus. The light also hurt me as I lay in the gloom of drawn curtains, semi-comatose… but still breathing.

Sabbath 11th November

After another restless night, I decided to brave the outside air. The day was overcast and freezing cold. I went up to the annex for the first time this week and managed to keep down a light breakfast of tea and toast. Nobody was about. The remaining Sonder-men were at work, and Muhsfeldt was nowhere to be seen. I'd not heard from Mengele either.

<u>**Sunday 12th November**</u>

I was anxious and prickly today. The irritability turned to
anger, then fury, as I ruminated on my present situation and
dire prospects of survival.

<u>**Monday 13th November**</u>

I awoke suddenly. I rubbed my face and removed the
crusted residue from my eyes. I'd just had the most hideous
of nightmares; both bizarre and disturbing, and leaving me
feeling agitated and confused. My God! It felt so real. I
remembered it so vividly and decided to record it at once:

It was dark outside. My curtains were open. A full moon
was casting its silvery light into my room. Standing before
me were two women. I instantly recognised them as Hannah
Fischer and Irma Grese. They were wearing lingerie and
stilettos. They whispered to each other, giggling coquettishly
whilst momentarily looking over to me and pointing with
their long, painted nails.

Grese broke away and walked slowly towards me. She
smelt like warm honey. She was wearing a black lacey basque
and brassiere, with sheer nylon stockings and red silk
knickers emblazoned in front with a swastika. She fingered
the end of a brown leather riding crop. Her golden hair was
slicked back, and her fair skin looked smooth and creamy.
Heavy mascara highlighted her pale blue eyes under long
eyelashes. Scarlet lipstick made her lips look plump, moist
and enticing. She grinned and ran her tongue over her white
top teeth that glistened like wet pearls.

Then Fischer approached. Both women stared at me
seductively, licking their lips and pouting. I ached to go over
and kiss them. But I wanted more... much more – yes, we'd
climax as one throbbing trinity.

I felt the warm licorice breath of Grese dance over my
face as she lent in closer. I closed my eyes and sensed her
lightly licking the skin around my throat. I was paralysed in

a languor of ecstasy. The moist tingling continued down onto my chest, my thumping heart, and nipples: and still that bewitchingly muscular tongue pirouetted and chasséd and stroked ever southward, traversing navel and abdomen.

A piercing sound broke the silence and shattered the illusion. It was the hard and sneering voice of my mother:

"József, you filthy boy! You're not good enough for these lovely Aryan ladies. You're too cheap, too dirty, too tainted. I am pure like them. Whatever possessed me to marry that Jewish father of yours? Bad Blood! And you're full of it!"

"Mother, please... forgive me... I was only..."

"Only what? You dirty little *drek!* You're disgusting!"

"But, Mother..."

"No buts... you're a puerile and circumcised piece of nothing!"

"No, please! Just let me explain!"

"No! You must first apologise to these exquisite Aryan ladies in all their fineries. Tell them there's been a horrible mistake. Tell them who you really are!"

"I... I... can't!"

"That's right, boy. You don't have the guts, do you? You always were a spineless loser!"

I could hear the unfriendliness of my mother's mocking laughter – taunting... derisive. Then a shrill cry followed:

"Go back to that Jewess slut from Munkács and your dirty little daughters! You can fuck them all if you like! Just leave the Aryan women to their own kind."

"Sorry, Mother... please forgive me."

"Never! You were the death of me, boy. You gave me those pills. You knew how ill I was; how desperate I'd become. Yes! You can finally add matricide to your long list of crimes. What a fabulous doctor you are!"

"Please, no more!"

"You're pathetic! I've seen you over the last few months, filling your veins with filth! I've watched you coming off the stuff – like some neglected animal, pissing and shitting all over the place. What a wretched sight you've been for your poor mother. Fuck Hitler's struggle – what about my own?

"I see you scoffing all that phenobarbitone! You like it don't you? Yes, you do: so much so that you gave it to your own poor Mother to top herself with! Yes, you know all about Luminal. It's been murdering disabled children since 1939. You Angels of Death must be so very proud."

"Please… please!"

"Don't be such a wimp! Now you're going to suffer. These delightful ladies will see to that on my behalf."

Grese suddenly shrieked and pulled back. Blood filled her underwear and began to leak out the sides. Another gush followed, heralding the appearance of a gestation sac that oozed up over her knicker line. Finally, it burst open, releasing a torrent of watery fluid and a small glistening fetus that quivered and writhed.

Fischer laughed derisively. She then squealed as a small naked infant emerged from between her legs. He turned to me and offered up a Nazi salute before beginning to crawl up the wall opposite. I recognised the child: it was the mouldering corpse of my own dead son!

"They're fucked up good and proper!" growled my mother. "And it's all your fault!"

I screwed up my eyes and yanked the bed covers up over my face. I cocooned myself in a damp swathe of blankets, like a swaddled infant. I just wanted the nightmare to end.

Thursday 16th November

Unable to write for a few days, I was pleased to wake up this morning feeling relatively normal. I was off the morphine and had broken the clinging addiction. Never again! Now a new battle would have to commence as I faced the hard reality of life, devoid of my comforting opiate cushion.

Friday 17th November

I was uprooted and transferred to *Krema* IV with the other remaining Sonder-men today. This will remain the only active crematorium. The other three will be demolished, although *Krema* III is in still in ruins following the Uprising.

An SS guard asked me to examine him this evening. I diagnosed gonorrhoea. He almost looked pleased:

"Have you got anything for the burning, Doc?"

I advised that he drink plenty of water and gave him an ointment of Protargol. As he made his way to the door, he hesitated and turned:

"Thank you, Doctor Sárkány."

I was astounded. He went on to inform me that there were to be no more killings across the entire Auschwitz complex, emphasising that the order had come from the *Reichsführer* himself.

Sabbath 18th November

Although initially heartened by yesterday's news, I have ruminated on this information overnight and begin to doubt its credibility. I suspect another ruse – and why not? The Germans are liars. Their pledges mean nothing. I know this all too well from my own bitter experiences.

A detachment of Sonder-men began demolition work on Crematorium I this morning; my home for the past six months. It was a cold, frosty day but the seventy or so men were happy to be doing this work. Jews built it, and by God, Jews were going to tear it down!

The years of bloodshed and genocide are to be wiped from the face of history. The past must be hidden: the incineration trenches filled in, the crematoria razed, and with them all traces of the gas chambers. But there is one more thing to be obliterated, and that must surely all participants in these factories of death. So, I must die: there is no other option.

Thursday 30th November

I took my meals in isolation these days. There were very few Sonder-men about the place now, and those who were not on duty were housed in a barracks outside the crematorium.

As I sat quietly supping at my bedside table, Muhsfeldt crashed through the door. He was flushed and unsteady on his feet, drunk as usual. As he staggered across the floor, I noticed that his feet were bare. He hovered over me and leant unsteadily against the table. His breath was rank and I estimated at least five days of stubble on his face.

"Good evening my boy!" he said, voice slurred. I wiped the spittle from my face.

"You're soon going to croak, you know. Yes, I'm sorry to say. The Bolsheviks are coming to get us all! Better to die, I suppose. I wouldn't wanna be bummed by Stalin's boys!"

I smiled to myself and offered the Ober some hot rum tea. "You've got rum!" he cried with utter delight. "My dear fellow, I'll take it straight if you don't mind."

He drained his cup and eagerly eyed up the bottle. There was probably enough left for four or five single measures. I emptied the remainder and he guzzled back the lot.

"Have you got any more?" he inquired meekly, like a child asking for more ice cream. I lied to his face and said that the rum was the last of my hidden stash. Looking disappointed, he wandered over to my bed and sat down, almost missing the edge entirely.

"The Reds are just forty miles away," he said. "All of Poland is on the move, retreating back to the Fatherland. They're animals, the Russians! Barbarian half-breeds from Siberia, most of them! Shall I do us both now? How about one in the neck for old times' sake?"

I politely told the Ober that he was currently unarmed. He burst into a fit of laughter before passing out cold.

Sabbath 9th December

Mengele paid me a rare visit in my room this evening. He did not stay long, but left a parcel on my bedside table.

"You may find this useful in the days ahead," he said rather awkwardly, hurrying out of the door. I quickly opened it, thinking it would be a loaded revolver. To my astonishment, I found an ornate *Menorah*, replete with nine candles.

Could this be true? Was I dreaming? Had Dr. Josef Mengele just given me my very own *Hanukiah* in which to celebrate the Jewish Festival of Lights?

As I lit the first *Shamash* candle and watched it glow brightly, I wondered how many other candles were burning throughout Europe. I thought about Éva and the girls. Were they also celebrating tonight? Were they even alive?

PASSOVER

Diary of Dr. József Sárkány, Auschwitz, Poland, 1945

<u>Monday 1st January</u>

A cold January morning dawned in Auschwitz-Birkenau. It was New Years' Day. The genocide of 1944 was now behind me. Only ashes and dust remained.

I wrapped up warm and ventured outside into the courtyard. A barren wasteland of deep snow stretched out as far as the eye could see. No smoke rose from the multitude of barracks chimneys, indicating that the stoves were unlit and the interiors unheated.

How much more could these wretched people endure? Must they all now freeze to death in the arctic winter of Upper Silesia?

<u>Sabbath 6th January</u>

O Éva! I am so sorry. I failed you as a husband and as a father to your children. I also failed to be your guardian and protector; impotent in keeping you safe, and unable to shield you from the Nazi predators. I was powerless to prevent the death of your parents. I did nothing as you and the girls were bundled onto that train. Yes, I eventually managed to secure your escape from this death camp, but at the cost of betraying my own people. I had to sell my soul to the devil and his minions. I assisted in their vile experiments. I mutilated the dead with knife and saw.

O wife! Even now, I am ignorant of your wellbeing and whereabouts. I even wonder if you're still alive amongst the God-forsaken ruins of this European apocalypse.

<u>Friday 12th January</u>

The Russian advance continued as a distant rumble of heavy

artillery fire caused the windows of my room to shudder and creak. The front line of Stalin's Red Army drew ever nearer.

I heard from the few remaining SS guards that the crematoria and warehouses were soon to be blown up. The physical evidence of the genocide – the undressing rooms, gas chambers, ovens and belongings – would be effaced from history.

But what of me? Would I ever leave this vast necropolis of graveless dead and get to see my family again?

I shuddered to think about the thirty warehouses of *Kanada*, crammed full with the spoils of extermination. I pondered over the hundreds of thousands of pillaged items – suitcases, shoes, overcoats, spectacles, wristwatches, combs, walking sticks, prosthetic limbs, glass eyes… hair.

Sunday 21st January

In the early hours of the morning, I was jolted from my slumbers by loud explosions and the stuttering of machine-gun fire. I leapt out of bed and opened the door of my room. I found a folded piece of paper under my door and picked it up without thinking.

Bright lights illuminated all of the corridors. The dead bodies of my remaining companions lay strewn across the floor. The guards were nowhere to be seen. My heart leapt with joy when I beheld the deserted guard towers surrounding the building. The SS had surely fled.

But why had I not been killed? I was certainly a secret bearer like the rest of my doomed companions. Had Mengele – or even Muhsfeldt – forbidden my execution?

I turned back. It was then that I noticed a patch of fresh blood smeared across the lintel of my door. I unfolded the paper and glanced at the note inside. The spidery hand was unmistakably that of Mengele's. It read:

'The blood of this lamb is without blemish, for it is my own. And the Angel of Death shall pass over this house of my loyal servant and friend. He has humbled his heart before me, and no man will touch even a hair upon his head. He will remember this act of kindness in the coming days, and repay the favour if needs must.'

So, Dr. Josef Mengele was to prove my savour after all? The final plague of Birkenau had smitten my companions, but Mengele's bloody mark allowed me to live on; untouched by knife, bullet or grenade.

I hesitated for a moment and then set my sights on freedom. I had ceased to be one of the *Sonderkommando*. I was no longer an untouchable and bearer of secrets. I did not have to die! I was now a simple number… a nobody.

I decided not to remain a moment longer in that infernal place. Waiting for liberation by the Russians was not an option. I was also worried about ending up in the murdering hands of the retreating SS men. Mengele's unsigned message was too cryptic and too vague to be of further use to me.

I got dressed. My room was freezing and there was a frost on the inner window panes. I had fortunately managed to procure some essential winter clothing for the sub-zero temperatures that regularly plunged below −20°C at this time of year.

I grabbed a few provisions – bread, cheese, sausage – and put them into my doctor's bag, along with this diary and the tattered journal of Michał Kowalsky. I also poured the last dregs of brandy into a hipflask and stuffed my pockets with all the cigarettes and Luminal I could get my hands on. The morphine was gone, but I didn't care. I was primed and ready for yet another evacuation.

SCARS

Diary of Dr. József Sárkány, 1945

<u>Wednesday 7th March, Mauthausen, Austria</u>

Auschwitz was burning when I finally departed on that freezing January night. I trudged through miles of snow in the company of at least 2000 other evacuees, accompanied by a small detachment of SS guards who had not bolted with the others. We marched for hours through the barren, black Silesian landscape. Strewn everywhere along the route were all kinds of camp paraphernalia – rusty spoons, cracked bowls, soiled blankets; even worn wooden clogs fallen from feet. Such pitiful items of former incarceration were rapidly joined by hundreds of frozen corpses lying crumpled and half buried in shallow ditches on both sides of the road. These were the unhappy bodies of the newly liberated; those who could not endure the cold, fatigue and extreme deprivation any longer.

After several hours, we arrived at a railway station in Racibórz. It was snowing heavily. Our number had already dwindled significantly, primarily through exhaustion and hypothermia. I was one of the lucky few who had adequate winter clothing and good footwear. Most people had little more than their flimsy striped uniforms and a pair of shoes.

The transport from Racibórz consisted of numerous railway carriages, assembled on a narrow-gauge track. Cries of anguish and despair went up when we realised that the rickety wooden wagons had no roofs and were fully exposed to the harsh winter elements. The loading went relatively swiftly, with an average of 50 people crammed into each carriage. It was standing room only in this open-topped meat freezer.

I dared not count how many frozen souls we dumped from the wagons during the course of that four day journey to Mauthausen Concentration Camp, some 300 miles south west of Racibórz, and perhaps a dozen miles east of Linz.

Mauthausen looked like a medieval castle, with its walls of hoary granite atop an imposing conical hill. A dreadful wind howled between the walls of that high stone fortress. We were on a mountaintop, in the foothills of the Alps. The winter here was very harsh.

During the first days in quarantine, an SS officer arrived accompanied by a camp clerk. He quickly surveyed my barracks with a look of disgust whilst his clerical assistant scribbled notes on a wooden clipboard. We were made to form an orderly queue and to present our tattoo numbers.

The officer looked at the list of some 200 prisoners and lit a cigarette. He then compared them to another list of numbers, presumably salvaged from the records of Auschwitz. Shaking his head, he ordered all prisoners who had worked in the crematoria of Auschwitz-Birkenau to present themselves immediately. My blood went cold. Did he have a list of secret bearers? Was this the end at last?

I thought it over whilst my heart thumped furiously and my legs began to shake. No, surely not. This was just a façade. These people had no idea about who was part of the Birkenau *Sonderkommando* in those final days. This was nothing more than a desperate trawling exercise.

I came to my senses, remaining perfectly still and avoiding all eye contact with the SS officer. If he truly had an accurate list, he would have picked me up by now.

In silence, I waited as the long and fretful minutes ticked by. At last, both officer and clerk departed. I was safe!

Friday 27th April, Mauthausen, Austria

Everything here was in a state of disintegration. The final collapse of the Third Reich passed before my eyes like a Hollywood epic. Defeated armies marched in endless columns toward their homeland, now reduced to ruins.

The murdering Nazi hordes were disappearing from the world stage in an inglorious inferno of defeat and surrender.

These fanatical pyromaniacs started such fires that no part of Europe was left untouched by their Fascist flames; but like some glorious *Contrapasso*, the Germans themselves – soldier and civilian alike – were now being consumed in the igneous onslaught of retribution.

The proud and patriotic voices that once sang *'Deutschland, Deutschland über alles!'* over Europe's radio waves had long gone silent. Ah, yes! 'Germany, Germany above all in the world' – I would have once believed this; even sang along to Haydn's merry tune. Now I almost choked over the irony of the words, 'Unity and justice and freedom…'

In this post-apocalyptic world, there was no brotherly love between fellow men. Hearts and hands were cold and murderous. The old and noble chimes of German culture were gone forever. For how could the world forgive them?

Wednesday 2ⁿᵈ May, Melk, Austria

Mauthausen was now behind me. The winter of Nazism was retreating from all over Europe. Spring was in the air and the snow had long thawed.

The elegance of Melk Abbey – a Benedictine monastery built upon a granite rocky outcrop – was a wonder to behold in the spring sunshine. The stunning beauty of the landscape lightened my melancholy a great deal. The Wachau valley of the Danube meandered below the camp, where the trees were once more adorned in their leafy green mantles. The great river was now swollen from the spring thaw. I realised that the mighty Danube was a Hungarian river too; making me feel at peace with myself, and giving me hope once more of a long-awaited homecoming.

Sabbath 5ᵗʰ May, Melk, Austria

A white flag fluttered on the tower as troops of the US 80th Infantry Division liberated the camp today. It was over. The Germans were defeated. We were free.

Thousands of prisoners came flooding out of the barracks, waving arms and banners. From around the camp streets, I heard Polish inmates singing *'Dąbrowski's Mazurka'* and jubilant Frenchmen chanting *'La Marseillaise'*.

For me and my fellow Jews, we simply cried. A small group in my barracks mumbled *'Hatikvah'*, but most of us just wept in silence. The quiet intoning of lamentation seemed a fitting liberation hymn for us. There was no real hope remaining in our Hebrew hearts and souls. The scars ran too deep. The millions of dead could not sing – and were forever silent. The living went on living, but the Jewish core, the very Jewish essence, seemed empty and forgotten.

Sabbath 16th June, Munkács, Hungary

I alighted from the train at Munkács railway station. It was midafternoon and the sun shone brightly in the cloudless blue skies. The train journey from Austria had been a sad but comfortable one. My carriage afforded me my own upholstered passenger seat, with windows, ventilation and an on-board service of refreshments. My compartment even had its own flushing lavatory.

My mind wandered back a year and I thought of that hideous death train with its crammed cattle cars, equipped with nothing but a pail of water and a privy bucket. I remembered the darkness, the suffocation… the indignity.

Now, at least, I was afforded the comforts of a civilised journey. I felt human again. But the bestial shame lived on.

I made my way on foot to the old family house in Munkács. The ghetto was long gone, but the rubble and ruins remained. I dreaded the reality that Éva and the girls would not be there to greet me: for I'd had no news of them.

I was wracked with remorse for the part I played in Mengele's psychosis and megalomania. Those dreadful deeds in *Krema* I continued to freeze my heart. I knew everything, but did… nothing.

I wandered through the familiar streets like a sunken

shadow of my former self. I was in a profound lethargy; a muted and nihilistic stupor that combined both indifference with futility. I felt no nostalgia, no relief.

I was changed. Auschwitz was behind me, but it still haunted me, day and night. I'd come a long way to get here, but I was still in Auschwitz. I would always be in Auschwitz.

The afternoon sunshine warmed my face as I finally arrived at the front door. I held my breath and knocked – once, twice, three times. My pulse was racing. Still I waited. Slowly the door began to open.

It was Olivia. We embraced and exchanged tearful kisses. It had been over a year since I'd seen her. She told me that her mother was out buying groceries with Emilia.

I entered the house and went into the kitchen. Lily was boiling water on the stove and made me a cup of tea. We sat at the table in silence. I eventually asked her about her time after Auschwitz in the months leading up to liberation.

Lily sipped her tea, but said nothing. I asked again. Then with great reluctance, she relocated her mind back into the concentration camp of Bergen-Belsen:

"It was horrible, Papa. Emilia got very sick and Mama was wasting away. There were withered bodies everywhere; dead and dying lying together. The corpses became their pillows, even their friends. Many talked to the dead... and the dead answered back. I saw babies born and wilt away. I saw children rake off their skin, and mothers pull out whatever hair they had left on their heads."

I learned that the camp was finally liberated in mid-April. Lily explained how the British doctors desperately tried to save the living. She recalled being given tinned beef and milk which only made her diarrhoea worse. Then they tried a kind of sweetened rice. They even added paprika to the mix in order to make it more palatable, but many were too fragile to even consume this. They attempted intravenous feeding, but this was soon abandoned as the sight of syringes and injection needles caused panic and mass hysteria.

Lily boiled more water and I cut some bread. We had

our afternoon tea like civilised people… civilised Jews. I glanced at my watch: it was just after three. There was still no sign of Éva.

~

It is past five when I heard the front door open and close. Footsteps approached the kitchen and I held my breath. Emilia entered first and ran over to me. We hugged and exchanged kisses. Éva peered inside. She was hovering by the door, holding a large cloth sack in both hands. She remained still, then quietly asked the girls to leave us.

My wife did not greet me, nor did she smile; she seemed restrained by conflicting emotions which glued her lips together and bound her tongue. Beyond the momentary surprise, I perceived a look of both calm anger and subdued disappointment that I knew so well.

Was she disappointed to see me? Perhaps she would have preferred an honourable martyrdom for her long-estranged lover. But I hadn't died. I survived, like many others. Was there shame in this survival? Were we also guilty for living? Had we been too selfish, ruthless… complicit?

I was all these things, and more. I was a living accomplice to the crimes of Doctor Josef Mengele.

The wounds of Auschwitz still ached and excoriated. Whilst the physical scars were dormant, the ignominious wounds of collaboration inside my head continued to break open and bleed. My survival was nothing about honour, bravery or human regard. I survived because of what I was… what I had always been.

And so, there was understandable disappointment in my wife's face; but it was more than this: there was shame in those now ungentle eyes – and perhaps a sense of disgrace even. For Éva recognised the real József Sárkány better than anybody else. She identified the vanity, pretense and self-regard. Yes, I was Mengele's assistant; his right-hand man: Josef and József, doctor and doctor – mirrors of the same poison compound, or two faces of a dirty coin.

Éva finally broke the awkward silence:

"Well, you're back then, that's good I suppose."

I nodded. She walked over to me and handed me the sack. She told me that she'd visited our former residence on Latorica Street. I untied the binding string and opened the bag. Inside was a small urn, together with a candelabrum and toy bear. At the very bottom, tied up in a bundle, were my old diaries dating back to 1938.

Should I now destroy these personal memoirs? They were testimonies of terrible secrets. They were channelled confessions into my inner self – my ego, my id, my primitive essence. If Éva were to ever read them…

~

Later that evening, I entered the gloom of the living room. Éva sat alone, staring silently at a *Menorah* that glowed on a sideboard in the corner. Next to this was the old *Steiff* bear sitting proudly on the urn. He still wore his *kippah*, but was crying no more.

Éva turned to look at me. I sat down opposite and asked her directly what was wrong. She replied obliquely, and it reminded me of her sleepwalking soliloquys of old:

"Within the bond of marriage, tell me, Brutus, is it accepted I should know no secrets that appertain to you? Dwell I but in the suburbs of your good pleasure?"

I told her that the past was behind us and that I wanted to move on and build our marriage anew. I explained that I was terribly scarred by my time in Auschwitz, in that infernal crematorium with the likes of Muhsfeldt and Mengele.

"I too have my own scars to bear," she replied. "I too bear the tattoo of perpetual servitude. I am prison number B-6789. The sorrows of death compassed me, and the floods of ungodly men made me afraid. In my distress I called upon the Lord, but He did not listen."

I dug around in my pocket and proudly produced her

wedding ring. I had somehow managed to keep it hidden during my months at Auschwitz and beyond. Éva forced a smile. As she showed no sign of accepting the ring directly from me, I placed it down on the table opposite her. She looked at it for a moment, but did not touch.

Desperately wanting to break the *impasse*, I remarked:

"That's been in some pretty tight spaces, I can tell you."

"I'm surprised it hasn't rusted by now," she replied.

"What do you mean?"

"Well, it's not real gold is it? We both know that. I would have expected all that base copper and tin to have corroded; especially as the thing's no doubt been through your alimentary tract on more than a few occasions."

We both grinned at each other.

"You seem disappointed to see me," I said.

"Disappointed – what can I say? Your past actions live on in my eyes. The mind may forgive and eventually forget, but the eyes always remember – always! Like tiny pinpricks, your transgressions are tattooed onto my irises. They bear the marks of your adultery and your years of neglect. They are branded by the abortion you nearly made me have, and the son you helped to murder. They are inscribed with your bribes, broken oaths… your association with criminals."

"I didn't have anything to do with death of our son."

"Stop lying to me! I've read your diaries. When I saw them hidden under the floorboards, I immediately turned to the winter of 1940. Your thoughts and actions speak for themselves. You can't deny what is written. Whilst *Kristallnacht* cost me my womb, it was your actions that took my only son from me."

There was a long silence. I felt angry, almost violated.

"But I honestly thought I was doing the right thing. I believed it was for your own good. I was trying to protect you; just as I protected you in Auschwitz."

"You should have left me to die. I cannot speak for the girls. I don't know what kind of life they can now lead; what future, if any, they will have."

"How can you say such things? You're clearly unwell."

"Yes, József – your wife is unwell. But that doesn't make her wrong."

"Look, my dearest sweet love: I ask… no, I implore… you to forget my past transgressions and learn to forgive me, for the sake of our marriage if nothing else."

"Twenty years of marriage to me has been the bitterest herb for you to swallow. I have freely surrendered unto you my body, my womanhood, my very soul. My love was pure, unwavering and self-sacrificing. But it was a Jewish love. Yes, I'm a Jewess, remember! I am Éva Székely of Munkács. My blood taints our children and everything we do. I am Éva the cockroach, Éva the maggot… who didn't even deserve a band of gold on her wedding day!"

"But you were happy, weren't you? I provided for you and the girls. You wanted for little."

"Happy? Wanted for little? You really don't understand, do you? What about the years of neglect, depression, self-harm and thoughts of suicide? I was wrapped up in my own guilt for trapping you into marriage; for poisoning you with my Jewishness, and ultimately destroying your life in Germany."

"What can I say? I'm sorry…"

"I will ask you one last time: do you love me, József Sárkány?"

"Éva, I love you… until the day I die."

She smiled. She knew. For this was surely the greatest of all my lies.

EPILOGUE

Report (abstract) of Dr. Manfred Portmann, Psychiatric Hospital, Burghölzli, Switzerland, Monday 7th January 1946

Dr. Sárkány's prison tattoo has been successfully removed. I examined the wound site which appeared clean and showed healthy scar tissue.

He persisted in his paranoid hallucinations. The negative symptoms of his *dementia praecox* dominated his waking state. I returned once again to hypnosis in order to circumvent thought-blocking and to explore memory sequences and repressed emotions. The language was invariably a hybrid of Hungarian and German in which the latter dominated when talking about Auschwitz-Birkenau. This was always spoken in the present tense, as if the patient was still there.

Recorded interview between Dr. Manfred Portmann and Dr. József Sárkány, Psychiatric University Hospital, Burghölzli, Switzerland, Monday 7th January 1946

Portmann: Who are you?
Sárkány: I am A-7938.
Portmann: What is your other name, A-7938?
Sárkány: I do not remember.
Portmann: You are Dr. József Sárkány, are you not?
Sárkány: Am I? Yes, I work in the *Lazarett*. But where are my patients? Ah, yes – they're in the *Sezierraum* with the eviscerator... what's his name? Ah, it doesn't matter; for they're all Mengele's *Meerschweinchen, zur sektion.*
Portmann: Where is Dr. Mengele now?
Sárkány: Mengele? Ah, *Herr Doktor Totenkopf. Es geht immer weiter, immer weiter.* My God! Éva!
Portmann: She is safe. Éva is safe. Your children are safe.

	But where is Mengele?
Sárkány:	Mengele? Mengele – yes! I know where he is.
Portmann:	Where is he? Where is Dr. Mengele?
Sárkány:	He's where he always is: on the ramp.
Portmann:	Mengele has left the ramp. He's left Auschwitz, run away. Where has he gone?
Sárkány:	No, never! *Alle Antreten! Mützen ab!*
Portmann:	*Arbeit macht frei?*
Sárkány:	No, it's a lie! Auschwitz is a *Vernichtungslager*! *Gib schon das Fressen den Juden!*
Portmann:	Mengele is not there anymore. You are no longer there. Auschwitz is no more.
Sárkány:	Auschwitz is my past, present and future. I live, breathe and sleep in Auschwitz. O *Judenstern!* Where is your guiding light for these poor, lost people?
Portmann:	You can leave the crematorium. Mengele has gone. Where did he go?
Sárkány:	The *Krema* are still here! Yes, I see *Zyklon* tins everywhere… *Blausäure*, never *Kohlenoxyd*. And we still have our *Drahtnetz Schiebevorrichtunge*. And these death-mills grind the grist in a relentless mechanistic rendering of fat, flesh and sinew; gear upon gear grinding on axel, like a clunking clockwork abattoir.
Portmann:	Let us try again shall we, from the beginning. Who are you?
Sárkány:	I am *Arbeitsfähig* – that is my name. I am *Untoter, Jüdischer Müll* and *Scheisse!*
Portmann:	You are Dr. József Sárkány from Hungary, are you not?
Sárkány:	I was perhaps made in Hungary, but wholly unmade in Auschwitz-Birkenau.

Recorded interview between Dr. Anatoly Brezhnev and Michał Kowalsky, Serbsky Psychiatric Centre, Soviet Union, Saturday 24ᵗʰ January 1948

Kowalsky: What's wrong with you people? I'm not sick. I'm completely sane. I know exactly who I am and where I am. I'm violent, yes. I might have even silenced a few Nazis, I admit. But insane? No, not guilty.

Brezhnev: Our agents estimate that you've murdered over twenty ex-Nazis between May 1945 and December 1947. Your most recent kill, Jonas Osterloh, was mauled to death in a shark attack off the coast of Brazil.

Kowalsky: No comment.

Brezhnev: Who are you?

Kowalsky: Michał Kowalsky, date of birth: 22/02/05.

Brezhnev: And your number?

Kowalsky: Fuck knows! Why don't you look yourself?

Brezhnev: And where are you, prisoner 61614?

Kowalsky: Some loony bin in Moscow. Look, I'm no threat to you people, politically or otherwise.

Brezhnev: I never said you were. Do you think you're paranoid?

Kowalsky: Probably, yes. But to survive Auschwitz and not be paranoid – that's insanity!

Brezhnev: If you are who you say, then you're also a Jew.

Kowalsky: Correction, I *was* a Jew. But after Auschwitz, after the genocide – no, I am no longer a Jew. I'm told you people found 348,000 men's suits and 836,000 items of women's clothing when you liberated the camp.

Brezhnev: Those are very specific figures for a man professing amnesia. But you are correct. Why are you no longer a Jew? Have you lost your identity, is that it?

Kowalsky: We bled from a thousand wounds. We howled

with hunger. We froze to death in unheated barracks. Bloodhounds tore at what flesh remained, and when even the lice forsook our shrivelled carcasses, the gas was our only liberation. But where was our Messiah in all this? Where was our Son of David, King of the Jews – come to lead us out of bondage? Bah! No, I'm done with God. Just like General Pompey did of old, I could stroll right now into the Holiest of Holies and not give a fuck!

Brezhnev: Yes, that's very good. But I would like you to share your time in Auschwitz with me. Bearing witness to the truth can be an act of self-healing, even purification. I don't expect every question to be answered. But I'm interested in the juncture between the said and the repressed unsaid; between what is told and what cannot be told.

Kowalsky: That's fine by me. You can psychoanalyse me to kingdom come. I'll tell you everything I can remember, which is very little.

Brezhnev: Excellent, then we'll begin. I'm going to induce a semi-hypnotic state. You won't feel any pain, just a sharp scratch.

Kowalsky: Hey, what the fuck was that?

Brezhnev: It's just a little serum to make you feel drowsy and to fully relax. Now, look into my eyes.

[Recording stops here and then resumes – time elapsed unspecified]

Brezhnev: Let me take you back to the beginning. You're on the train. You've just arrived at Auschwitz. You leave the boxcar. What do you see?

Kowalsky: I see dogs, ferocious fucking Alsatians. And SS guards, they're shouting. *Komm raus! Alle runter! Geh raus Juden! Ordnung Halten!* And there are bald matchstick prisoners in striped pyjamas; sacks of hessian that we Poles call *Pasiak*. I feel sick, vulnerable… confused. There are shouts. Mengele is there on the ramp, selecting whilst filing his nails. *Zwillinge, komm raus! Links! Rechts! Männer hier und Frauen hier. Wie alt?*

Brezhnev: You hate Dr. Mengele, do you not?

Kowalsky: I hate him with every bone and fibre of my body. I ache for vengeance!

Brezhnev: Yes, that's right. You want to track him down, kill him and exact your sweet revenge.

Kowalsky: Yes, I'll drown the bastard, slowly of course.

Brezhnev: That's good. We shall return to Dr. Mengele in a moment. But first tell me what happens after the ramp.

Kowalsky: We are stripped and processed like animals. My hair is shaved. But this is no comfortable barber's chair, no polite chitchat, no mirror. The clippers are blunt and the dull razorblade cuts and chafes without the lubrication of soap or water. Ha! I joke about the lack of wax, pomade and brilliantine. A guard smacks me round the face. Fucker!

Brezhnev: Then you take a shower, yes?

Kowalsky: The shower's not so bad. But there's no towel; you just stand around, ball naked, and drip-dry. Then they tattoo us. I ask what the dye is. It's a mixture of carbon and nickel in methanol. The pricking stylus hurts like fuck as it injects the black muck under my skin. Then I'm just a number!

Brezhnev: And after this, then what happens to you all?

Kowalsky: They herd us into horse stables teeming with vermin; twelve poor sods to a berth. They feed us on stewed weeds, sawdust and lignite. Life is arbitrary. It's another world, another planet almost. There are no fucking rules. There's no justification in survival, in carrying on.

Brezhnev: Survival can be warranted if justice is meted out. There is always retribution.

Kowalsky: That's what keeps me going. Nuremberg was a joke of course. It was a glorious piece of televised theatre, a show trial, nothing more. Most of the real cunts got away!

Brezhnev: Come now, what about Streicher? We also got Höss and Moll. And Muhsfeldt was hanged today in Kraków.

Kowalsky: Ha! Maybe there is a God after all! Muhsfeldt – what a sadistic fucker he was! And yes, I was so relieved when you got *Malahamoves*.

Brezhnev: *Malahamoves?*

Kowalsky: Otto Moll.

Brezhnev: Ah, yes. Anyway, *Mossad* will deal with Eichmann, that's not our concern. But Mengele, well yes, he is ours. Yours if you want him.

Kowalsky: You bet! But why not *Mossad?*

Brezhnev: Your old acquaintance, Dr. Sárkány: *Mossad* believes that he's protecting Mengele, but will not touch him. We've thought about taking him out with an assassin's bullet, but the late-stage syphilis is now doing the job for us. The correct microbe is indeed a powerful weapon, especially when delivered by a grinning blonde executioner wearing silk underwear.

Kowalsky: I've never trusted Sárkány. He was Mengele's Bitch alright, and no doubt played his own treacherous part in the October Uprising.

Brezhnev: Precisely. We know all this because our Soviet agents had the entire camp wired. We are still going through the hundreds of hours of recorded material.

Kowalsky: Clever! So Sárkány was saved by Mengele, and the traitor is now repaying the favour.

Brezhnev:	Knowing the war was now lost, Dr. Mengele specifically kept his corruptible Jewish pet alive; first as a means of witness insurance in the event of capture, and then as a source of information and protection whilst in exile.
Kowalsky:	I mustn't come near Sárkány then. The last thing we need is for Mengele to get wind of my survival. The Angel of Death was only too aware how much I hated him.
Brezhnev:	Mengele — you're sure you would recognise him now?
Kowalsky:	Of course I'd recognise him! What is this shit?
Brezhnev:	That's good. Just take a deep breath, count to three and calm down. I'm going to give you another small injection – that's it. Now, tell me more about camp life.
Kowalsky:	People work, people get sick and people die. In a nutshell, it's a carefully calculated extermination through labour. I'm lucky. I work for a while in the *Kanada*, but I see enough *Muselmänner* to know what camp life means for most. You dry up like a prune. The skin hardens and crusts and flakes before finally breaking down to form running sores and fungating ulcers. Your head becomes elongated and heavy as lead. Cheekbones appear chiselled, the nose pinched and eye-sockets deeply sunken. The muted *Muselmann*, the human hourglass, waits patiently for death. For the infirmary blocks are no more than waiting rooms for the gas chambers. Daily selections take place in the barracks where the feeble and emaciated have to perform like circus animals in front of Mengele and his selection committee.
Brezhnev:	And what of the other people that don't pass Mengele's selection on the ramp. What about

the pregnant women, the children and the elderly?

Kowalsky: They all go straight to the crematoria. They're crammed into a gas chamber which soon becomes a corpse cellar once the Red Cross disinfection squad is done. They use cyanide, always cyanide. They pour the poison granules through holes of death in the roof. Mengele is often there. Sometimes I can still hear the *Sh'ma Yisrael* amongst the screaming.

Brezhnev: And afterwards, what happens to the bodies?

Kowalsky: The doors swing open and the warm mountain of entangled bodies spills out like a human waterfall. The corpses are hosed down. The vultures then swoop – the shearers and tooth pullers. The bodies then go to the furnace room. The Sonder-men poke and stoke the crackling meat that pops and hisses; loading shovel after shovel of coke into some sort of gasifier chamber.

Brezhnev: And what is your role in all this?

Kowalsky: At first, I work on the ramp. After a brief spell in Buna, I'm sent to *Krema* I where I'm part of the *Sonderkommando* and also assist Dr. Sárkány with Mengele's autopsy work.

Brezhnev: And how do these autopsied people die? Are they gassed like the others?

Kowalsky: Most are killed with injections into the heart.

Brezhnev: What sort of injections?

Kowalsky: Anything really – phenol, chloroform, petrol even.

Brezhnev: Does Dr. Mengele administer these injections?

Kowalsky: You bet he does! But there are others psychos too – Oberhauser, Vetter, Klehr... in the experimental barracks. Mengele performs all kinds of sick experiments on twins, Gypsies, dwarfs – anybody who might be useful in confirming his theory of racial degeneracy. There are pickled specimens too, in some kind of warped pathology museum next door in *Krema* II. And skeletons… I hear they have lots of skeletons, including many Russian commissars captured at Stalingrad.

Brezhnev: We know about these comrades, thank you. And where does Erich Muhsfeldt fit in?

Kowalsky: The Ober is in charge of the two large *Krema*. The forest *Krema* – numbers III and IV – are overseen by Voss. Muhsfeldt is our neck-shooting specialist.

Brezhnev: Go on.

Kowalsky: Well, it's like this. Mengele likes to sweep out the hospital blocks with his posse of selectors. We get all the women, the hourglasses, waiting for the sands to run out. And then there's Mengele's whore, Irma Grese. Such a beautiful sadist, she glides about like a perfumed blonde spectre. Other times, she's like a stomping mare with her steel-studded boots; but always immaculate, always untouchable. Dreschel is invariably with her mistress, wearing the white coat of a doctor, which she most certainly isn't. She's the antithesis of Grese: bony, vulgar and ugly; her buckteeth jutting forward, even when her loathsome little mouth is closed.

Brezhnev: And what happens to these women – these 'hourglasses' – when they arrive at the crematorium?

Kowalsky: The tipper truck unloads them onto the ground like muck being poured out of a cement mixer. They crash to the ground in a naked heap of undignified flesh. Muhsfeldt finishes them off with his small-bore carbine he stole from a Katowice slaughterhouse. We have to hold each woman by the ear, at arm's length. Then the Ober shoots her in the back of the neck. Before she collapses, we have to take great care to lower her head so as not to cause blood to spurt and soil the executioner. Then we let her gently fall, before dragging her off to one side to make room for the next.

Brezhnev: This must be traumatising for you.

Kowalsky: That's a fucking understatement! It's hideous! Muhsfeldt leaves a horrible mess behind. A pile of women's bodies, an enormous pile, dreadful and disgusting and horrid to behold. Argh! The stench grabs you by the throat. The horror of the croaking death rattles; the bodies that writhe and squirm all over each other in a final *danse macabre* – choking, vomiting, defaecating, defiling. I can never forget this, never compartmentalise and suppress such haunting, harrowing images. I wake up every night and I'm in Auschwitz again; that dreadful sick smell from desecrated human beings, devoid of dignity and dying horribly like pieces of worthless meat.

Brezhnev: And then they are cremated?

Kowalsky: Yes, just like the rest. There are no memorials, no graves. There is nothing. They all die hideous deaths but nobody hears their cries of despair except me! The world is silent. How can one speak of liberation in this epicentre of annihilation?

Brezhnev: But you revolted. There was an uprising, yes?

Kowalsky: Yes, that's when I escape. Resistance is that final act of desperation; a decision about how to die, not how to live. And so, here I am, sane but mentally broken: liberated in body, but certainly not in mind.

Brezhnev: Thank you, that will be all for the moment.

Oath (invalid) sworn by Éva Sárkány on behalf of Dr. József Sárkány, Munkács, Soviet Union, Friday 31ˢᵗ December 1948

"I hereby swear this new oath as set out in the Declaration of Geneva. I, Dr. József Sárkány, solemnly pledge to dedicate my life to the service of humanity. The health and wellbeing of my patient will be my first consideration. I will respect the autonomy and dignity of my patient. I will maintain the utmost respect for human life. I will not permit considerations of age, disease or disability, creed, ethnic origin, gender, nationality, political affiliation, race, sexual orientation, social standing or any other factor to intervene between my duty and my patient. I will respect the secrets that are confided in me, even after the patient has died.

"I will practise my profession with conscience and dignity and in accordance with good medical practice. I will foster the honour and noble traditions of the medical profession. I will give to my teachers, colleagues and students the respect and gratitude that is their due. I will share my medical knowledge for the benefit of the patient and the advancement of healthcare. I will attend to my own health, wellbeing and abilities in order to provide care of the highest standard. I will not use my medical knowledge to violate human rights and civil liberties, even under threat."

Diary of Éva Sárkány, Munkács, Soviet Union, Sunday 7ᵗʰ October 1954

Today my husband was finally laid to rest. He was just 48 years old. Despite his premature demise, József was ready to die, although he never found his faith in God again. He was old for his years; very old. He tried to rebuild his life with me and the girls, but he could never really leave Auschwitz.

Amongst my husband's writings I have found a separate collection of tattered papers in a scrawling hand. They appear to be the writings of another inmate by the name of Michał Kowalsky. His diary entries end abruptly on the day of the uprising, exactly a decade ago today. I guess he never made it.

Letter to Emilia Sárkány, dated Wednesday 7th February 1979, São Paulo, Brazil

I read in the paper recently of your mother's passing and recognised the name Sárkány. You do not know me, but I believe you may be in possession of some personal documents of mine. They date back to 1944 when I was a prisoner with your father at Auschwitz-Birkenau. Although we did not always see eye to eye, I respected your father and was his technical assistant. We parted company in the October when I managed to escape from the camp. I was assumed to have died with several others in an explosion that rendered identification impossible. Before I escaped, I left your father my private journal. I am therefore writing to inquire whether you or your sister still has it.

I am currently in South America on some unfinished business which will conclude tomorrow. Then I shall fly back to Europe and attend the funeral of your mother. Although I did not meet Mrs. Sárkány, I would like to pay my respects in person to both of your parents at the graveside. It would also be a privilege for me if you could perhaps spare me a few moments of your time on the day.

Yours sincerely,
Michał Kowalsky.

Transcript of a student tutorial given at the Institute for Forensic Medicine, University of São Paulo, Brazil, Wednesday 16th March 2011

"Behold the cranium that once encased a brain tutored in science, medicine, philosophy and anthropology. Behold the orbits that housed the eyes of a soldier, decorated for bravery. And here hung those lips that spoke words of comfort to the sick and dying. Behold the highly skilled hands of a physician and surgeon, long trained in the healing arts. But why are they not buried with dignity in some marble tomb or family mausoleum?

"The bones before you are a century old today. These desiccated old bones were once packed with marrow and blood; glued together by ligaments; fleshed out with sinew, fascia and skin. They are the exhumed remains of a doctor, yes. They are the bones of a decorated soldier, yes indeed. So why are these bones here? Why were they taken from the cemetery of Nossa Senhora? Why are they stored in an old plastic bag, locked away in a dusty old cabinet? Where are the pleas and petitions from family and friends to repatriate these bones in the land where they were born? What heinous crime or crimes could these bones have committed to deserve such ignominy?

"So, who was this man? Was he Wolfgang Gerhard? Was he Josi Aspiazu? Perhaps he was Fausto Rindón. Some even called him the Angel of Death.

"His real name was Dr. Josef Mengele. He died on the afternoon of 7th February 1979. He supposedly suffered a stroke, and drowned whilst swimming in the sea at Bertioga. But my father, Michał Kowalsky, knew better.

"Here is the head of Josef Mengele. What perverse sculptor shaped this skull? Behold the cranium that once encased a brain obsessed with racial hygiene and human experimentation. Behold the orbits that housed the eyes of a mass murderer. And here hung those lips that spoke words of such deceit. Behold the highly skilled hands that murdered children with lethal injections and directed thousands to their deaths in the gas chambers.

"Damn you, perverse man! Why were you not hanged for your crimes at Nuremberg and incinerated into oblivion like the others? How did you evade capture for so many years? No wonder your family has abandoned you. Even Germany finds you repugnant.

"These bones are a hundred years old today. But this is no centenary celebration. This is neither sanctification nor ritual cleansing. They are the exhumed remains of a criminal doctor. They are the relics of an unrepentant psychopath. So why are they here? The world does not want them."

Extract from autopsy report labelled 'Operation Mengele', dated Thursday 8th February 1979. The document is signed by D. Lebedev and stamped 'Komitet Gosudarstvennoy Bezopasnosti SFSR'. Dossier discovered in top secret archives, Moscow, Saturday 20th April 2019. (Translated from original Russian)

Caucasian male, late sixties, in hessian shirt & trousers with faded blue stripes. Medium build, right-handed, height 170cm, weight 74kg, head circumference 56cm. Shaved head with grey-white stubble. Sclerae red & brownish discolouration to irises. Conjunctival petechiae, lips cyanosed, blood in mouth. Lingual frenulum tear.

Contusions (recent) to oropharynx with gun-muzzle oily residue. Loosened teeth x3 containing gold fillings. Scarring of tympanic membranes, mastoid sinuses & maxillary sinus.

Superficial ligature marks over neck (recent). 6mm ballistic wound in suboccipital triangle (recent); blackened powder burns; no exit wound. Lead bullet impacted in skull base, 3mm lateral to brainstem.

Fresh venepuncture marks in left antecubital fossa. Absent fingernails on left hand (recent avulsions). Number '61614' tattooed on left forearm (recent). Six-pointed star branded on chest (recent).

Bilateral rib fractures (recent) with surgical emphysema. Old fractures to pelvis, left clavicle, left scapula & right thumb. Left leg surgically defleshed postmortem (thigh & calf musculature). Scalpel blade marks over left femur, tibia & fibula. 4cm gluteosacral pressure sore (recent). Surgical castration (recent).

Sanguineous pericardial effusion (179ml). Fresh 7mm

contusion with superficial pinprick over the left ventricular free wall, 5mm inferolateral to distal LAD. Needle tract trauma (fresh) to myocardium (depth 4mm). Heart 378g. Concentric left ventricular hypertrophy (LV 190g; free wall thickness 1.7cm). Severe coronary artery atheroma. No myocardial infarction or scarring. 1.2cm adherent thrombus in left atrial appendage. Valves normal. Complicated aortic atheroma. Congested venae cavae & tributaries.

Right pneumothorax & elevated right hemidiaphragm. Bilateral serosanguineous pleural effusions (R 380ml; L 260ml). Partial atelectasis of right lung (764g). Left lung 782g. Bilateral pulmonary oedema & congested cut surfaces. Anthracotic mottling & apical emphysematous bullae (R>L), with minor pleural adhesions. Bronchial tree mildly ectatic. Patchy mucosal erythema, no suppuration. No pneumonic consolidation. No endobronchial mass lesions. No thromboemboli.

Chemical burns to hypopharynx & oesophageal mucosa. Hay, straw & silage bolus in dilated stomach. Gastric mucosa inflamed. Patchy erosions. Pancreas (88g) normal. Normal small bowel loops. Sigmoid colon diverticula. No ascites or peritoneal adhesions.

Congested liver (1786g) with nutmeg change & early cirrhosis. 1.9cm mixed calculus with gravel in gall bladder & cystic duct. Mild mucosal inflammation & cholesterolosis. Biliary tree otherwise normal.

Moderate splenomegaly (372g) & perisplenitis. Congested splenic pulp. No diffluence. 1.6cm splenunculus between splenic hilum & upper pole of left kidney. No lymphadenopathy. Thyroid & parathyroid glands normal. Adrenals normal. Vertebral marrow unremarkable.

Kidneys pale with adherent capsules (R 98g & L 101g). 3cm staghorn calculus in right renal pelvis. Right hydronephrosis & proximal hydroureter. Urinary bladder empty. 1.2cm bladder stone adherent to trigone vesicae. Mild mucosal trabeculation. Nodular prostatomegaly (79g).

Skull, dura mater, falx and dural venous sinuses normal.

Moderate atheroma in Circle of Willis. Normal pituitary gland. Brain congested (1465g). Normal myelination. No cerebellar coning. Part-clotted extravasated blood (~40ml) in subarachnoid space. Medullopontine/intraventricular tracking (third, fourth & sylvian aqueduct). CSF bloodstained. Old gliotic left cerebral infarcts (1.5cm frontotemporal; 0.8cm globus pallidus).

Cause of Death: 1. a   Accidental drowning.
                          1. b   Subarachnoid haemorrhage.

The End

ABOUT THE AUTHOR

Dr. Mounter has three intellectual passions: medicine, history and literature. At forty-nine years of age, he is a full-time Histopathologist working on the Isle of Wight.

The opportunity to develop his other interests – history and literature – came about when he was in his early forties. His two sons were no longer young children, and he had managed to secure a permanent consultant position. This led him to write his first novel, 'Bitching Bits of Bone'. Published in 2016 by Austin Macauley, this dark comedic retelling of Chaucer's 'The Canterbury Tales' enabled him to explore aspects of fourteenth century medicine.

Five years on, his second novel has permitted him to fully flex his medical muscles and to concentrate his acumen upon arguably one of the darkest places in human history: the pathology laboratory of Dr. Josef Mengele at Auschwitz-Birkenau.

Select Bibliography

Annas, George J. (Editor). The Nazi Doctors and the Nuremberg Code: Human Rights in Human Experimentation (Oxford University Press, U.S.A., 1995)

Appelfeld, Aharon. Badenheim 1939 (Penguin Classics, 2005)

Arendt, Hannah. Eichmann in Jerusalem: A Report on the Banality of Evil (Penguin Classics, 2006)

Binding, Karl. Hoche, Alfred. Allowing the Destruction of Life Unworthy of Life: Its Measure and Form (Suzeteo Enterprises, 2012)

Borowski, Tadeusz. This Way for the Gas, Ladies and Gentlemen (Penguin Classics, 1992)

Braham, Randolph L. The Geographical Encyclopedia of the Holocaust in Hungary (Northwestern University Press, 2013)

Browning, Christopher R. Ordinary Men: Reserve Police Battalion 101 and the Final Solution in Poland (Harper Perennial, 2017)

Cesarani, David. Eichmann: His Life and Crimes (Vintage, 2005)

Conroy, Melvyn. Nazi Eugenics: Precursors, Policy, Aftermath (ibidem, 2017)

Czech, Danuta. Auschwitz Chronicle, 1939-1945 (Henry Holt & Company, 1997)

Dov Kulka, Otto. Landscapes of the Metropolis of Death: Reflections on Memory and Imagination (Penguin, 2014)

Earl, Hilary. The Nuremberg SS-Einsatzgruppen Trial, 1945-1958: Atrocity, Law, and History (Cambridge University Press, 2010)

Epstein, Leslie. King of the Jews: A Novel of the Holocaust (Other Press LLC, 2003)

Fenelon, Fania. Musicians of Auschwitz (Sphere, 1979)

Frank, Anne. The Diary of a Young Girl (Penguin, 2012)

Friedlander, Henry. The Origins of Nazi Genocide: From Euthanasia to the Final Solution (The University of North Carolina Press, 1995)

Gerstein, Kurt. The Nazi Slaughter of the Disabled: The Euthanasia Program T4 (American Bibliographical Press, 2017)

Gerwarth, Robert. Hitler's Hangman: The Life of Heydrich (Yale University Press, 2012)

Gilbert, Martin. Kristallnacht: Prelude to Destruction (Harper Perennial, 2007)

Hilberg, Raul. German Railroads, Jewish Souls: The Reichsbahn, Bureaucracy, and the Final Solution (Berghahn Books, 2019)

Höss, Rudolph. The Master of Auschwitz: Memoirs of Rudolf Hoess, Kommandant SS (American Bibliographic Press, 2016)

Lengyel, Olga. Five Chimneys (Academy Chicago Publishers, 1995)

Levi, Primo. The Drowned And The Saved. (Abacus, 2013)

Lifton, Robert. The Nazi Doctors: Medical Killing and the Psychology of Genocide (Basic Books, 2017)

Lower, Wendy. Hitler's Furies: German Women in the Nazi Killing Fields (Vintage, 2014)

Marwell, David G. Mengele: Unmasking the 'Angel of Death' (W. W. Norton & Company, 2020)

Mendelsohn, Daniel. The Lost: A Search for Six of Six Million (William Collins, 2014)

Mozes Kor, Eva. The Twins of Auschwitz: The inspiring true story of a young girl surviving Mengele's hell (Monoray, 2020)

Muller, Filip. Eyewitness Auschwitz: Three Years in the Gas Chamber (Ivan R Dee, Inc, 1999)

Nyiszli, Miklós. Auschwitz: A Doctor's Eyewitness Account (Penguin Classics, 2012)

Perl, Gisella. I Was a Doctor in Auschwitz (Lexington Studies in Jewish Literature, 2019)

Posner, Gerald L. Berenbaum, Michael. Ware, John. Mengele: The Complete Story (Cooper Square Press, 2000)

Ringelblum, Emmanual. Notes From the Warsaw Ghetto: The Unflinching, Classic First-Hand Account (Milk & Cookies Press, 2006)

Sakowicz, Kazimierz. Ponary Diary, 1941-1943: A Bystander's Account of a Mass Murder (Yale University Press, 2005)

Speer, Albert. Inside The Third Reich (W&N, 2009)

Spitz, Vivien. Doctors from Hell: The Horrific Account of Nazi Experiments on Humans (Sentient Publications, 2005)

Trunk, Isaiah. Judenrat: The Jewish Councils in Eastern Europe Under Nazi Occupation (University of Nebraska Press, 1996)

Vági, Zoltán. Csősz, László. Kádár, Gábor. The Holocaust in Hungary: Evolution of a Genocide (Altamira Press, 2013)

Venezia, Shlomo. Inside the Gas Chambers: Eight Months in the Sonderkommando of Auschwitz (Polity, 2011)

Wiesel, Elie. The Night Trilogy: Night, Dawn, Day (Hill and Wang, 2008)

Online References

A Jewish Community in the Carpathian Mountains. The Story of Munkács

www.yadvashem.org/yv/en/exhibitions/communities/munkacs/ghetto.asp

A People's History of the Holocaust and Genocide

https://remember.org

Auschwitz-Birkenau – Virtual Tour

https://panorama.auschwitz.org

Axis History Forum

www.forum.axishistory.com

Fritz, R., & Novak-Rainer, C. (2015). Inside the Ghetto: Everyday Life in Hungarian Ghettos. The Hungarian Historical Review, 4(3), 606-639

www.jstor.org/stable/24575808

Harvard Law School Library. Nuremberg Trials Project

http://nuremberg.law.harvard.edu

Holocaust and Genocide Studies. University of Minnesota

https://cla.umn.edu/chgs

Holocaust Education & Research Team

www.holocaustresearchproject.org

Holocaust Forgotten

www.holocaustforgotten.com

Holocaust Memorial Day Trust: Learning from genocide – for a better future

www.hmd.org.uk

Honey, Michael. Research Notes on The Hungarian Holocaust, 2008

www.zchor.org/hungaria

Jewish Calendar 1944

www.hebcal.com/hebcal/?year=1944

Jewish Virtual Library

www.jewishvirtuallibrary.org

Memorial and Museum: Auschwitz Birkenau

http://auschwitz.org/en

Ofer, Dalia. Weitzman, Lenore J. Women in the Holocaust. Jewish Women's Archive

https://jwa.org/encyclopedia/article/women-in-holocaust

The Beth Shalom Holocaust Web Centre

www.bethshalom.com

The Holocaust Explained.

www.theholocaustexplained.org

The Holocaust: Key Notes from the National Archives

www.nationalarchives.gov.uk/education/resources/holocaust

The Nazi Concentration Camps: A Teaching & Learning Resource

www.camps.bbk.ac.uk

The Nizkor Project

www.nizkor.org

United States Holocaust Memorial Museum

www.ushmm.org

USC Shoah Foundation. The Institute for Visual History and Education

https://sfi.usc.edu

Walden, Geoff. Third Reich in Ruins. Birkenau (Auschwitz) Concentration and Extermination Camp

www.thirdreichruins.com/auschwitzbirkenau

War Crimes Trials - Vol. II The Belsen Trial. The Trial of Josef Kramer and Forty Four Others

www.bergenbelsen.co.uk/pages/trial/TrialFront/TrialFront_01.html

Wiener Holocaust Library

www.wienerholocaustlibrary.org

Yivo Institute for Jewish Research

https://yivo.org/Encyclopedia

www.ingramcontent.com/pod-product-compliance
Lightning Source LLC
LaVergne TN
LVHW041331080426
835512LV00006B/393